ANGLO-SAXONY
AND ITS TRADITION

THE MACMILLAN COMPANY
NEW YORK · BOSTON · CHICAGO · DALLAS
ATLANTA · SAN FRANCISCO

MACMILLAN AND CO., LIMITED
LONDON · BOMBAY · CALCUTTA · MADRAS
MELBOURNE

THE MACMILLAN COMPANY
OF CANADA, LIMITED
TORONTO

ANGLO-SAXONY

AND

ITS TRADITION

By

GEORGE CATLIN

1939

The Macmillan Company

NEW YORK

Set up and printed. Published August, 1939.

FIRST PRINTING.

PRINTED IN THE UNITED STATES OF AMERICA
AMERICAN BOOK—STRATFORD PRESS, INC., NEW YORK

To
HU SHIH

WHO PERHAPS ALONE AMONG
MY FRIENDS CAN READ THIS BOOK
WITH DETACHMENT

FOREWORD

For some time it has been my conviction that, if we are to stand firm in the days that are coming, we must consider well the rock whence we are hewn and the root whence we are sprung.

The substance of the following work on that theme was delivered in the form of lectures in Washington, D.C., during March 1939, by the hospitable invitation of the Bureau of Economics of the Department of Agriculture, conjointly with the Graduate School of the American University. Needless to say these hosts, who made my stay so pleasant, are in no wise responsible for the opinions here expressed. I would nevertheless wish to put on record my gratitude to them; to the general audience that patiently listened to my remarks; and, not least, to the graduate students who cross-questioned me, to my profit, about those views. They will recognize the chapters addressed especially to them.

It was further of interest, as it was a pleasure, to me to find some sympathy for the views of more topical relevancy—here stated in the 'Open Letter' which, by his benevolent permission, I have inflicted on Mr. Wells—in areas so far apart as the shores of the Great Lakes and the Deep South, and to listeners as diverse as the academic audience and the business men's lunch club.

Mr. Wells, I believe, and the common reader, I hope, will pursue with me, beyond the momentary applications, into those chapters where I have discussed those issues as cardinal to the Anglo-Saxon Tradition as his philosophy was to Marx. If some are tempted to complain that my applications are too popular, I trust that others, forewarned and with finger-posts erected for their guidance, will not complain that my principles are too "deep".

I am not responsible that this age has raised for discussion the basic issues of thought and not merely the simplicities of popular party politics, or that Marx, Lenin and even Nietzsche are not every man's mental fodder. I have endeavoured to relegate these issues, such as What is Truth? and Is Mussolini God? My Class Right or Wrong and Is The State All?—issues abhorrent to the healthy common reader—to the minimum space and to the remote recesses and crannies of this book. I warn him, however, in his pilgrimage that they are there, ready to leap out upon him from dark places, fiercely gnashing their teeth.

I am well aware that there are many themes, not irrelevant to the Anglo-Saxon Tradition, that remain undiscussed here. They have been adequately dealt with by abler pens. There is the spirit of the Common Law, alive on both sides of the Atlantic, that has engaged the attention of Dean Pound and of the late Lord Haldane. There is the common Language on which Professor Lloyd James, with his preference for the American 'a' and distrust of British affectations, speaks with authority; and there is that great future of the basic international language towards which Mr. C. K. Ogden pioneers. There is the spirit of Constitutionalism which has been a theme from the days of Bagehot, and Lord Balfour's introduction to Bagehot's *English Constitution,* to Woodrow Wilson's *Congressional Government* and Professor McIlwain's recent *Constitutionalism and a Changing World.* There is the spirit of liberalism that has occupied attention from the writings of Jefferson to the distinguished survey by the present Warden of New College. The similarity of what I have to urge to that which, in full administrative detail, is urged by Mr. Clarence Streit, will be patent to everyone. Above all, and kernel of all, there is the theme of Natural Law, fundamental law of human kind, to which on some other occasion I hope to return. But discussion of it is inappropriate here and at this hour and for the general reader, to whom rather I would recall more urgent words which I will dare to use:

> "To every Middlesex village and farm,—
> A cry of defiance and not of fear,
> A voice in the darkness, a knock at the door."

I would light two lights again in Boston steeple for a new cause and not a lesser, for an old cause of Englishmen.

For the rest, I hope, as the godson of the once incumbent of the Old South Church, Boston, cathedral of New England Puritanism, that over fifteen years as a sojourner but never as a stranger in the United States, and, during the same period, two political campaigns in England may make my venture in interpretation not too rash.

One last word. This book declares the existence of a threat. It is yet dictated by no malice against the German nation. Once in a lifetime to hear about 'the Hun' and 'the Bosche' is enough. Germany is for me always the land of the simple village people with their fair-haired children; and of the voices chanting midnight Christmas mass in the great minster at Cologne; and above all, of the Germans, with their graves along with the French soldiers—'Français inconnu mort pour la France'—buried together at St. Romagne, beyond Verdun, that of Friedrich Vögel, "aus Geislingen", with the inscription from his company "to their gallant officer", and the other by it, "Here rests in God their unforgettable son and brother, Jacob Weickert." Perhaps to you, Jacob Weickert, I should have dedicated this book and to the day when we and those who follow you will meet in conference of peace together. Here is the truer German people, because the truer humanity. To the meeting of that Conference we look.

ACKNOWLEDGMENT

I have to thank for permission to quote from UNTO CAESAR (copyright, 1938), Mr F. A. Voigt and G. P. Putnam's Sons; from GERMANY, MY COUNTRY, Mr F. Sieburg and Messrs. Jonathan Cape, Ltd; from SCIENCE AND THE MODERN WORLD, Professor A. N. Whitehead and The Macmillan Company; from RETREAT FROM REASON, Professor Lancelot Hogben and Random House, Inc.; from THE SOCIAL FUNCTION OF SCIENCE, Professor J. D. Bernal and The Macmillan Company; from ON ENGLAND, the Earl Baldwin of Bewdley and Messrs. Philip Allan & Co., Ltd; from COLLECTED POEMS of the late G. K. Chesterton, his executors and Dodd, Mead & Company, Inc.; from POWER, the Earl Russell and W. W. Norton & Company; from REVOLT OF THE MASSES, M. Ortega y Gasset and W. W. Norton & Company; from a review of Professor MacMurray's book, THE CLUE TO HISTORY, the editors of *Time and Tide*.

CONTENTS

III

CONCLUSION

I

PROLOGUE

"Energetic men . . . perceived the attractiveness of the suggestions of the formulae, and that they wanted to exploit that attractiveness with an uncomplicated directness. . . . To qualify or criticize was enfeeblement of effort, sabotage, downright treachery. It would mean having to reconsider, instead of getting on."

H. G. WELLS.

"There are masked words droning and skulking about us in Europe just now . . ."

JOHN RUSKIN.

AN OPEN LETTER

§ i

Introductory: The Grand Tradition of Humanism

MY DEAR H. G.,

'Twenty years after,' August 1938—as well as September
and October; the Berchtesgaden, Godesberg, Munich con-
ferences—have come and gone. Those who warm their hands
before the very imagination of war's flames, explaining the
while that they wish nothing better than peace after their
own designing, must wait again. Others, who claim the advantage that the inner processes of history and its future have
been revealed to them, must transfer their fatalist, ill-omened
prophecies of evil to some other date. And yet these months
from May 1938 were beyond a doubt more critical than any
yet, not excepting the Military Reoccupation of the Rhineland. No sane man, acquainted with the situation, can view
with other than contempt the suggestion that the war-risk of
those months was all 'bluff' by the German Führer or a 'put-
up job' by Mr. Chamberlain. The tension, relaxed in October,
was keyed up anew by the occupation of Prague, in March.

We have now for the moment a breathing space. This
pause is more decisive than any of the fifteen decisive battles
of the world. We have perhaps time in which to decide where
and with whom to take our stand. There will be an interval
before the Reichsregierung, the German Government, takes
the next step in a plan faithfully followed. That next step
need not be for war, if we have national will and vision,

3

whether on the English side of the Atlantic or on the American, to see and take our own right steps in relation to it. Of such vision I cannot claim that I see bright signs. The times are growing late; and the new spirit may not attend us before the hours have sped and the time of decision is upon us in our sleep.

If dead statesmanship is in so many vital quarters to be in charge, despite the labours of a Roosevelt, during these coming months while the sands run out, then the prospect is indeed black. I don't know whether Sir Thomas Inskip or Lord Stanhope in the front line of defence, or the Townshenders in the back trenches, fill you with confidence. They don't encourage me. I deplore the slack mood that leads to the appointment of a London food-controller, resident in Belgium. I submit that the old heroes and saints are more alive and more likely to help, if we recall them, than the new, dead politicians. This is no new concern of mine. Shall I tell you that, since December 1918, outside Mons (I still have my manuscript written there), it has been this notion of the next war, of the rôle of war in human affairs and *Realpolitik,* of the science and philosophy of politics, that has spurred and reined the body of my thinking? The hours of daylight are perhaps now few during which a man may labour. And surely a people without vision will perish.

Such different persons as Mr. Justice Frankfurter and Señor de Madariaga have said—the one to me in the lighted room of the Supreme Court Building, there on the one side of the Atlantic; the other on the other side, as we looked out over the Thames—that we, in the West, need clear concepts of the values for which we stand; that there is a chaos of ideas and purposes in the Western world and that the prime imperative is to order this chaos. Should war come, one of the decisive forces in moulding the future of human civilization will be the opinion, ideals, resolution of the ordinary American and of his nation. And the middle-class American, the average, middle-income-level American of the average American Middletown, is more at sea than any man about what he stands for—although, besides words about Jefferson and Lincoln, there has been some hard thinking in the last six months.

If war comes, followed by a Peace—and that Peace is to be a peace indeed, and not a broth of passion poured from the alembic of hell, maddening men for yet one more Bigger, Greater War in 1960 [1]—then the sole hope is that some men shall coldly discover the values, the scheme, the human ideals that Democracy, while still dispassionate, can be supposed to wish to prevail in post-war Europe; and that these men shall install themselves early in such seats of power that by no clamour can they be unseated therefrom when the hour comes. It is due for Democracy sober to install them there today against the days of Democracy drunk. The immediate task now is the discovery and decision of these values.

It does not for a moment follow—the thesis of this book is the opposite—that the world is to be divided between two ideologies, or even split between three. If peace can be maintained on the basis of "keeping pact," in the mood of equity, then the imperative duty is so to maintain it, without detaching ourselves because of the uncongenial domestic ideology of others. I do not doubt that our athletes would be prepared to give cheerfully the Communist 'clenched fist' as they did the Fascist 'Roman' salute.

It does not follow that a flaccid acquiescence is tolerable before the hostile doctrinal penetration of others, with their "world outlooks"; or that the duty of choosing values and objective can be shriked, as distinct from the purely selfish

[1] As Marshal Foch, in the 1920's, prophesied World War for 1935.

defence of frontiers and empires, once peace were lost. We, in the English-speaking world, cannot abdicate the task of creative political thinking or disclaim any permanency of value in our own tradition. If we do so, that thinking will be done for us by more vigorous minds.

Today the civilization of Europe, that has meant so much in the preservation of values—not, indeed, meant all, as you yourself have shewn who have displayed the panorama of the East, contributions from Confucius to our own days—this civilization is a garden in disorder. The cultivated plants of Liberalism are giant stalks, long seeded and in decay; weeds luxuriantly spring up. The gardeners, many of them, as Julien Benda in his *Trahison des Clercs* has pointed out, have deserted for new, more fashionable masters. It is time that some band shall be found—and here you have indeed led us— who will take off shirt and vest as even dictators can do—as Mussolini did down there at Aprilia—and who will hoe that garden in the summer sun. They should hoe it, not with a melancholic face, but thanking God that we are blessed to be confronted with such problems and confident of new seed-time and flowering, if not for us, then for our children. The democracies are dying of defeatist talk. It is a cursed fate for some that they should be born in this age, when they would have decorated so elegantly another, quieter epoch. But it is yet an age that, for the magnitude of its enterprises, has seen no parallel; and it is a glorious time, for those who would be men, in which to live. Is there not, perhaps, somebody among us who will cry 'courage'—like another Danton, happy even *que son nom soit flétri et que la patrie soit sauvée.*

Our primary need at the moment is to discover and to affirm values which make it worth while to live in these days. We have also to discover values which make it worth while maybe for a second time in a generation to sacrifice ourselves. Talk of wars to end war and dictatorship can be dangerous enough. War in fact produces dictatorship. Peace requires for its making and maintaining more intelligence and moral courage —the moral courage that the statesmen of 1918 lacked—than war. Nevertheless it was out of the oppression of the old Czardom and out of the agony of humiliation of post-war Germany that the militant faiths of those countries have sprung.

These present days of crisis may produce something beside ill if, out of them, springs for us too a faith that shews our own ways of life to be affirmative and very far from effete. Such a discovery and faith is indeed not to be produced over-night. It will find its background in the history of the people. In searching for it we can possess our souls in peace, knowing that, whether in peace or war, either way it will be required; and, if in war, it will be equally required in victory or in defeat. Our first moral duty is to avert war, not to chatter like the Marxians of its inevitability—but these things are yet contingent, and the faith must be such as to be the core of our souls.

There is, let us be sure, such a reality as civilization—and this as a pattern of values described through the ages, which is a witness against the upstarts of each generation and an enduring measure of the stature of great men. That should give us confidence, even in the blacker hours, as we labour.

In writing recently my *Story of the Political Philosophers,* which was a kind of story of mankind reviewed from the peaks of those major minds, on which the light of full consciousness shines amid the valleys of ignorance and confusion, I have had one great comfort. I found no sure evidence at all of progress in moral vision since the earliest days, any more than in poetry since Homer or in sculpture since Pheidias or that unknown sculptor of the head of Akhenaten's queen.

There was progress in aqueducts and sewers. Man, above all, is the Instrument-Maker; and there was progress, if wavering, yet effective, in all the conditions of tolerable, decent, dignified living for the many. But I discovered, I believe, a Grand Tradition in human values.

There is a pattern of values, seen by the major minds as permanent like the constellations even during the greatest darkness, and at times known to blaze with certainty like the noon sun. Nor, despite the misery that men invite upon themselves, even in Dark Ages does this pattern perish. It is no strange, exquisite speculation, but very plain that, as Aldous Huxley says, the great seers of mankind have spoken with no babel of voices, but with quite singular unanimity, upon the ends and final values of humanity. The customs of men may vary, as the first anthropologist, Herodotus, shewed: men in some places holding it the greatest piety, and in others the greatest impiety, to eat the bodies of their parents. So, too, Catholic and Protestant revere or abhor bones and books in the name of religion. But far more singular than the diversity is the startling unanimity of the great seers, Confucius, Buddha, Socrates, Christ, arising separately in climates so diverse.

These isolated speakers of *logoi* and maxims stand at the threshold. Later the Grand Tradition of the West—the steady Chinese Confucian tradition is separate but certainly not in conflict: you will recall how, even in art, the most striking figure in the recent Exhibition displayed acceptance of the canons of Greek taste—the Grand Tradition was formed with system and beauty by the Greeks. Those who in modern times sought to restate that tradition, purified from barbarisms, we call the Humanists. I quite decline to put the traditions either of Judaea or of Rome into mutually exclusive antithesis to that of Greece—certainly the Humanists did *not* so put them—but rather see a syncretism and fusion. And I am unable to be persuaded that notions and beliefs, fanaticisms and bigotries that flout this tradition, and are schismatics from this heritage, although all the battalions of Sisera are on their side, are likely to prevail. To this I pin my faith.

I talk of faith and will to believe. I do not state or believe that there are absolute truths now known to us—save of the platitudinous tautological order, as that what by definition is such, is such by that definition; or copies of fact, as that the Battle of Waterloo took place in what Westerners (but not Mahomedans) call the year 1815. I neither affirm nor deny the possibility of absolute knowledge, alike of truths or values. But neither you nor I, being human, evolved creatures, have it. Faith cannot now be dissolved in final knowledge. The faith of the scientist leads him to affirm, from partial knowledge, the value of science. Moreover, faith resting on partial experience proceeds to the adventure of new experience, and thereby makes new truth—which pragmatic faith in science we call working hypothesis.

Our faith is not a dogma but an adventure. So I too hypothetically affirm, as faith, *the value of Humanism,* and demand for Humanism a creative, moulding faith among those who would lead into the future. All that aids, even if indirectly, to that end we must encourage. We must, for example, attend to the revival of Catholic Humanist civilization. I attach the utmost importance to French Humanism and to the work of such men as Maritain. All these cultural forms we must foster on the way to the civilization of the World Commonwealth. Let us be clear that Christianity, both Protestant and also indeed Catholic, is today on the defensive in a fight that threatens death, against resurgent paganism and against dogmatic materialism.

The curse, however, of today is the political religions in

which men affirm themselves to know absolutely that which
they cannot so know. These are the new bigotries. Under their
saturnine, intimidating sway, men will not have the high courage and inventive initiative to scale the stars—literally to scale
them, as you yourself have said in *The Shape of Things to
Come.* The fruitful spirit of science will die down when dogmatism prevails, just as, after the efflorescence of the Renaissance in experiment, from Leonardo da Vinci to Galileo and
Torricelli, it died down into the deadness of seventeenth-
century Italy. Men become sodden in religions that, with
quick, spying, jealous eyes, demand obedience as of faith and
cut the nerve of resolution. For the bigots it is enough for a
truth that it is 'my truth,' convenient for race or class or fatherland—thereby denying the claims alike of humanity, civilization, science, objectivity and the idea of Truth itself. The
denial that Truth exists is the peculiar quality of the passing
epoch. The observable degeneration of morals follows in its
wake. Men no longer 'keep faith.'

There is an ancient rule or test, known to the Churchmen,
and ascribed to St. Vincent of Lerins: *Quod semper, quod
ubique, quod ab omnibus*—"What is received always, everywhere and by all." It is my reading of history that we draw
from it examples of values so received in rough through all
ages, in all places and by all thinkers. That unity, that Tradition, by abbreviation I refer to as the Humanist Tradition. It
is that of our Western Christian civilization, but it is also
wider. The builders and master artists of this tradition are
added to by co-option. Not trusting myself to judge good
music, I yet trust myself to judge who may be the great mu-
sicians who can judge good music. Not trusting myself to
know the truth, I yet trust myself to know who are more
sensitive to it than I and than most others.

Advancing slowly in affirmation, I acknowledge the central

contribution to this tradition of Hellenic civilization and, Judaea entering in, of Catholicism. I detect indeed a perceptible community of affirmation in Confucianism; I think we are entitled to recognize Kung as also among the masters. In this chorus clearly I detect Plato, but not less, as antiphonal, Aristotle ... Socrates also, if we may distinguish him ... certainly Dante, Erasmus, Goethe ... and Voltaire (ringing with a more flawed sound). Equally slowly, tentatively, yet with some confidence, Rousseau I would reject.

As Voltaire said, the cult of the simple life almost is so attractive that one is tempted to run around on all fours, but, perhaps unhappily, one has abandoned this for too many years. There are some who ask us to reject the Hellenic tradition and (so Professor Macmurray) to return to the Hebrew alone. And if we ask why, they reply that we must return to the primitive. That cult also, as enough for our maturity, I reject. My object is not to suffocate thought beneath the stuff cloaks of great names, cloaks fallen from dead men's shoulders. The object is to clarify our concepts of values by arranging some convenient hierarchy among those whose judgements normally we would, with every confidence, accept as those of our soul friends, or differ from with trepidation and heart-searching.

Does not then history shew change? Must not this very material progress or spreading of the instruments facilitant of the good life among the masses, of itself influence the thought of the guiding thinkers and materially condition and determine them? Of course. Does not this then vitiate the attempt to descry some tradition of civilization—the core of what we *mean* by civilization—or even a Humanist tradition, as providing a canon for modern thought, aspirations and values? I do not think so.

It is not the values that change, but the ways and means of

expressing them—the cultural forms under which they become incarnate. The thinkers' views about these ways and
means of course must change; and perhaps now this and now
that aspect of the total, non-self-contradictory tradition of
right-living becomes more important than another.

That shift of emphasis happened during and as a consequence of the High Renaissance, the Age of Exploration following that of the, as it were, excavating humanists, polishers
of antiquities. If not the Reformers, at least the typical men of
the Renaissance, were concerned with the 'objective,' the discovery of facts. And both were concerned with the discovery
of the individual. A change of mood took place—actually related to the Platonizing past as experimental and Aristotelian;
but often believing itself to be anti-Aristotelian because opposed to Aristotle, the Schoolmaster. Signally, in the very attack, it illustrated the saying, so emancipating and so rash, of
the great 'master of them that knew,' inscribed at the beginning of his *Metaphysics:* "All men by nature desire to know."

That new mood was the Empiric: It was strong in its scientific, practical and moral stresses, but frankly weak in the mystic or religious, as distinct from the moral, consciousness. It
was undogmatic and tolerant. That is why it is under criticism
today from the new bigotries. If there be a 'recall to religion,'
let us pray it to be to the religion of mercy and goodwill
known to the masters of our Tradition, and not to such as
these.

Let us, however, have patience. The stress of the classical
world, since the days of the Stoa, was on Natural Law. That
of the individualistic Renaissance and *Éclaircissement* was on
Social Contract. Today there is a new shift of emphasis. We
live in collectivo-totalitarian times. The myth in vogue is that
of Social Organism. The ecstatic bigotry of some of its devotees is no new sign, but characteristic of men desperate with

scepticism and secularism and seeking incontinently any new religion, be it Leviathan or another. In the decline of the Ancient World, before the religion of Christ was found, men in Rome and in Alexandria were impelled to turn to 'primitivism,' to strange corybantic dancing cults of Serapis and 'the barking Anubis.' They do it again today.

We have our choice. Is civilization merely an aggregate of the achievements and convenient views, imposed for their own political *interests* by strong men of action, chance 'organizers of victory,' *sabres organisés* (as was said of Napoleon), 'men of destiny,' ruling classes, 'Disciplined Vanguards,' self-conscious of class or conscious what this or that economic factor determines, or self-conscious of their own arbitrary wills? Or is civilization the material expression and recorded imprint of a culture, limited by its vehicle, but moulded by ideas of *value,* of historic permanence, even if not of metaphysical eternality, and shaping our destiny—ideas, not indeed unformed by their temporary environment; but also springing from primaeval vital energy; not without creative effect on that environment and not unmoulded in action by their integral relation to each other. Out of that relationship springs the notion of better or worse, more or less in value, whereby alone we are entitled to an historically valid judgement of right or wrong. Let us take our stand here with Plato and against Thrasymachus, the believer in 'action' or in the success of the big stick and the empty spirit. The great men of action are but the seers—or the victims—of ideas. And the ideas—earth-born, I grant you, not heaven-sent, if it gives anyone pleasure arbitrarily to assume earth and matter more 'real' than heaven and the cosmic (it is a quarrel of words); born indeed of our own real natures in impact on wider reality—the ideas have an inherent life and capacity for adventure of their own. "Revolution," Napoleon said, "is an idea that has found arms."

As poets, these ideas rule the world. It is indeed the prophets, the poets, who, for its good or evil, in fact do rule the world. A man must be blind who does not see that ideas are not remote, 'unpractical,' but are indeed deluging our world with human blood here around us, this year, this day. . . . Unhappily, today these prophets are too often persecuting theologians or fanatics of a Book, be it *Das Kapital* or *Mein Kampf,* who resist judgement before the Tribunal of History and by an age-long Truth, unveiled in history, that they deny. Nevertheless, *securus judicat orbis terrarum.*[1]

§ ii

The Anglo-Saxon Tradition

The Empiric mood of the sixteenth century found peculiarly full expression in England. It is no especial merit, since many of the Englishmen most typical of the spirit were true Europeans, and many most hostile to the mood were to be found in England. Fanaticism and internecine war—in Germany, in Italy—happened to render the practical conditions more difficult elsewhere, and at least the temper of the people was not hostile to toleration and its child, experiment.

A land of great poets and of no mean philosophers, its masses were too sluggish and too little romantic to desert, for long, common-sense in favour of enthusiasm. The mood of compromise, impossible in the lands of the Thirty Years' War and of the Counter-Reformation, was voiced in the pages of Hooker. Empiricism itself was formulated as a philosophy, not by the Cartesians, but by the Englishman, Francis Bacon, Lord Verulam. Even in his distant namesake, Roger Bacon, and in Duns Scotus, *magister Duns, doctor subtilis,* there shone authentic far-off pragmatic lights. The philosophic foundations of this Anglo-Saxon Tradition were laid. They were

[1] "Secure, the world judges"—the dictum of St Augustine, quoted by Newman. I would prefer the inversion, *secura, judicat orbes terrarum.*

built up by Locke into the structure of a coherent system. They were added to by the Utilitarians and later by the pragmatic school of James and Dewey, and indeed by Russell.

An intellectual weapon was forged, alone competent to meet the dogmatic suppositions of the French school of Descartes, and of Spinoza, or to meet the German dogmatic schools of Hegel and of his successors, Fascist and Marxist. Here were suppositions congenial to the experimental technique which provided progress in the natural sciences. An 'open world,' not a closed, dogmatic system, was their common assumption. Here was found a natural soil of tolerance and of personal liberty. This book that I send you is designed to show the nature and shape of this philosophy offered to the world, which is yet quite peculiarly the heritage of the Anglo-Saxon peoples.

As much as Thomism—as much, nay far more than Marxism—it is a completed and thought-out philosophy, with its own distinctive attitude towards experience. The relations between the Catholic Humanist tradition, with its stress on personal value, within the framework of natural and divine order, with its respect for moral choice and for the voluntary basis of the social order, and the Anglo-Saxon Libertarian tradition with its history of politically mature and sober discipline, are matter for a separate study that should prove fascinating enough. It is perhaps one of the most important intellectual tasks of our time—the discovery of the 'buckle' or common values between the two.

The Anglo-Saxon Tradition has not remained, even in the hands of its metaphysicians such as Locke, only a metaphysic. It has always had a markedly ethical note. It has shaped its own political philosophy, ranging from the empiricism of Burke to the libertarianism of Mill, which has had more influence on the continent of Europe than any other single school of thought save Catholicism. This political philosophy of ours has received authentic expression in the writings of Jefferson and in the speeches of Lincoln. It has impregnated the political institutions of the Anglo-Saxon world on both sides of the Atlantic; and has provided patterns—which those derived from Rousseau and the French Revolution alone rival—to all Europe and to the lands that look to Europe. It has ever been a political teacher and leader, not some mean follower of the Germans. This present decade has indeed turned away from its principles and leadership—but then, this present decade, in the record of civilization, may well be ashamed of comparison with the darker Middle Ages. My work is done if this book helps to re-expound, re-clarify and re-vindicate that tradition, and to indicate it as a basis for new political formations.

This philosophy, of which the outstanding representative is John Locke, and from which half of the intellectual heritage of modern Europe traces, is the illuminating sun of our common culture, not solely ours, but chiefly and authentically ours. It is not centralized institutions or even monarchic glory which holds this Commonwealth together. A common tradition of law which our sceptred democracy shares with the great Western Republic, and a common language, have more significance. The significance of this spirit of the Common Law has been elaborated by abler pens than mine. It is indeed entirely impossible to separate the United States from the rest of Anglo-Saxony in these matters of culture. What is called the tempo of living may be different—although here the line of division rather lies between Great Britain and the greater trans-Atlantic Dominions—but the heritage and the presuppositions in living remain the same. They remain sharply distinct from those of Germany and of Russia. The culture, with so much in common, remains definitely distinguishable from the classical culture of France. It is neither better nor worse, but different. *When we speak of the Anglo-Saxon world we speak, not of a*

State or indeed of an Empire, but of a civilization, a culture which carries, latent in it, a philosophy and an outlook in living.

In a famous passage in his *Gleanings of Past Years,* the great Liberal Premier, Mr. Gladstone, after prophesying the economic rise to dominance of the United States, and enumerating common elements in the culture of that country and of Britain—love of self-government; a settled idea that force must be backed by thought; a belief in "governments, not by force only but by persuasion"; a belief in equality combined with liberty—continued:

"Many more are the concords, and not less vital than these, of the two nations, as expressed in their institutions. They alike prefer the practical to the abstract. They tolerate opinion, with only a reserve upon behalf of decency; and they desire to confine coercion to the province of action, and to leave thought, as such, entirely free. They set a high value on liberty for its own sake. They desire to give full scope to the principles of self-reliance in the people, and they deem self-help to be immeasurably superior to help in any other form; to be the only help, in short, which ought not to be continually, or periodically, put upon its trial, and required to make good its title. They mistrust and mislike the centralization of power; and they cherish municipal, local, even parochial liberties, as nursery grounds, not only for the production here and there of able men, but for the general training of public virtue and independent spirit. They regard publicity as the vital air of politics, through which alone, in its freest circulation, opinions can be thrown into common stock for the good of all, and the balance of relative rights and claims can be habitually and peaceably adjusted. It would be difficult, in the case of any other pair of nations, to present an assemblage of traits at once so common and so distinctive, as has been given in this probably imperfect enumeration."

Professor Lancelot Hogben has said that "English politicians are probably the most expensively uneducated class of people alive at the present day." I do not feel, however, that this charge is relevant in the case of Mr. Gladstone. A quotation from a very different quarter has bearing on the same theme. Herr Hitler, in *Mein Kampf,* speaking of the advantage of concentration of territory, says:

"Even Britain is not proof to the contrary against this advantage, for we are apt to forget the nature of the Anglo-Saxon world in its relation to the British Commonwealth. If only on account of her community of language and culture with the American Union, England cannot be compared with any other State in Europe."

It is for us today to decide—and the decision is urgent—whether we still believe in this characteristic culture; and believe that it, and through it we, may contribute something of note to our common human civilization and to the wider stream of humanism. For if we are to contribute worthily, our contribution must also be of the mind and spirit, and not only of sports and plumbing and variety humour. The Anglo-Saxon peoples are, in the mass, neither noted as emotional nor logical. Nevertheless, along with that practical temperament that produces great architects and engineers, they have gifts that have made them second to none as touching the scientists, but also the painters, the poets and the philosophers whom they can boast. The lands of Boyle, Newton, Darwin, Michelson, Edison, Kelvin; of Reynolds, Gainsborough, Constable, Turner and Whistler; of Shakespeare, Milton, Wordsworth, Byron, Shelley, Keats, Longfellow, Whittier, Tennyson, Browning; of Duns, Occam, Bacon, Hobbes, Locke, Berkeley, Hume, Bentham, Mill, James, Dewey and Russell, need fear comparison with none. Nevertheless, at present this notion of a grandeur of Anglo-Saxon culture, not as empty words but as a spiritual reality in which chiefly lies the hope against the servile state, has scarcely yet entered upon the fringe of consciousness of most of our citizens. Within four years, if we are to be saved, it must become a blazing conviction.

It is for us to decide whether this culture and tradition matters . . . and whether we will found our wills on the decision. On the historic record, as record of benefits to human progress conferred, I say it does matter. I would say with some confidence that this is the general opinion among the citizens of the democratic states of Europe. We hear with monotonous reiteration that one-sixth of the human race is under the control of the police system, now nearly twenty years old in sin, of Stalin. It is forgotten that the British Commonwealth has the responsibility for a quarter of the world's area and more than one-quarter of the world's population. I extract the information, however, from an American year-book, and I cannot recall the Englishman who has ever told me this.

That rule may be, and has been, in some places, characterized by an imperialism of which the career of Cecil Rhodes shews the evil as well as the good. It is yet deeply federal, rather than imperial and fascist, in its governing idea. I have yet to learn that the peoples of India prefer federation with Germany or with Russia. If we talk in terms, not of administration, but of culture, if we are to put on one side India, we must add in the American Republic (and its Old Dominion of Virginia), around which the British Dominions shape in a half-moon.

I do not profess to understand the meaning when Victor Hugo said: "England, thou art humanity" (de Madariaga has been no less emphatic in his phrases). But I am confident that this Commonwealth is doing less than its duty if it declines to confront its own responsibilities in leadership, not—like gross Carthage—in wealth and material goods alone, nor in an imperial might that is devoid of idea, but in spirit.

With France, it must be in the forefront in contributing to the enriching of a new epoch of humanism and human decency. To do this, however, it must first *know what it itself stands for* spiritually—not accidentally and incidentally, but against the background of four or more centuries of its own history.

There are those who are so impressed by the totalitarian might of modern Germany, sprung up like a phœnix out of defeat, that they regard these Anglo-Saxon countries and France as already as good as worsted. They would therefore throw up some Maginot line of defence in the first place they can find, and then dig themselves in, in panic disregard of all international equity or of the principles of Wilson which alone justify the Peace settlement.

Others have confidence, no less precipitate, that Germany and Italy—but not Russia—must speedily disrupt from within, and that we have but to circle them thrice, blowing trumpets of Jericho. Both appear to me to be idle opinions. Germany has experienced a mighty revival under a very singular man, a kind of Wagnerian hero, sincere as Lenin was sincere, who once swept snow with blue hands on the streets of Vienna and now is Caesar—a revival incredible ten years ago, although not yet proven to be more successful or beneficial for Germany than that which would have resulted if Stresemann or Brüning had received even a glassful of cold encouragement from the monstrous Poincaré, with his policy of weak strength, or his successors—Poincaré who knifed Briand. In Clemenceau, who used 'peace as a means of waging war,' great Satan was reborn; in the attorney, Poincaré, a mean Beelzebub.

It is not our concern to interfere in that internal régime of Germany save in so far as our own is interfered with. It may happen to be my personal hazarded opinion that that régime may well go the way of those of Sulla and Tiberius and Domitian and Bonaparte, as that of Stalin will go the way of those of Marius and of Marat. These are matters for the auguries of history.

My concern is chiefly, absorbingly, with my own country. Assuredly, a totalitarian organization, German or Muscovite, cannot be met by sixpence extra on the income tax to pay for another battleship, or grocering calculations. Not battleships are wanted but heroes, men of a new mould. This Commonwealth is indeed degenerate unless it can rediscover and make articulate its own soul, as the first step to reshape its life in a fashion equal to the magnitude of the times.

We cannot confront Germany, and scarcely Italy—the modern Roman Empire as it is called, and is—until this is done. We have seen with our own eyes in these few months a mighty portent. An *imperator* in Rome; a placing of hands on the imperial *regalia* in Vienna—we have seen no less than the symbolic and would-be refounding of the Roman Empire, as usual with two emperors. Under the statue of the Emperor Francis II Augustus, Holy Roman Emperor, descendant of Julius and Charlemagne—Francis I of Austria—in the Hofburg in Vienna, runs the inscription—I read it but the other day—"aequus, fortis, justus et pacificus." [1] Will the new empire also be pacific, also bring a Roman peace? I, at least, have no desire to see it built up as an empire of aggressive fascism. That empire—some scheme for Middle Europe—will be built up thanks to the goodwill alone of Great Britain. We may not be able to prevent its initiation: we can ruin its success. Our attitude towards that scheme dominates the situation in Europe and in world politics today.

In deciding upon that attitude we must not presume on our own position or adopt an attitude of elderly selfishness. If the

[1] "Equitable, strong, just and pacific."

British Commonwealth in one aspect is the heir, along with the United States, of a great tradition, the Anglo-Saxon Tradition, in another aspect the British Empire is but one more ramshackle Habsburg Empire of which the Windsors are the Habsburgs and London the Vienna. It is a distant Teutonic legatee of the old Roman Empire. What has our vast Black Empire got to do with Anglo-Saxon culture? What is it more than an administrative and money-making (or money-losing) appanage? What common citizenship, what *ius connubii,* right of inter-marriage, can there be unless we wish to see a race of mulattoes? If we handed over these black colonies to Hitler tomorrow, from the point of view of our *own* nation and culture, it could be argued to be a beneficial and self-advantageous act.

If it were a betrayal of natives, then we must look to our own native policy, whether of 1918 or of today, in some areas. I recall . . . but let it be. . . . It is not ourselves who take chief interest in colonial scientific research or spend most money on African linguistic institutes. Lord Hailey's *African Survey* gives the answer. Let those look who like. What folly indeed to fight about Togoland or Walfisch Bay. . . .

Until international control comes we must, I believe, provisionally administer these lands; there are immense opportunities for native and for European civilization, hitherto undreamed of, in this administration. This Black Empire is a responsibility of trusteeship which we have not yet begun to face; and a liability to our culture and to our souls which we have not yet begun to calculate. Nor can India, with its ancient civilization, ever be part of our culture. Where there is no inter-marriage there is no community. It was the triumph of raceless Roman Imperialism to have recognized that basic fact. India remains with us only and solely in terms of the Federal Idea of which Anglo-Saxony—not Germany: no, nor Russia—

is, for the present epoch, the guardian. The common basis is that of interest alone. Africa also remains with us in justice solely in terms of our idea of trusteeship.

I should not, my dear H. G., be writing this letter to you were it a plea for some new narrow racialism, some new boastful nationalism. True, you coined the phrase, "a Liberal Fascism." Let me change it—for you will agree that 'Liberalism' must be the substance, not, like 'Socialism' in some countries, just the label. I don't like Fascism. Will you accept an improvement—"Liberal Discipline"? Good, then: that liberal discipline or habit of life rests on principles, historical principles, capable of being recognized by us as a people.

I add this, that this Anglo-Saxon culture has been built up by Irishmen and Welshmen as by Englishmen and Scotsmen; and this alike in America and Britain. The mood of the Dutchman in South Africa is too similar to set him apart. Nor, despite deliberate national and religious and even linguistic separatism, do I exclude the French *habitant* in Canada, and the Jew who has long made here his home. Racialism, nationalism, and the thesis that to each nation belongs sovereignty, instead of the thesis that to *no* nation belongs full sovereignty, must disrupt our Commonwealth in a decade as it Balkanized Europe after 1918. The true racialism is biologic and seeks the improvement of the *whole* human species to a better breed. Of that more later. Our nationalism is real but federal. It is one *culture and tradition that unite us;* and loyalty to their principles—yes, let us say, to their ideology—is the test loyalty.

Our tradition—the rendering articulate of that tradition— much more so indeed than the civilization of France, offers hope, and almost alone offers hope, in the world today of the policy of a Middle Way. That policy, and the abhorrence of class war, is good Aristotelianism. But Aristotle has been long dead. And our tradition, which has absorbed so much Aristotelianism, alone offers today a philosophic background for that choice of the middle course. It alone offers a core of resistance to such an armed faith as that of the Reich. The amazing cohesion and success of the Jewish race has been due, through the millennia, not to blood alone but to a well-comprehended tradition obstinately adhered to. Let us take a leaf from the book of this People—a Book of Prophecy and Covenant that has come true. Let us not be guilty of the deep treason of shame of our own tradition. Let us be nationalists, not in terms of square miles on a map, but as the Jews are nationalists, looking to a mission of ideas to the world. In this connection, I would call your attention to the *Civitas Dei* of Lionel Curtis, which, for all its difficulty, seems to me to have much more than flashes of inspiration.

It is not the case that truth or philosophy—even empiric, 'anti-metaphysical' (i.e. anti-dogmatic) philosophy—can be reduced to terms of some national dialect. Truth is not so. But it is true that particular historic traditions have in fact more completely or less completely expressed certain facets of truth. And it is further true that no people can re-achieve belief in itself so long as it abandons its own characteristic ways of thinking and endeavours to think in the fashions set by an alien philosophy woven of an alien experience, worn like borrowed clothes.

Every philosophy of living, even Christianity itself, must be presented, at least in detail, in a texture that is home-spun. Conversely, our own empiric, tolerant and free *tradition,* although, like our *institutions,* it can influence other peoples, can only do so when adapted and made-over to suit their experience. It can guide; it should not regimentate. Of its nature it is *not* a dogma infallible *in fide et moribus.* The influence of English or Anglo-Saxon *policy* must be of precisely the same relative, empiric nature.

§ iii

Marx-Stalinism and Russia

We shall, however, have to ask ourselves whether there is not a dogmatic philosophy—tracing, be it noted, from the opposite school from that of Locke, the father of English liberalism—of materialism, the 'materio-dialectical' interpretation of history, surplus value and inevitable class war, in brief, Marxism, which alone deserves attention and which over-rides all other considerations whatsoever. We shall have to ask ourselves whether this militant atheistic materialism is not—for some eminent men say so—the true Christianity. We shall have to consider whether the true picture of history be not the Magian picture: that of a struggle of Ormuzd and Ahriman, of light and darkness, of Stalin and Hitler, of oppressed and oppressors. Many today have become new primitive religionists, devotees of this mythology. Compared with this battling of the hosts of heaven, which arouses their idealism and fanaticism, nothing else counts. The stars fight in their courses for Materialism and Anti-God, or for the Hooked Cross of the Sun-worshippers. There is a great dichotomy, a final dualism and forceful struggle of titans, until the coming of the classless society and the end of that dialectic movement in history. Messias then will reign.

That is not my reading of history. The Kingdom of Heaven comes slowly and stilly within the hearts of men. There is good reason to deplore the fatalistic and cynic psychology, tracing back from Marx to Hobbes, that is pessimistic about human co-operation and potential reasonableness as operative political factors. The principles announced from the beginning are spread by education and conviction, and take social shape, as widening circles rise to the height of human dignity —or if not to that dignity, then at least to human decency and power, the multiplication of the mechanical instruments of civilization lending external support. It does not, of course, follow that this conviction may not rise to a revolutionary resolution in applying the appropriate pressures upon those who are obstacles to advance.

All Europe today is a gaming-table of Red and Black. Anxiously Marxist and Fascist alike proclaim that there is *no* Third Way. Spaniards, Chinese, Indians later, are to be thrown into the fray. The late Premier of Czechoslovakia, M. Hodza, welcomed Russian aid while imploring with tears that he should not be sent a Russian army to befriend him— odd alliance. Spaniards explain that the true Spain of their loyalties has been destroyed by this warfare of foreigners in their land—Prussian agents and Italian soldiers; and Spain will awake to hate every calculating alien and to massacre them if it dares.

As the *Manchester Guardian's* correspondent, F. A. Voigt, says in his *Unto Caesar:*

"Nothing would suit Russia better than an Anglo-German war. Her conception of the 'indivisible peace' is one that conceals the wish to transfer the potential battlefields of Europe from the East to the West. Germany, even if undefeated, would then be weakened for years to come and Russia would have security in Europe."

If I were a Russian, even as an imperialist I should seek to involve on my side the great Western Powers and to make then on the Western Front—as strategically it would be made —the cockpit of battle and the main theatre of war. If I were a Communist I would try to provoke a protracted war as being the best hope—as Lenin said it was—for a successful Communist revolution in the West. A good decisive war might settle the future of civilization—or, at least, the colour of such civilization as could arise from the wrack. What, then, can be worse than a non-Marxist pseudo-peace?—this bourgeois armistice between wars? If I am a Russian Communist, what will turn me back from these better things?

Since, however, I am not such, I can only comment that the thing at all costs to avoid is a Russian-German understanding against the West—an understanding not utterly impossible, and, at the present moment, the gossip of the Government departments of Washington. I should estimate its probability at a five per cent chance. In some diplomatic quarters it is placed far higher. Russian high military officials have spoken of a great war coming, in which Russia would decline all bourgeois alliances. That, under certain conditions, Stalin should prefer to remain on the side-lines and await the exhaustion of the combatants, is intelligible. If the Western Powers, in Palmerstonian fashion, will defend their territories, he will defend his—and his régime—until *his* time comes, either to receive German thanks or to march across a world devastated to build his new world.

It is necessary to be clear, then, that we do not mean merely the defence of our every outlying territory, and our own territories alone, by one of the Anglo-Saxon Powers, or the protection of citizens' pockets, and that alone, by the other. Minds have got to be made up, on both sides of the Atlantic, whether one is protecting 'interests' or *that* interest and *that* principle which is the right to the democratic way of living within one's own borders and within lands essential to one's own powers. Confusion here has produced endless misunderstanding, not least in the American Press and in British interpretation of that Press.

There are, then, three objects of Anglo-Saxon policy: (i) to prevent war at all; (ii) to see that, if war comes, it is fought successfully; (iii) to establish a system that will guarantee the rule of law between states and of liberty among persons. Our task is—to adapt Stalin's words—to maintain, fortify and develop at least one democracy.

For the sake, indeed, of the genuine advance of the common man, for that united front, I would be prepared to tolerate even international schemings and brewings of the broth of strife. The notion of the rising of the oppressed peoples of the world is one that stirs me, as I suppose, my dear H. G., it stirs you too. Is there not a pathos and a tragedy in those who looked to see the long light of liberty streaming over the world from Russia, as the sun of justice arose? Such a rising, however, of those kept under, must be intelligently led, unless it is to end in chaos, in a blood-bath of revenge and in the mud of self-seeking. How, then, will Marxism and a Marxist revolution succeed in Britain or in America?

Let us imagine the underpaid cobbler; the unemployed man whose wife is trying to bring up a family on the means test; the Irish navvy who sleeps with four others in some rat-infested basement bedroom; the artisan dismissed at fifty because of some crisis on the other side of the Atlantic. Is it enough, my dear Wells, that they should ally themselves with Mr. Victor Gollancz, the publisher, and with Mr. John Strachey, late of Eton, and with other proletarians of the hereditary ruling class? Or with the intellectuals of New York? It is not enough. Nor will I bleed England to replace our ruling class, called lords, by another, with scorpions of Rehoboam, called commissars.

What prospects, then, of success, have the Marxists? That in these Anglo-Saxon countries some peaceful means may be adequate is a thesis explicitly and in so many words repudiated with contempt by Lenin himself.

Lenin, also, it is, who explains to us the conditions of success. These are: (*a*) the existence of a revolutionary class—we have it; (*b*) the revolutionary pressure of the masses—granted rising unemployment we may have it; and (*c*) the moment when "the activity of the vanguard of the people is greater, when the fluctuations among the enemy and among the weak and indecisive friends of the revolution are strongest." Further, "no great revolution has happened, or can happen, without the disorganization of the army" or an 'anti-patriotic' government.

These are days of international crisis and menace of war. Let us translate these conditions into other words. The concrete conditions of Marxist success *here* are (as in Russia in 1917) an international war in which this country is involved; which war is protracted and unvictorious; in which, consequently, there is revolutionary discontent even in the national army; and in which, consequently, revolution is possible at the price of defeat and of a Brest-Litovsk peace. These are the conditions. Let us note them. These conditions mean, further, either international stalemate, exhaustion and chaos and international revolution, favourable to Russia, or they mean German Fascist victory. Just as Tukhachevski is alleged to have been betrayed by the Germans to Stalin because the Germans preferred Stalin and the terror in Russia, so Germany might well prefer, *for the time being,* Marxist revolution, anarchy and material breakdown in Britain and the breaking up of the Commonwealth. After that, attention would be turned to immigrant minorities in America, disaffected or capable of being made so; or to Latin discontent. Those are the concrete conditions. To aid in the fulfilment of these conditions I decline utterly and finally to set my hand. I would ask all who contemplate them, often well-intentioned persons, very sincerely to consider what is involved in such a new Lenin-Zimmerwaldian policy. Decisively I do not regard it as the sole path of social justice.

On the contrary, if war comes, its length must in large part depend upon the attitude of the German people to the régime. The common people of Germany, in the days of free voting, tried Marxism and rejected it. If it would enable them to contrive the overthrow of a hated Britain and France, along (if fate left no choice) with their own country, they might, as a last throw, adopt Marxism. Otherwise not. But the German people never had a quarrel with the principles of Wilson; but only with their non-enforcement. The American people has, then, got to make up its mind, and decisively, what prescription it will prescribe for Germany—and for itself. For it is the American people that will probably be called upon to make the determinant choice.

Of all corruptions the worst is that which brings the best into disgrace, which dishonours liberty, democracy, equality and justice for the common man. I am free to admit that Stalin's terror sticks in my gorge as much as Streicher's pogroms. Both are affronts to civilized living.

The Communist Party member undertakes to abide by his Party rules. Among the rules is to be found this: "The Communist Party of Great Britain is a section of the Communist International and is bound by its decisions." I need not explain who does control the Communist International. What was the comment of Marx, as a German, on the International, in the days of its first incarnation? "It would be sheer folly, we might almost say it would be an outright crime, to allow that central hold to fall purely into English hands. . . . England cannot be treated simply as one country among a number of other countries. She must be treated as the metropolis of capitalism."

I will not pledge away the liberty of the country to the Moscow Foreign Office. I well recall being told by a departmental chief in the Russian Foreign Office, that there they believed in Collective Security, "but realistically . . . the armies must march." When I questioned whether British public opinion would approve, the comrade said: "Is that a matter for public opinion? Is it not a matter for Governments?"

Shall we hold our tongues about what we see or hear of Russia? No.

Shall we, then, do anything for the worker and the common man—for those who, some of them, had such high hopes of that red dawn? Yes. What, then, do we choose to do to shew that our ideals and talk of liberty and democracy are not *mere* ideals and fine talk, but are actual and resolute intentions? To the discussion of that we will return.

If one chief achievement of Marxism on the record has been to produce Fascism in most of the major countries of Europe, that does not mean that Russia has not provided an experiment that, not in some points but many, has got to be imitated. Even Mussolini has seen that. If war comes in Europe, after war, beyond peradventure of a doubt, will come Revolution in at least the losing, and maybe in all, countries. That is the prime fact. (Whether that Revolution will end as Marxist or Fascist it is premature to say.) The capitalists and employers will be very fortunate if they come through such a decade with their heads on their shoulders, let alone with their money in their banks. Collectivism, whether in Russia or in Germany, has shewn that it can initiate as well as capitalism. The admirable increase of *material production* in Russia after the corruption of the Czardom—an industrial production increased sevenfold—is so amazing that it has no parallel of development save in the individualist opening up of the Middle West of America. On the other hand, the standard of living of the *industrial worker,* intolerably low to begin with, has only doubled, and that of the agricultural worker has not increased so much.

The collectivist experiment of Russia has succeeded best—and brilliantly—where capitalism has succeeded best—in material production—and worst where its leaders claimed most. Nevertheless the experiment commands allegiance. It sets the pace of reform for the world. And those who will not have the wit to reform and guarantee from their riches security for the worker such as he has in Russia (however regimented; however poor the rate) will be superseded, possibly painlessly, probably painfully. It may be to accomplish that change by reform is the work of genius; but the genius must be there or we turn the page of our land's history. Let us repeat, a miracle of St. Januarius has got to take place with our society so that its customs liquefy and flow. In the alternative, reform will be forgotten before the onrush of Revolution. The issue of Revolution is never a simple one: it is a question of the proportion between the number of people contented and the number of them discontented.

Russia, on the chess-board of politics, is a great Power, and one of the greatest. The correct way to regard Russia is precisely as such. There is no spiritual kinship between Bolshevism and the Anglo-Saxon Tradition. There is no moral compulsion to alliance. That Tradition, however, is no doctrine to be forcibly injected into the political system of other countries. If the rulers of Russia choose to regard it with contempt, and to prefer factories regimented by loud-speakers, it may be their peoples' loss . . . and that is all that remains to be said. Conversely, Marxism has not been so successful in Russia in raising the condition of the worker to the Western level that alliance with Russia *necessarily* involves Marxist revolution throughout Europe and America, granted war conditions, within a decade. . . . That revolution is, of course, the Marxist hope; but its achievement is conditioned by belief in our own distinctive ideals; the compulsory removal of selfish and obscurantist obstructions to reform before it is 'too late'; and our own resolution.

Military alliance with Russia is a matter solely of convenience and interest, save so far as common action, of a reliable quality, is possible—without presuming universal civil war—to build the peace of the world. If Germany moves East, according to the plan in *Mein Kampf,* and Russia fails in her policy of seeing that the Western Powers become involved in war *first* and *before* she herself becomes involved, then Russia is the main object marked out for attack and she requires *our* co-operation, on our terms—not we, hers. An attitude of celestial detachment, with folded arms, would be hastily abandoned. This is true even although I believe her to be, as in the days of Napoleon, almost impregnable in defence unless (which is the German calculation) there is a revolt in the Ukraine so soon as the common folk, as distinct from the Red Army, have arms.

If Germany, abandoning her immediate territorial hopes or confronted with unexpected resistance or recognizing impregnability in the East, moves West, then a Russian military alliance may become necessary for the Western Powers as well as an alliance with the Little Entente group. Which Germany will in fact do will depend, if she determines upon war, upon the height of the barriers of resistance that she will meet from the one side or the other—it is an issue of strategic opportunism.

A pact with Russia should be welcomed in the West (i) if it is part of a system open to all to join; (ii) if it binds Russia in the East to action as immediate—not mere supplementary action—as Britain and France are bound to it in the West; (iii) if it does not commit Britain to send conscripts to war on some issue conveniently picked by Russia to involve the West; (iv) if it does not produce an intransigent resistance to all change in the *status quo* and all revision, for the benefit at least of a liberal Germany, of the Treaty of Versailles. If Stalin refuses this, then defences must be raised so high in the West that Germany will turn aside to consider other plans. But I see no reason why Stalin should not be approached with the same good faith (perhaps all too trusting) as was shown to Germany at Berchtesgaden, if not to the Czechs at Munich. It is merely necessary to recall in these dealings what we must suppose, as an honourable Marxist, are Stalin's own principles of policy—just as Herr Hitler is an honourable Nazi.

Profoundly as I agree with Mr. Sinclair Lewis that the secret of political wisdom is that human nature does not change, I am not prepared to go so far as he is in his further recent remark that "the Stalinists" are "the greatest enemies of socialism that would interfere with their autocracy." I give credit to some officials in the Kremlin for wishing to see a World Socialist Soviet Republic at some convenient future time.

I will go further by saying that, if the bourgeois powers, challenged by renascent world Caesarism, are too flaccid or too jealous to establish a Sovereign League without civil war, then I wish good fortune to Joseph Stalin when, calling on the apocalyptic horses of war, famine and plague, he rides westward to establish that League. For the present, however, I retain faith, if we can but establish an escalator downwards for dead men still walking, that we can construct, without war foreign or civil, a new world picture and a pacified Europe in which even the great and courageous German people, with or without the régime, will also find a just and contributory place. Such hopes are perhaps Anglo-Saxon sentiment, but they remain, not unlinked with power, the best guarantees in peace or war of a clear conscience and of a duty performed by what is more than nations—civilization.

Whether Germany will choose war and thus play the Leninist game of sending up Europe in flames, with Russia on the side-lines, remains to be seen. It depends upon the visions and ambitions of the Führer; upon the willingness of the German Government to indicate clearly that it will be satisfied with economic breathing space in the South-East, which expansion it can obtain; and upon the willingness of Germany, turning around on its course since it quit the Disarmament Conference and the League, to collaborate in building a new world of organized peace. If a Russian alliance is forged, Germany, by the old 'too-clever' diplomacy, by fear of *Macht-politik,* will have forged it. She must give her concrete guarantees.

§ iv

Germany

The Germans are a civilized people. They are more—they are middle-Europeans, not Eur-Asiatics, suspended between the civilizations of China and Europe. Nevertheless, their concentration camps at Dachau and Buchenwald are a scandal to civilization such as puts in countenance again the Dark Ages. It makes Edward I of England, expelling the Jews, a monument of progressiveness in his administrative methods. It is true that the Jews and the opponents of the régime have been treated better than the middling farmers of Russia and as well as the Russian Baptists. It is no excuse: the Germans are not Russians, but the countrymen of Goethe and Kant.

(Or are we to remember his ancestors, and call Kant a Scotsman?) The British in India, in Ireland, in Africa, have been very far from blameless: there are many things, not at all pretty, that stain the record. But it is not the British who are judging Germany, but civilization that is judging us both.

The National Socialists have the excuse, beloved of certain intellectuals of the British Marxist faction, that "no omelettes can be made without breaking eggs." Röhm and Matteotti and Rathenau and a hundred others, it is said, are small sacrifices for the ends of national restoration, unity and advance. The Jews are aliens with whom Germany is at war, and can be asked to leave the country like any other alien nationals in time of war, or be put in concentration camps. That is the argument. It does not cover the case; enemy prisoners of war are not (or one hopes are not) treated so.[1] The malignancies, great and petty, in the treatment of minorities is something that one condemns, as in Russia so in Germany—and more in Germany than in Russia because the world expects more of Germany.

The persecution is alleged to be pursued in the name of national unity and of the Fascist revolution. A measure of tyranny, it is said, is necessary for revolution. Lenin himself said: "Nothing is more authoritarian than revolution." What this revolution is, socially, is still uncertain. Krupp von Böhlen, Siemens, Thyssen and the like remain in the Supreme Economic Advisory Council, and the old names recur among the governors of Italy. Has there, then, been any transfer of power—or transfer of benefits? The test lies in the condition of the common man.

---

[1] Condemnation of the treatment of Boer prisoners of over forty years ago will naturally have more weight when emanating from the Premier of the Union of South Africa or his colleagues than from Berlin. Ground for indignation there doubtless was and is: the reparation was not unhandsome.

One notes exhortations to him to tighten his belt. But this, we are told, is for the sake of the great national effort. Above all nations is humanity. The issue is whether the sacrifice be for national military glory—or, as with Bonaparte, just for military glory—or whether it be for the good of the common German, or the common man, physical and spiritual, in the sequence of the generations. With all allowance for the admirable system of family endowment and for the real achievements in health and medicine of modern Germany, as also in transport and building and such bricks and mortar, the answer is not yet clear. The intention towards the upward drive of the average level, if not the absolute performance, is clearer in Russia, pitifully low although its level is and wide though the divisions be in the rewards for different grades of employment. At least Russia is not, like the West, the land of the millionaire.

Will Germany not be such a land? Perhaps, with our millionaires of inheritance not service, it is not for us to ask. One notes, however, Mr. Keynes's definition of the German economy as 'armaments finance capitalism.' The sacrifice of the worker, in common happiness, for armaments is no greater than in Russia. But the distribution of the profits is not quite the same. In Russia we ask: Is this indeed the classless, free society? In Germany we ask: Is this indeed the common good put before private acquisition? We have to see.

It is within the meaning of our Anglo-Saxon Tradition that we utterly repudiate Totalitarianism, Red or Brown or Black, root and branch. We do so for ourselves; but we believe that in voicing this philosophy we voice something in humankind, wherever it is found. A Roman totalitarianism founded on the divine emperor is repugnant. But a Roman universal totalitarianism which is yet founded on one dominant race or nation is insufferable. German race-theory, however, places (at least the Führer himself has said so) a close limit on German imperialism. It may yet be the lesson of history that expansive nationalism, political ambition, imperialism, always in the long run take precedence, at least with Great Powers, over mere ideologies, however fanatical. If this be true, then our argument is but reinforced that Communism and Fascism are to be watched as but the cat's paws of Foreign Offices, adverse to our realm and state.

Let, however, the *advocatus diaboli,* "the devil's advocate," speak:

The Roman Reich, of the German People, he may say, has been refounded before our eyes. The Roman Empire is in process of being refounded. To this, as a commonwealth and as an Atlantic civilization, an Anglo-Saxon world, we have got to decide our own relation.

Will it be a crime crying out in history if we (like the Papal States against United Italy) obstruct the building of this unified Europe again? Briand's scheme of a United States of Europe was either impotent to come to birth or was aborted by the evil genius of our generation, Poincaré. Have we here, in the Reich, a reality, backed by executive power—instead, it may be said, of the maxims of Geneva, with the vain mendacities of its assembled statesmen, decorous as the devil when they go to church, never abating their national sovereignties? If Geneva cannot be midwife to a United Europe, why should not the Reich try?

Do we wish World-Peace or not? If we do, must it not be organized? Does this not require a World-State? If so, can Geneva any longer be believed capable of compelling such a State to come into being? Is there not a moral categorical imperative to rebuild the Roman Empire? Is not the independence of little sovereign states a fundamental evil and another name for international anarchy? If so, why do we

oppose this compulsory unification of Middle Europe, save
from imperialist jealousy?

Here at least are deeds, and centralization, not words and
covert fomenting of jealousies. *Heil Duce, heil Führer: Asse
Roma-Berlin*. The two Emperors not only reign but rule. The
map of the old world-empire set up in the Roman Forum
comes concretely nearer to realization. What shall we do
about it?

What is the conclusion of the argument? Should we, then,
look with favour on the establishment of this German-con-
trolled Mittel-Europa, the growth of this new Roman Empire?

Should we invoke against it, as some selfish stepmother to
the new Europe, the doctrine of the Balance of Power? Or,
patching the old with new clouts, speak of the Balance of
Power and Collective Security? Was not the Balance of Power
designed rather, for our own selfish peace, to keep us out of
Europe, unentangled, and not because war is 'indivisible'?
Must we for ever be building up new alliances against a unification of Europe? Would it not have been far better for
mankind had Napoleon succeeded? Were not our campaigns
against him a vast mistake, encouraging the new evil nationalism, the new anti-international tribalism?

This picture, however, of a new Roman Empire as a serious
attempt to make a United States of Europe is too simple. The
account of Bonaparte is too simple. The Germans, as they
penetrate down the Danube, will have to decide whether they
will follow the raceless Roman idea or whether they will follow *Rassen-theorie*. Will they follow the Roman idea of a
state based on Law, or is there a mere cult of Power? At
present Herr Hitler appears to use an argument, shaped like
Cardinal Morton's famous Fork, of which the two prongs
are 'self-determination' and 'the overriding interests of security'—against the Poles in Danzig 'self-determination' and

against the Czechs military 'security'. He must be careful lest the only permanent element in the argument is not that "Germans are always right." The arguments of force and of equity make ill partners unless the force is that of a recognized court and judge.

Herr Hermann Rauschning, in his book, *Die Revolution des Nihilismus,* maintains the theme that National Socialism is a version of Bolshevism; even a power cult, not for a class through class-war, but for power's own sake through war in disregard of any restraining rational scheme; a national abandonment to the revolutionary tempo for its own sake. "Nothing gives ground to suppose that Politics and Understanding have anything to do with each other . . . [Hitler] will and must work out his revolutionary Temperament which spells the destruction of the old order. There is a drive to domination." This is a partial and suspect interpretation which ignores a more respectable heritage for National Socialism, coming from Fichte, from Bergson and even from Nietzsche, as Bolshevism has its own respectable heritage through Marx from Spinoza and Hegel. But it is, nevertheless, a possible index of practical action which can only be disavowed by the record of events and by the energy of Germans themselves who recall the great classic heritage of the *Kaiserzeit* and of German Humanism as well as the Gothic-Romantic heritage of Wagnerism (with Parsifal left out) and of *Sturm and Drang.*

Sir Archibald Sinclair says that *Mein Kampf* has "never let him down." His judgement is right. And *Mein Kampf* makes it plain that Germany looks for territorial expansion to the East, not the West. That policy may shift from year to year or month to month, according to diplomatic opportunity. The tactics may change. The strategy will remain constant. As Germany presses East, her troubles will not diminish. On the contrary, like those of Austria-Hungary, they will increase.

She will consolidate the divided Slavs against herself, even in the act of 'emancipating' them. Her race-theory must do this and commit suicide by very success.

Nevertheless, will she still not be powerful enough to dominate the West? That depends upon ourselves. . . . It is for Germany to decide whether she will challenge a decision in the East; whether she will find it *too costly to challenge one in the West is for ourselves.* Which Germany will do, I can only suppose, will be a matter of tactical calculation.

If there is to be another Migration of the Nations, it is our concern that it does not move West. If there is power in the world to establish a reign of law on the basis of a World-State, it must start with a modicum of cultural homogeneity, and it is for us to take the initiative, thanks to our own integrated strength, towards establishing a sovereign assembly of free nations.

And why not have a war today to prevent a war tomorrow? Or why? *Cui bono? Qui tertius gaudens?* Who will pick the chestnuts from the flames of Western Civilization?

If the Germans pursue the course of stressing race privilege, then the further South-East they go, the greater will inevitably become their difficulties with all the Slavs. The difficulties that brought down the old Austro-Hungarian Empire will be nothing compared with it. It is enough, then, for prudent statesmen to consult their own strength and then to wait. If, however, the Germans put first the advantages of economic imperialism, then they must compromise; the fire of the old fanaticism will abate; the only question becomes whether we can contemplate with patience a world constituted of three great blocs, the Russo-Chinese, the Anglo-Atlantic and the Middle-European, of which the last will also be the least. I am more concerned to develop an Atlantic civilization with command of the sea and effective parity in the air than to answer this question in the negative. If we are impotent to create the second, the Anglo-Atlantic integration, I am not sure that we are competent to prevent the third, Middle-European control by the Reich. And such an Anglo-American integration is alone homogeneous and powerful enough to act as an effective lever in compelling the establishment of a World-State.

German expansion down the Danube is inevitable. Here are her natural markets, the hope of her common folk and their living. Here is her *Lebensraum*. As M. Bergéry explains, in his paper *La Flêche,* in France: some safety-valve for Germany must be left. (He was a Communist, and was in London in connection with the Dimitrov anti-Nazi counter-trial: but in France they have the habit of seeing clearly.) It may not be an expansion under the flag. It may be enough if it is economic.

The opposite policy, repudiating 'a-peacement,' overshooting the words of the *Daily Worker* that "appeasement threatens peace," must alienate even the German or Italian common people, who will grasp that it is *they,* in their numbers and central position, *not* their Government, who are regarded with jealousy as a European menace to be crushed back and bound down. Sound policy here must be adequately generous to a great people; absolutely firm with their rulers; inspired by an energetic spirit of justice; backed by an overwhelming strength. The strength is there. The task is to organize it.

Let us look at the matter in another perspective. Let us first distinguish the German people from the present German Government. The German people is entitled to expansion of its markets in the Danube basin. That is natural and should not be checked by French and British finance. While that economic policy is admitted, which allows Germany economic *Lebensraum,* there can be no serious question of encirclement.

The South-East is the German sphere of influence. Further, the maintenance of democracy does not involve, as I stated some years ago, the encouragement of Poland and Rumania, which are certainly not democracies in the everyday sense, in a blunt refusal to discuss issues of trade and minorities. Merely such discussion must take place within the framework of peaceful negotiation and of respect for Polish and Rumanian independence, pending some voluntary scheme of European federation.

The tragedy of modern Europe is that the Weimar Republic was not supported by the Entente statesmen and that no German Talleyrand was invited to Versailles. The responsibility lies squarely on the shoulders of Clemenceau and Bertholet, who rejected Fleuriau's suggestion that the Germans should be present. The mood of Clemenceau and Bertholet has got to be fought even at this present day.

(Above all, if there is war, this mood has got to be fought at the Peace Treaty, unless it is to be a Great War to begin yet a Greater War. My personal belief, however, is that the Peace would be engulfed in general Revolution, of which the chief issue would be the destruction of all national sovereignties in favour of Soviets, Caesardom or Federation.)

The German people, however, is actually represented by the German Government. Here the first issue is whether it wills peace—and that can only be judged from its conduct. Germans deny to me, as being anti-German propaganda, either that the Führer has Napoleonic ambitions or that the German people aspire to impose themselves upon the rest of the world as a superior race. They further tell me that Germany has no primary ambitions as touching colonies overseas. The test again is the practical one of conduct. Does economic expansion down the Danube satisfy Germany? If so, it may be feasible. Will

Germany give an *immediate gesture* of willingness to return to conference—a Five-Power Conference with American initiative?

As the issues between Germany and Western Europe are primarily psychological and economic, will the German Government respond to Chamberlain's statements about a conference by a speedy reply that will instantly lower the psychological tension? Will she exchange persons, books, broadcasts that will prepare the way for understanding, before the momentum of the war-machine becomes too great? As I told friends in Berlin, in 1934, Germany, I believe, made a fatal mistake in 'walking out,' not only from the Disarmament Conference but also from the League. Can the retracing of these steps be regarded as a goal? Amid many utterances of another nature, the Italian Dictator has declared—and indeed truly enough—that, in the interests of European civilization, a protracted period of peace is required. Will the German and Italian Dictators practically collaborate in steps for that end? Or are the Western Democracies to be put in a position where it becomes politically impossible for them to make any accommodation whatsoever without their action being construed as a symptom of weakness and decadence?

The prime task is to outline, before war breaks, the objects of peace in order that by that very action war may be prevented now—and, if not, that the war-obsessed may be ousted from control at the Peace by a scheme clearly laid down and with determination pursued. Before the war, let us have the Peace Conference.

If that scheme involves not only the satisfaction of the equitable demands of states including Germany, but the union of states, then we have to take our choice between a Caesarian and a Federal unification. The philosophy of the Western Democracies commits them to the second plan. That decides their relation to the smaller Powers. But it places upon them the obligation to favour and produce that unification as effectively as was done in the Roman Empire by Caesarian methods. Without unification, there can be no true Court; no law properly so called; and (as Kant shewed long ago) no justice.

Patent and admitted injustices in the *status quo* must be adjusted—errors of settlement which every man in his calmer moments knows and admits to be errors of settlement. Those members of the British Labour Party who produced, in 1923, the official manifesto of root and branch condemnation of the French occupation of the Ruhr, in that year, have much to be proud of. Some relics of the old temper, in obstructive financial interests, remain still. Either readjustments must come by discussion and pressure on those Powers who accumulated ill-gotten gains by the inclusion of minorities, or readjustment will be settled, at the cost of civilization itself, by world war to decide the fate of some area the common man has perhaps never heard of. Further, and concretely, Germany can expect economic breathing space in Yugoslavia and South-Eastern Europe. Some of these South-Eastern Powers, so responsible for the catastrophe of 1914, seem almost to welcome this future. Germany can aspire to a federal system there. It can *not* be suffered to propose the marching of its troops into capital after capital, with its legacy of accumulated hate.

The categorical imperative is peace. It is that for Germany as for Anglo-Saxony. That imperative spells the *organization* of peace so that he who breaks it will surely lose by armed might. It involves the will to arbitrate, as also (this is noteworthy) the will to equity. Equity itself, however, is *subordinate* to acceptance of due process of arbitration. It has been accepted for a millennium in domestic law that he who will not submit to a court has no case in equity. States are not

here different from individuals. To deny this is to maintain anarchy. If a new Roman Empire to keep peace is to
be established, it will not be established so. A World-State
is inevitable, and the end of sixty-odd sovereignties—but not
such a World-State as is a Caesarian despotism.

The question is simple: whether, following the Chamberlain gesture and request for a counter-gesture, Germany is
prepared to accept the principle of coming into conference,
or whether Germany is not, here and now, prepared—while
the situation still depends upon psychological factors of confidence and while the good will to peace, indubitably and
pathetically, still holds among common folk—to make that
gesture.

It would be a pity were the dreams of Herr Hitler of good
for his people to be, like those of Napoleon, left to be mere
dreams to be idly written down after war, slaughter, defeat
and exile. Let Herr Hitler settle in conference, before war,
the Peace terms and, as Napoleon did not, in conference make
in time his bargains with Fate. So perhaps his name will be
remembered among his own people for good. No one will
deny him, any more than Lenin, the name of patriot. No
one will forget the justification of his cause that he found in
the humiliation of his people—if maybe not the justification
for his humiliation of other peoples. Under the cloud of war
few statesmen will be suffered, by their peoples, to play the
cattle-dealer on Germany or to defraud her of her place. Will
Herr Hitler not recall the spirit of Thoiry? Which is it to be:
conciliation or the faithless Frederickian policy that waits for
its moment to dart—and then gets caught in a net? A *Macht-
philosophie* has no justification save success: it will deserve and
will receive no sympathy. There is so much to be done for
civilization within the confines of peace; nor can war do
other, even were the Führer victorious, than wreck the forces

of his great people and expose them to the enmity of more populous lands. In war are no final victories. Will he not consider this before the finger of history has written on?

§ v

Anglo-Saxony

The Anglo-Saxon idea is federal, not totalitarian. If the Roman Empire or United States of Europe is to be constituted or reconstituted, it must come to terms with that idea. Basically we *cannot* on principle give up the idea of Wilson, the idea of Geneva. That remains. Germany, because of her peculiar totalitarian race-theory, cannot—even from the Vienna Hofburg—rebuild a centralized Roman Empire. In theory, because of her racialism, she must recognize the formal autonomy, political and cultural, of other races and nationalities. She will be expected in practice to recognize the actual sovereign independence and cultural autonomy, if not economic sufficiency, of these countries. The fear, nevertheless, will not abate among them that, hastily swallowing her theories, some new Bismarck will destroy this autonomy of theirs and that 'racialism' will become merely the new and more assertive imperialism of a 'superior race.'

The nature of German policy, facing both ways, makes a political formation inevitable in which half Europe—its small countries—must look to Britain, as outside Europe and without ambitions territorial or military, to uphold with them, until the day of its final realization, *the Federal idea*. Here, and here alone, is Britain's natural function on the continent of Europe, between the Channel and the Vistula, save that she also must act as guarantor of the Rhine alike to Germany and France.

I put above the basic query: "Can Anglo-Saxony achieve

any adequate vision of herself?" What is called 'bourgeois democracy' is taxed by both Marxism and Fascism with one fatal flaw: it is alleged that it lacks both courage and imagination. Have we, in fact, either? Either our minds have got to stand still, content with the idea of sixty-odd sovereign states—final for ever, like the Nine Muses and the Seven Lamps of Architecture—and as chaotic as the three hundred odd states of Mediaeval Germany. Either, that is, our minds have got to abandon all attempt to take the international idea and the organization of peace seriously. Or we must acquire courage and vision; liquidate the cake of custom; and contemplate quite new political formations. The goal—reversing Austin Chamberlain's phrase about "a free assembly of sovereign nations"—must be "a sovereign assembly of free nations." Or, to use the phrase of a German friend still resident in Germany: "One Big Government." We must abolish the unanimity rule which wrecked, first, the old Polish Constitution and, then, the Geneva League. We may have to contemplate also direct taxation. With this framework I do not regard even an International Air Force as impossible. There have been successful multi-national professional armies in the past. Sovereignty must, however, clearly inhere in this League. That is the kernel of the matter.

This Sovereign Supra-National Federation, from China to Peru, cannot be achieved at one step, however. An adequate common culture and moral consensus are still lacking. We must proceed where there is power, step by step and regionally. If regional fusion is impracticable, *a fortiori* world-wide federation, as more than a sham, is impracticable. That regional fusion cannot expect in the first case to surmount profound cultural barriers. That places a limit to what can be done between Anglo-Saxony and Latin America.

I wonder whether you have read Lionel Curtis's *Civitas*

Dei? If you have, I expect that you have put it on one side, all three volumes, on the ground that it puts forward the kind of idea of a British Commonwealth that led you astray when you were younger, but which you have now abandoned for a wider humanism. Certainly I do not go with Lionel Curtis all the way—do not profess fully to understand him. The notion, however, is admirable indeed of taking the World-State seriously and of asking small nations to join up. Curtis says, New Zealand and Australia to begin. I suppose Curtis knows the New Zealanders better than I do. I have heard some things. . . . But Iceland and Scotland? The Icelanders like the idea at this moment, and maybe the Danes won't object. And would Denmark join up itself? And if there were a chance that Britain would join America (will Canada object? . . .) I'd favour it tomorrow.

Let us be plain. I happen to be a patriotic Englishman, sentimentally attached to England. England, however, is a political unit, extinct, as sovereign, for these two centuries. We are ruled by Scotsmen or Welshmen. I am driven on, then, to a wider allegiance beyond my sentimental one. It is a matter of free choice to me whether my sentimental attachment is to Great Britain or to the British Commonwealth or to what, following a good usage, I will call Anglo-Saxony.[1] Were I a Virginian or Nova Scotian I should be in the same case.

We need not look back upon Rhodes' idea to grasp the fact that this federation would assure absolutely the peace of the world. We live in days when nothing is impossible—when Sir Robert Borden has stated that, in the event of war, Canada may become the centre of the British Empire. You

---

[1] Writers, and not least French writers such as André Siegfried, have for long used the adjective 'Anglo-Saxon.' The noun was coined some years ago by Mr. Wyndham Lewis.

yourself have pleaded in Australia that the function of that
land is to bring Britain and the United States together—
shall we say to re-unite into some kind of Atlantic-Pacific
Verein or association (perhaps like the old *Nord-deutsche
Verein*) England and America? It is not impossible to conceive of the forty-eight states of America, including the Com-
monwealths of Pennsylvania and Massachusetts and Kentucky
and the Old Dominion of Virginia, entering into political
confederation with the thirty-odd units, states and provinces
of the British Commonwealth and so undoing Lord North's
evil work. The Commonwealth is a lax confederacy as it is.
The confederacy can be extended, and the Irish of Ireland
and Massachusetts, the Dutch of South Africa and Pennsylvania, not to speak of the English and Scots, can be re-
united. We must think ourselves back to the times and problems of the Articles of Confederation of the United States,
not to speak of those of Madison and Jay.[1]

[1] Since the above was written, my attention has been called to the brilliant book of Mr. Clarence K. Streit, American and correspondent of the
New York Times, entitled *Union Now* (1939). At the time of writing I had
not heard of it, although we owe a common debt to Mr. Lionel Curtis, and
at the present (March 1939) my knowledge is derived from the favourable
comment of Mr. Edgar Mowrer, the well-known American correspondent.
Mr. Streit's proposal is for a 'North Atlantic Confederation,' which would
include not only the United States and Great Britain in a 'union now,' but
also France and various smaller countries. Mr. Streit, in the words of a
certain New York hostess, sees no reason "why all you small countries
do not join up . . ." (In brief, the Briand-Coudenhove proposal.) He stresses,
as I understand it, that nothing less than unions of peoples—instead of the
Genevan federation of *states*—would be adequate and effective. Although
my approach has been from the angle of tradition and culture and of the
imponderables, whereas Mr. Streit's is from that of precise political organization, I am in the profoundest and most cordial sympathy with his plan.
From my personal knowledge it has been well received in America—and,
indeed, obviously the objections must come from the European side. My only
comment would be that Mr. Streit by proposing (very properly in the name
of internationalism) to straddle in his union several disparate cultures—
including so marked a one as the French—rather, I submit, sketches the
second than the first stage of a movement driven forward by the great

There are practical difficulties. Of course there are. There is, however, in all practical affairs, a time to discuss difficulties and a time to ignore them and rather to ascertain what it is that men *wish*. Thereby the dynamic flames are released that melt difficulties away. If Adolf Hitler in 1922 had sat down to discuss with all and sundry, as a matter of 'common sense,' the 'difficulties' in the way of being Reichschancellor or of the *Anschluss* of Germany and Austria, he would never have left the tables of a Bavarian beer-house. If Lenin had adopted the same tactic, as touching the Russian Revolution, he would have ended his days in jail. It may be that the "bourgeois" lack both courage and imagination, but there is no reason why it should be said of Anglo-Saxons as a people. Instead, therefore, of *talking* about internationalism and the World-State, let us take the first steps towards actually building it up in a fashion that shall be irrevocable. Such action alone ends the division between "us" and "them." Or shall we wait for the Union of World Soviet Republics to do it for us?

By this I do not mean at all that I wish—and this I hope I have made plain—America to follow British policy. I wish British policy to be more like American in its European scheme. That is perhaps a thing difficult for England and Scotland, but almost too easy for the British Commonwealth. If England involuntarily and geographically has concerns in Europe, the United States has like concerns in Latin America. These facts must be taken into account. But stock and culture matter more, in a world of changing communications,

---

historic forces of hope and interest. (Anyone in sympathy with my proposal, outlined in the text, should communicate with me, care of the publisher, Messrs. The Macmillan Company, 60 Fifth Avenue, New York City.) At the lowest, Mr. Streit's scheme might eliminate—and its economic possibilities seem to me most helpful—the disastrous Anglo-American trade rivalry in Latin America.

than geography. The British Empire itself was certainly not brought together by necessities of geography. The airplane brings Europe nearer to America—all too near to South America. The Monroe Doctrine, enunciated to "keep peace in a hemisphere"—Jefferson's words to Monroe—must be re-adapted to the new situation. The future centre of gravity of Anglo-Saxony, however, culturally and geographically, lies outside Europe.

I am indeed so little a propagandist seeking to persuade America into commitments, that I am less an interventionist than most American citizens—whose fingers itch to fire the British naval guns. Ardent anti-Nazis must complain against the pace set by the Middle West. I cannot fight for America to the last British child until I know whether American ideas go beyond food ships. The American must know what democratic values he is fighting for as well as that, if the British Commonwealth is demolished, the turn of control in Latin America comes next. I will go towards mixing in European affairs as quick as that pace of the West permits—which, mark you, is getting quicker. Of that, the statement on the 22nd December 1938 by Senator Pittman, of Nevada, Chairman of the Senate Foreign Relations Committee, is eloquent:

"(i) The people of the United States do not like the Government of Japan.

(ii) The people of the United States do not like the Government of Germany.

(iii) The people of the United States, in my opinion, are against any form of dictatorial government, Communist or Fascist.

(iv) The people of the United States have the right and power to enforce morality and justice in accordance with the Peace Treaties with us, and they will.

Our Government does not have to use military force
and will not unless it is necessary."

What the American people will, in fact, commit themselves
to do, we must wait to see, and set our pace according to their
commitments. It would be arrant folly for Mr. Chamberlain,
or any other, to set a quicker one than the American Senators.
It may, of course, be that there is no immediate danger of
this. . . . The corollary of this speech of Senator Pittman's
would appear to be to make a colonial and commercial offer
to the people of Germany in return for the abdication of
Adolf Hitler in favour of, e.g., Otto von Habsburg. In like
manner, Napoleon abdicated under the pressure of Talleyrand. If the Germans seek to make conditions as touching
the personnel of the domestic governments of the Western
Powers, such conditions of negotiation should be instantly
made in return, through all the channels of propaganda. But
we have no right to presume the making of these conditions
or to decline to negotiate with the recognized and acclaimed
heads of any great peoples, these our modern prophets and
Caesars, so long as they are prepared to negotiate in good
faith for peace with honour.

Many of the objections to emphasis on this common Anglo-
American outlook are factitious. It is amusing and significant
that the popular author of the Britanno-phobe, satirical *England Expects Every American to Do His Duty,* acted as coun-
sellor and *amicus curiae* on Ellis Island to John Strachey, the
Russo-phile Communist Left-Winger and propagandist of the
world-indivisibility of war. The common factor is minority
disgruntlement, carping and 'knocking.' It is more noteworthy
that Republican Party speakers—although Mr. Hoover's remarks to me on Britain, in a long conversation, were the
reverse of unfriendly—have served notice that America can-

not commit herself to a Britain that finds its ally (or ally's ally) in Russia, *except* within some far wider framework than one of merely military alliance. The framework must be genuinely one of co-operation in terms of law, order and equity, with a power bloc competent to enforce these things.

Here, then, is an *Anschluss* to write home about. In these matters let us go as good as Hitler, if we believe in what we stand for. Let us crusade through the world, if the world wants it—but first let us be strong, in ships and ideals, belief and dry powder, ourselves. . . . Herr Hitler may indeed have set in motion a force beyond all his or our power to calculate. He may be the creator, though involuntary, of Anglo-Saxony, just as Versailles was—along with Bismarck and Houston Chamberlain—of Adolf Hitler and his Third Reich.

Is then the old Imperialism to be revived—the Nineteenth-Century Imperialism of Black Empire or the new counter-Imperialism of Race Theory? It is not.

It is Dean Inge who, in his customary caustic manner, provides a definition of a Nation. "A 'nation' is a society united by a common error as to its origin and a common dislike and contempt for its neighbours." He continues, however, with a quotation from Isocrates: "Hellas is the name of a culture, not a race." Its application to the Anglo-Saxon world is striking and complete. The organizing principle for this world is not race theory but a tradition of values. Of those values some indeed are common to the seers of all the human race—in the words of a great historian, "no more confined to race or frontier than a rainbow or a storm"—whereas others owe their shape and formation to the characteristics of the people.

That tradition which exists, and has so long and so definitely existed, it is necessary to render vital again. The recitation of the ancient pieties or incanting the words 'Liberty, Liberty' or 'Democracy, Democracy' is assuredly not enough, nor shall we thereby enter into any Kingdom of Heaven. It is significant that Lenin was prepared to sacrifice Poland, Finland, the Baltic States, even the Ukraine, in order to have at least one area in which a homogeneity of ideals—even if imposed by a limited group—might be able to sway and control the country. Out of that determination all the triumphs of the Soviet Union sprang. Similarly, Adolf Hitler, invited and tempted to enter into coalitions, with one famous exception when he was checked by Goering, steadfastly declined to adulterate his ideals by admixtures and party alliances. As a direct consequence he was able to shape modern Germany, whether it be for good or evil. Mussolini is able to get his Blackshirts shouting that, for them, "Nothing is impossible."

The Anglo-Saxon world will perish as Carthage perished unless, instead of becoming a pleader for alliances involving mutual commitments to lean up against this or that support, it first seeks world unity and adequate power by finding principle in itself and in its own vitals and by the putting down of the men who find most things impossible—the "better-not-ers."

We must stand on our own feet. The Anglo-Saxon peoples must do this. If they will, they can.

In our Atlantic civilization, if the Anglo-Saxon Republic of the Western Atlantic, centred in Washington, and the Anglo-Saxon Commonwealth of the Eastern Atlantic, centred in London, can stand together, the decisive responsibility for world affairs becomes theirs. Their advantage in area, man-power and wealth, including the raw materials essential in war, is so immense as to be invincible *when organized*—so decisive as to make this responsibility for peace in the world, for liberty and democracy, theirs and unquestionably theirs, on their shoulders and none other's. Overwhelmingly they still have power if they will organize it.

The issue is whether they have the resolution to organize it, as Cromwell once had the resolution to organize. If not, the historic answer is plain and their day is by—the issue is between Reich and Soviet. It is for these people, united by a common tradition, language and culture, severally to decide whether by disunion they will make an historic renunciation and take their place as have-been Powers, or whether they will assume leadership by their own example, in the cause of world federation. Assuredly, if we cannot get such a confederation, then a Sovereign League of Nations, a World-State with direct taxative power—which is the only League that matters—is *a fortiori* out of the question. Is it necessary, like Germany before Hitler, to be defeated before we learn the lesson?

We must stand strong during this night of civilization, in order, when the light of humanism dawns again, to be able to move forward. This is our first, our chief, our only duty. We must maintain freedom for at least one people. We, we also, have an international faith.

The time is coming when the national State will fall. Its function and justification have been that it, the sovereign national State, has welded the several countries each into unity, suppressed feudal anarchy and maintained domestic peace. But the national State has not attained to be the expression of the nationalist ideal of Mazzini, who visualized a comity of nations in which all made their special contribution. Briefly, Mazzini was a supra-nationalist, and what we now instantly require is supra-nationalism, as 'the Shakespeare of our age'—at least not blind of vision—Mr. Shaw, has seen.

Nor has the national State, from its local, regional character, been able to perform the supreme function of maintaining peace. On the contrary, the doctrine of absolute sovereignty, owning no superior, has bred war as it bred it when feudal lords claimed to be "sovereign in their barony." And there have not been lacking some who have seen, not war as a function of the State, but the State as an instrument peculiarly fitted for the waging of war in an unceasing struggle. They have glorified war as an expression of bloody heroism, like the Spartans of old, who perished. War will not end until there is an authority, able to maintain peace by armed force, that overrides and subjugates all states, while freeing all nations. The function of the State is to maintain peace. That is what it is for. The nations of the earth and their peoples have other and richer functions. The perfect State, as Hans Kelsen shewed, perfectly does this; and the State merits allegiance as a necessary form of that nobler thing, Society, just so far as it can do this. The tragedy is that the national State—desirable and noble although Nationalism may be—cannot, from its very nature, maintain peace. It can maintain it against robbers within, but it cannot, without cyclic crises and armageddons, maintain it against robbers without. It is an exhausted social form. It yields to some species of collective organization.

If Adolf Hitler or Josef Stalin, or a Parliament of Man, can re-establish the Roman Empire, maybe he or it will deserve thanks. The prospects of effective action by a Parliament of Man do not at the moment appear bright. It was, as I have said, perhaps a pity that Napoleon was not permitted to carry through this work of compulsory unification, this work of a new Julius. For it is the re-establishment of a World-State, such as Rome was, for which the world longs, and which alone can ensure peace. It may be that we need a new Charlemagne. It may be that in Adolf Hitler we have him. There is reason to suppose that Adolf Hitler thinks so. As he has said: "the old Roman Empire stirs again"—and soon this ghost, armed, sceptred, alive, will seize us with crowned might.

There is, however, another, freer possibility. Supra-nationalism is not anti-nationalism. The Anglo-Saxon world provides, as we have said, a working model of federalism or confederatism, with its bonds as close as those between London and Edinburgh or as lax as between London and Washington or Dublin. This model is inspired by a principle. How shall we make articulate and missionize the gospel of this principle to willing hearers?

Anglo-Saxon civilization, as we shall seek in this book to shew, has a tradition that displays this federal liberty as *no mere opportunism but as in the very texture of values* to which the English-speaking peoples have held for centuries. It is a tradition consonant with scientific experiment, industrial initiative, personal choice. It fits in well with the background of the wider Humanist tradition and of Christian civilization. Anglo-Saxon and Catholic civilization today draw together in the discovery of common ideals of the value of the human being as end in himself.

There are many alive who have spent their time picking flaws in Christian theology or in pointing out that the ethics of the Old Testament or of St. Paul is not beyond criticism. They may have been so objective as to discover "much good" in Nietzsche, just as one could find "much good" in Marx. It does not follow that even these intellectual critics, let alone common men, do not regard the Christian faith as eminently expressing the values and decencies in outlook that mankind would most wish preserved, or that they would not deplore having substituted for it the religions of Wotan or of Dialectical Materialism. If so, they must co-operate to maintain against attack, open or insidious, this Christian civilization, which is one not of war and militarism but of co-operation, presupposition of goodwill and peace. Those who stand for this kind of civilization, from Catholic Legate to Quaker Friend, must also stand together.

It is possible to seek to understand causes of enmity and desirable to encourage friendship between all nations and to enter into full diplomatic relations with their chosen governments. Blowing upon the embers of ill-will works not the Will of God or the good of man. It is, however, necessary that we preserve ourselves clearly, sharply and resolutely distinct, without entanglement with totalitarian schemes. We are entitled to preach this rejection of alien principles among our own people. We must carry the war into the other camp. The time has gone by to be apologetic. Nothing can be more dangerous than for the young people to come to believe that they are being asked to fight for what nobody really believes in, mere *talk* about Democracy, and Liberty, parroted phrases, dead creeds.

I am aware that many wise men, from Plato down, including Hegel and Marx, have been held—sometimes, I think erroneously, and sometimes rightly—to have vindicated such totalitarian régimes as right and to have acquitted them philosophically of the stigma of being bloody tyrannies, imprisoning body and spirit. It may be held that Russia has been developed strikingly under Stalin, and the Reich under Hitler, as Louisiana under Senator Huey Long. I am aware that these human ant-heaps, *because* they are such, have—or may have (since German efficiency is dubious)—unparalleled military striking power. I am not sure that they have staying power. The comparative history of Athens and Sparta does not bear the belief out. I am aware of the justification that, had the dictatorships trusted to sweet reasonableness and justice against imperialist and capitalist, and not to armed might, an hypocritical Britain and an ever-wakeful, jealous France would have devoured their substance, alike in Russia and Germany, while chloroforming them with fair phrases. The dictators have not sprung up from the ground without cause and explanation, and the explanation is in tears and blood.

There is, however, no obligation to let the ideology of their rulers—even were it appropriate for their respective peoples, nurtured in lands of Slav and Teutonic authority—infect ours. There is an instant obligation to prevent it by counter-affirmation. Brüning and Dolfuss pursued the policy of persecuting the persecuting—of sending both the factions of physical violence into concentration camps and both into the same camps. It is to be hoped that in Anglo-Saxon lands the same policy may never be pursued. It is to be hoped that a constructive, not a repressive, policy may be adequate—and that this is no mere pious 'good Christian' aspiration. If, however, the necessity arises, then the policy of enforcing law against political brigands will be pursued. In an issue upon which may turn the history of freedom there will be no timidity. We shall not be taught our political A B C by the emissaries of lands that have never known democracy—and still less so if they attempt intimidation.

Let us be clear. So great is the mass-power of the United States and of Russia that, in the event of all institutions being put into the molten furnace of war, the future of the world after war (and not that of individual countries alone) will be moulded on one of these models only: the Russian, the German or the Anglo-Saxon. I see no further possibilities—no possibility of a world remaining of diverse and insulated systems, not an interconnected world. Americans especially will do well to reflect on this choice of systems—this alternative with which they, as well as the rest of the world, are confronted in this crisis of civilization.

For those who love peace and believe that peace is the mother of democracy and progress, and power-lust is the chief determinant of war, the only available course, the only practical compromise, would appear to be to raise high the defences behind which, undisturbed by the warring ideologies of hate on principle, the democracies of the West can maintain themselves in the development of their own traditions, while lending their effective support to the rule of equity and law elsewhere.

If we, or those who deliberately and fully join with us (not merely according to the old diplomacy), are then attacked by the dictators of modern superstition and the priests of political voodoo and witchcraft, we shall strike back. I do not use these words against men, men who are heroes of their own peoples, engaged in the honourable task, which I praise, of building up the self-respect and even prestige of their own countries or of the workers of the world in the context of civilization, but against those who knowingly turn, from love of cruelty or cynicism of truth, against the values that the saints and heroes have honoured throughout the centuries of striving of our race.

If, moreover, we strike, there is a wrong and a right way of striking. The wrong way is the slap on the face, the provocation, the weak, hysterical calling of names: weak diplomacy. The whole of our attitude in Spain has been made fatuous by that. We never decided whether the classical policy of Richelieu—"no Germans on both Pyrenees and Rhine"—was right or wrong. The right way is the blow of an organized nation, organized and disciplined in all its parts, falling as a steam-hammer on iron: effective, strong policy. If we are incapable of that discipline and energy in organization, we merit to lose and go down. And the record of history by examples is that we shall.

This policy of self-defence within our allied lands is a policy less than ideal in a world so patently less than ideal. But it is not a policy of despair. Our fortress of defence is still indubitably strong enough—it is potentially the strongest in the world, not excluding Russia, if we choose to make it so. And we can raise its portcullises and throw open its gates in co-operation with other peoples, so soon as there are indications that this co-operation will be welcomed on terms that do not involve destroying our own tradition and letting the ideological enemy within the gates.

Let us summarize. The policy here advocated is a commonwealth policy, *not* an imperialist policy, as the Nineteenth Century understood it. Further, it is not a policy of concession to intimidation, but of equity with strength—resolute, self-disciplined, organized, efficient strength. It supposes that as Germany moves East, her embarrassments with conflicting national claims will grow greater, not less, and that the leadership of small nations with equitable claims is there to be had at Geneva for the asking. (I do not deny that Germany, she also, has equitable claims, e.g. in Danzig, as Italy in the Suez, nor would I lift a finger to support the lethal policy of denial of equitable economic claims persistently pursued during the deplorable and criminal 1920's and only escaped from, too briefly, at Thoiry, at the Stresemann-Briand-Chamberlain meeting.)

It supposes that Russia always needs Western support more than the West needs Russia, and that our attitude to totalitarian Powers that desire to break each other—Russia, Italy, Germany—must be dictated solely by interests in democratic security. I will support full alliance with a Russia which can actually be supposed to contribute to that security, even although it be for internal reasons of stabilizing the régime.

I would do the same with Germany did I suppose the intentions the same.

It supposes that we will fight, at need, on the Rhine and in all the lands we expect to see organized, and can organize, according to our own democratic standards, or whose support conduces to that end elsewhere. For the rest, our terms are peace with any régime whatsoever that will respect international law and that will prefer its equitable claims within the framework of respect for the self-determination of its fellows, as units in the comity of nations.

It supposes the indissoluble alliance of the Atlantic Powers and the accommodation of the pace of each to the pace of all, with no commitments that involve not keeping step.

This is a great task. Finally, therefore, Conservatives must swiftly decide whether they will put country before privilege, nation before party, and make the patriotic sacrifices necessary for a social policy requisite for unity. I hope so. Will they? Or will they continue to be mere money-changers, buying and selling parliamentary seats in the hour of decision for their people?

Is commonwealth to come before private wealth, and the advantage of the common man, in the succession of the generations, before that of the possessing few? That is the issue. If the right answer is not given, faction will multiply upon faction, and an ideal of disciplined liberty competent to confront totalitarianism is hoped for in vain.

Recently we have seen Mr. Macmillan, at Westminster, struggle with his Conservative conscience to produce a scheme for a Milk Board which should aid in securing a minimum nutritional standard for children in England. How many Republicans in America, confronting the New Deal and accusing it of waste, have not been also faced with the same **problems** of conscience? We have not, however, seen Conservatives rally to Mr. Macmillan's support. We have seen criticism of his scheme on the ground that this regulation and centralization disturbed the system of capitalism and the successful working of the principle of private property. The public health, however, of a nation is the responsibility of that nation; and before private wealth comes commonwealth. Let us not be like the man who, having for years been attended by servants who lived in some remote region of the house, was scarcely aware of their existence until a burglar broke in, when he called down: "Come up; let us defend *our* house."

Let us be clear. A people must be regarded not as those brothers for whom we are *not* keepers, only shopkeepers, but as members with us in "a contract between the living, the dead and the unborn"—a contract of liberty in ideals of conduct but of co-operation in natural and established necessities. There must be no more talk about 'the working classes' in the old style: it is to be hoped that we all belong to 'the working classes'—and those who do not, had better make right good haste to become members. If dictatorial countries *can* afford to provide, not 'bread and circuses,' but those minimal economic things essential to citizen health and dignity, and if capitalism under democracy *cannot,* then it is so much the worse for capitalism. I withdraw my words and raise my hat to the dictators of all colours. The test is a concrete one: the results. It is no good pleading "the system." We are concerned that democracy, not the big man with his big profits, masquerading under the hat of democracy, shall survive. We are concerned to wage war on anti-social effete snobbery, as also on 'shopkeepery'; to set the child of the rich man in the schools at some time in his life down beside the child of the poor; to concern ourselves with citizens as citizens in a community, function-differentiated indeed, but by intention class-less, recognizing common clay; to concern ourselves with eyes, teeth, stomach, health and fitness of this generation and for future generations. One major source of social infection in Britain is the decaying relics of a money-class system, divorced from public service, that clogs sound values and impedes decisive leadership. As Dr. Arnold of Rugby wrote: "I lay a particular stress upon this separation of tastes and feelings between the rich and the poor in England, because I am sure that it is the peculiar curse of our own state of society." The comment is fortunately not equally true—yet—of America.

It is impossible to give unreserved support to any party within Anglo-Saxony that gives out an uncertain sound in these matters of justice and practical patriotism. It is the task of some group or club or public movement to press for a better view—of some who are like-minded to discover instantly a less selfish vision in these years of corporate danger. Is it necessary, I repeat, *to be defeated* before we learn our lesson of dedication, organization and commonweal? Let us do it now—volunteer for such a movement and insist, against the bureaucrats, on being accepted. It is *our* land and *not* only theirs. How shall we ask common men to fight, if we accept no common obligation? The man who fights not only *owes* a duty, but a duty is *owed* to him. And it is the common man who fights.

There is a priority at the moment in foreign affairs. And here, as indeed at home, the sole proper course is that of our own Middle Way, disentangled from the underbrush of poisonous ideologies and envenomed hatreds-on-principle—disentangled not in theory only, but in diplomatic practice also. (That does not, of course, preclude correct relations when there is correct reciprocity—or the intention of establishing broad-based peace without being led aside by hatred of words. It does mean non-absorption in alien *blocs*.)

Our own tradition is anti-doctrinaire from conviction, bred in the bone, tolerant, honouring a golden mean, free, concerned with social justice, respecting initiative, valuing the individual as end in himself, empiric. The Middle Way of our tradition we need to follow *alike* in home and in foreign affairs. At the moment we are asked to take *either* the slack selfishness of those *beati possidentes,* propertied gentry, along with 'moderation,' *or* social justice, with a weak and ill-organized bellicosity.

We need creativeness and imagination in the State Department; organization and dry-powder in the Defence Ministries. We need strength in justice at home and strength in peace and war abroad, based on our own folk and those whom we understand and who understand us. Shall we have it before too late?

We shall only have it by putting the *common* cause first, and the common man's cause. Under these circumstances, there is a moral compulsion for individuals to renounce party parliamentary ambitions save so far as is consistent with freedom of utterance, and to go to their countrymen, seizing such opportunity as there may be to give warning in time to this nation and its fellows. Let us stand by the principles and forget the politicians; and appeal to the country, certain of its common-sense.

Anglo-Saxony is strong *if it chooses*. Does it choose? It is strong in acres, in population, in material wealth. The mind is dazzled by the vistas of opportunity. But the men equal to the grandeur of the opportunity appear lacking. The comparison has many times been made between the British Empire and the Roman Empire. Let us be careful lest the true comparison be not with the Carthaginian Empire with its wealth and its commerce, and its inequalities and its inner rottenness. Carthage is now a ruin, set on a hill. Rome stands.

Another comparison, more contemporary and more full of portent, is with the ramshackle Habsburg Empire. It also, held together by a crown, strove to tie to itself peoples among whom there could be no possible cultural sympathy. It fatally turned its interests from the native Rhine to the alien Danube. And all the world could see that the cultural heterogeneity was such that the task was hopeless; and the fall of the House of Habsburg and its Empire (however economically disastrous) was sure. But the task of the Habsburg Empire was easy compared with that of the British Empire. Little although the national sympathy may be between German, Rumanian and Czech, at least there is greater cultural community than between an Edinburgh Scot and a Nigerian. The great African Empire is still conducted on the principles appropriate for the age of Metternich—that what matters in politics is not loyalty to nation but allegiance to an administration, a bureaucracy under a crown. In India the issue has become incandescent with national angers. In Ireland, in Arab Palestine, the old mechanical assumptions have been rejected.

The British Empire is a colossus without nerve or muscle until it discovers some principle of energy to pull it together and to stand it on its feet. I reject the term 'imperialist.' Imperialism is the bad, mechanical system, without soul or imagination, that I am attacking. Shall I say, then, that I am speaking, in a new sense, as a commonwealth man? I am speaking as an unashamed commonwealth man.

What then shall this new principle be? Not blood. As Daniel Defoe said, over two centuries ago, the British are a mixed people. The Anglo-Saxon tradition is an Anglo-Celtic tradition with Dutch and French and Danish admixtures. The common principle is culture, common civilization and this common tradition. There is no reason why others—Icelander, Norwegian, Philippino—should not adhere to it. With those more remote two arrangements are possible—the arrangement of conscious advantage and the arrangement of trusteeship. As touching India, if it can see that advantage, it will remain in the Commonwealth, and, if it cannot see it, it will move out. Assuredly the line to India can and must *never* be the life-line of the Commonwealth.

If no better reason need be given, there is one final one: English and American on the one side, and Hindu on the other, do not inter-marry. No common empire is possible when that is the case. Rome found that out. At present, the line to America and Australia is the life-line. Inspection of the map will shew that America is in the centre of the Anglo-Saxon *bloc;* and that the rest lies in a crescent moon around it. The total comprises two hundred million souls—as much as Russia and France combined, nearly three times as much as Greater Germany. If those politically controlled be included the total makes over 600 millions out of a human total of 1920 millions.

Our concept of 'empire' as cultural is alone adequate in the Twentieth Century, be it Russian Empire or German or British. It is that of commonwealth with common tradition. There alone is the bond of union. Men will not much longer as dupes bleed for *interests,* not *their* interests—if bleed they must, they would rather do it for class interest. It has to be seen whether the bond of union, of tradition, values and culture, need be that of blood and blood-nationality. I believe not.

At least that is our gambit in this Anglo-Saxon polity, and, if that loses, we too are lost. In the alternative, the Germans, with blood and a Führer, or the Russians, with class and the bureaucrats, win. It has also to be seen whether the issue must be that of class against class. That will depend upon ourselves and our enforcement of classlessness against *snobisme* with vigour and even brutality, since our need in these years is so urgent. It is not in the Anglo-Saxon tradition that, as for Marxism, the only bond should be uncompromising class placed before historic community. But it is in that tradition that this community can be extended by prudent stages federally out, until it embraces all humanity, French-speaking, English-speaking, that accepts our intention and ideals. The task of the present is this: To make it yet plain that that intention must not be forgotten or ignored, but accepted; and that that ideal shall be clear.

§ vi

The New Commonwealth

I care for England. I am not, however, interested in putting England into opposition to Great Britain; or Great Britain to the British Empire; or the British Empire to the British Commonwealth; or the British Commonwealth to Anglo-Saxony as a leader in human progress. How are we, then, to make the most of the heritage that, in trust, is ours? Shall we hide our talents in some clout from cowardice?

Not the severest critic of Russia can deny, or should wish to deny, the development of that country since the Revolution. This does not mean that a condition of economic equality prevails there. On the contrary, as Max Eastman points out, managing directors in Russia may receive up to eighty times the wage allocated to the lowest-paid worker. It does not mean that the worker is within sight of being as well off in Russia as in the Western Democracies—let alone better off. I can say from personal experience that, in 1935, the pound sterling was unofficially exchanging at 170 roubles. In that year, by the official figures, the *average* wage of the Russian in work was 225 roubles *a month*. To this, such authorities as the Coates would add 34 per cent. in respect of social services. Nor do any figures such as I took down, of shop prices—which tally well with those of Citrine—give cause to modify one's obvious conclusions.

This does not mean that there is no begging in Russia; there is . . . because they can sometimes make more by begging than from wages. It does not mean that there is no unemployment in Russia. In 1928 there were admitted to be one and a half million unemployed—I say nothing of famine and starvation before and later, five million in 1920–21 dead of starvation, and a minimum three million in 1933. If now there are no unemployed, it is just the same in Germany. It may be a triumph for totalitarianism, but is no especial triumph for Marxism. And in both countries there is busy employment for the 'political criminals' on gang-work.

Russia has worked out certain blue prints, in industrial insurance, in kindergarten education, in free medical attention (in practice often without anaesthetics) for the workers, which are not so much creditable to the Soviets, although they are this, as disgraceful to rich democracies that have not adopted them long ago. Russia has given to the workers the sense (however fantastic in relation to the reality, and however become daily more uncertain as mutual suspicion increases) that it is *their* country, just as in Germany the workers have the sense that Hitler is *their* Führer. This is the strength of totalitarian religion. Russia, moreover, has made an immense material advance, which indeed sets up no standard for general imitation among the civilized democracies of Western Europe—who have led, are entitled to lead, and should lead—but which is remarkable and almost miraculous in a Euro-Asiatic state.

As I travelled across the miles of plains to Rostov-on-Don

I asked myself what was the ground for this advance, which, to many minds, is the decisive testimonial to Lenin's course, however many millions of lives that course may have cost, in civil war, to Russia and the world. Was the explanation Communist ideals or Marxist ideology or State-Capitalist planning, or true co-operative Soviet planning?

The explanation, I submit, is none of these things. Since the days of the opening up of the American Middle West, which drove the United States at a bound from a third-class to a first-class Power, there has been no area of equivalent size and richness developed until the opening up of Russia, and especially Siberia, since the Revolution. This has been done by the industrial methods of the Twentieth and not of the Nineteenth Century. The Revolution released forces latent but rendered inert by Russian apathy and the corruption of the *ancien régime*. The Russian people have inevitably benefited. The new bureaucracy at least was not interested in filling the pockets of the nobility and of cotton kings and timber kings, although it squandered as much upon building up the most gigantic military machine in the world as a first instalment of the new Utopia.

If the Anglo-Saxon political system is to be commended to the electorate of England and Scotland, of America and Canada, as better than the Russian, how is this commendation to be made? Assuredly the test that this electorate will apply will be the pragmatic one of *results*. These Western countries are very rich countries. How should they shew to the common man *better* results?

So far as the British Commonwealth is concerned, a clear answer can be given.

There is now, on the entire earth's surface, only one space capable of startling development comparable to that of the American Middle West and of modern Russia. That space is the Colonial areas of the British Commonwealth. Some of this space, such as Jamaica and British Honduras, is rotting from lack of forethought. It would be better to pay off honourably our American Debt by leasing for 999 years an area for an American naval base in this region. In Kenya and Nyasaland, lack of an adequate agricultural policy may turn a colony into a desert. It is high time we abandoned the petty-minded provincialism of Lord Palmerston, who sincerely thought that only Europe—the area that Jefferson called "lands of eternal war"—mattered.

The last decade in Europe saw the vogue of catchwords, 'rationalization,' 'planning.' Some of them were due to the impression made by Lenin's Russia, with its slogan of "co-operation and electrification." There were the Russian Five-Year Plan, and, later, the German Four-Year Plan, and, all along, the Webbs' Plans, as well as de Man's and others. They had this kernel of truth, that anarchy and *laissez-faire* have been shewn by experience, in our contemporary, complicated, large-scale civilization, not to be the most satisfactory guarantees for the liberty and economic security of the common man. On the contrary, in many fields, public control is the appropriate guarantee of this security. With many people, however, planning—however essential in the right place—became a substitute for thinking. The habits of the country, its morally legitimate individualism, its existing co-operative associations, its voluntary organizations, may well all be resistant to this variant of the proposal that the State is All, and the plansters its masters. At home, planning is necessary, but its scope is limited and its objects must be precisely defined.

The Colonial situation is abruptly different. Hitherto the British people in the Homeland, and, to a lesser degree, in the other British Dominions, have regarded the Colonies as 'possessions,' areas perhaps for profit but also for apology, about which the less said the better. Such an attitude is morally and politically irresponsible. Any people that adopts it deserves to lose its colonies and has small claim to a sixth of the earth against the expectant millions of Poland or other lands of rising population. It is not the case that any country which adopts a deliberate policy of increasing population, without regard to standard of living or civilized well-being, is thereby entitled to claim its neighbour's lands. On the contrary, it is only increasing the numbers in the world of the derelict proletariat, victims of anti-social ambitions. It is the case that Britain has the choice between being another Habsburg Empire, the first victim of any virile people, and a totally new and imaginative Colonial policy. The nature of that policy is indicated by Lord Hailey's *African Survey*. We must, however, go well beyond these indications.

The British people and Anglo-Saxon democracy have one great chance, and only one, of leaving even the Russian experiment in development far behind in the shade. They hold the only part of the earth where this chance is possible. It is not an opportunity that, bungled now by timid statesmanship and a confused public opinion, will recur. The alternative is the conventional treatment of colonies as 'possessions'; the deprivation, bit by bit, of those colonies on the basis of the equal right of other Powers to share in the 'exploitation' or to settle their own teeming populations; threat of war to a heterogeneous, nondescript empire of the old, Nineteenth-Century type; and the collapse of the British Commonwealth in ignominy, compared with the future-looking, materially successful Russian Dictatorship.

The moral duty of Anglo-Saxony is to develop, with the resources that only Anglo-Saxony possesses, this vast area until the time comes to transfer it, as a substantial basis of wealth and power and as a *peculium,* to the direct rule of Geneva or a

World-State which requires such sovereign possession to give it dignity.

The British neglect of the Colonial Empire is an abomination that smells to heaven. Much of this empire is a dictatorship, of which the dictator is the British electorate. That electorate is so notoriously indifferent that it is a source of worry to his friends when a Member of Parliament devotes much attention to Colonial issues: he will lose votes. Already the day of reckoning is coming. Not only is Germany demanding the return of her colonies, but responsible voices in America are suggesting that the handing over of the West Indies would be better for all concerned. In the event of Anglo-Saxon confederation that particular issue at least could be brought to some satisfactory solution.

The guilt lies with the British voter, the irresponsible democratic sovereign, not with the British administrator. Lord Hailey's survey, itself the work of a distinguished administrator, is a monument recording opportunities lost or not yet utilized. It is the most effective study by far since Dr. Raymond Buell's. Each layer of problems presupposes and is conditioned by one more fundamental until we reach the soil itself, and such issues as those of soil-erosion.

If the great African continent is to be developed without wastage, and without more than the misery of the European industrial revolution, there must be a planned co-ordination between the physical development and the economic, and between the economic and the governmental. In the Sudan, as in Fiji, in the Katanga, and in some abortive projects in South Africa, such co-ordination has been attempted. For the rest, it has been too conspicuous by its absence—and this, as touching production and marketing, more so in the British colonies than in the French. The lack has been due, in part to want of finances, in part to want of ideas. Lord Hailey's book is a massive plea for this co-ordinated development.

"The task of guiding the social and material development of Africa gives rise to problems which cannot be solved by the application of routine knowledge. . . . This study must be pursued in the field of the social as well as in that of the physical sciences. But for this purpose assistance is required from the Imperial Government."

The policy of material development combined with promoting health organization: this is recognized—by the Belgians. The issue of local government for the de-tribalized native: "it is a problem which so far has engaged more attention in the Union and the Belgian Congo than in the British colonies." The necessity for stimulating the cultivation of subsistence crops: "the Belgian Government may be said to have taken the lead in the study of questions of this type." There is the need for scientific research—in which the Germans did excellent work. "The British Government has hitherto given *less* support to institutions devoted to the study of African languages than, for instance, has the German Government." Rhodes is dead, very dead.

In a primitive continent, in transition in the inevitable process of opening-up, public plan, social planning, may be the *best possible protection of the native* from private exploitation. There is one sole area in the world where, by co-ordination of scientific and geologic research, of transport, of mining and crops, of sanitation, of population movements, a result more startling may be attained even than in Soviet Russia, a result that can put Germany and Italy, avid for colonies, in the shade. That area—this imperial cloak of cloth-of-gold about us—is the British Colonial Empire, a section of a Commonwealth that controls a quarter of the world. Mr. Neville

Chamberlain might reflect that this is opportunity—including opportunity for our own unemployed engineers and steel industry—beyond the dreams of Joseph. Lord Hailey, as an administrator, should know well that by preference we are a nation that chooses to do nothing—a nation that, if God is just, deserves to lose. Perhaps Lord Hailey will succeed in dynamiting this nation into action.

§ vii

Anglo-Israel

It is a matter of common knowledge that, if the Commonwealth is to be maintained, it must be populated. It avails nothing for the politicians of this or that Dominion to explain that the Almighty has given them this or that portion of the earth so choice that they wish to share it with no one else. It is still true that frontiers are held by power, and by man-power —and this rightly, since it is hard to argue, in justice, that a dwindling nation should obstinately stake property rights to rich lands when other peoples have a low standard of living in the crowded areas of Japan and the teeming Yangtse, shut out from these wide spaces.

A baby-race to win wars is a prospect of horror from which any man must recoil who holds that above all nations is humanity. The Oxford moralists of the last century used complacently to explain poverty as a punishment inflicted by nature (and providentially promoting virtue and thrift) upon those classes who had no foresight and prudence in the rearing of over-large families. The tune has now changed. I am prepared to believe that this country is still over-populated, and to suspect those who desire more cannon fodder. But the Commonwealth is patently under-populated, and its downfall is certain if it cannot provide itself with the human basis of wealth and power.

Into the far places of the earth go the Finn, the Slovak, the Swede, even the Dutchman. The Englishman only appears as a "member of the upper classes," a salaried manager with wife and no children, a consulting engineer keeping to his own society. The unwavering message of history is that such aristocrats die out.

If, however, in the British Dominions and Colonies there is an unwillingness to accept an Englishman or even a Scotsman as an immigrant—and I trust that before long we may change all that—and if the mood of pioneer and pilgrim has passed, which was a mood of rocky individualism and contempt for neighbourhood convention and leaning up against each other, there is an alternative. There is a race, without a home, with reasons for being loyal to this Commonwealth, that is not afraid of hard work. And Matthew Arnold was never tired of pointing out that if our Western European tradition in part traces from Hellas and its culture, it in part traces from Palestine and this race.

The Jewish people has three choices before it. It may become assimilated, as the Goth and the Lombard have been assimilated, with the surrounding folk. In some measure, this policy has been followed in France. It is for the Jewish people to decide. It is my belief that with a nation—and Jewry is not only, or even chiefly, a religion but a nation, and much more pronouncedly a nation than most nations—with a nation of such ancient and distinctive traditions this course is never likely to be more than partially successful.

Secondly, there is the possibility of finding a national home to which all Jews in the world can feel attachment and about which they can feel pride, as Welshmen do in Wales and

Scotsmen do in Scotland. I declare myself a convinced pro-Zionist.

Thirdly, there is the too easy but entirely disastrous course, root of anti-Semitism, which is to be always sojourners among nations but never to be of them. Even were the world still an eighteenth-century humanistic world or a true internationalist world, it would be difficult that its peoples should be taught internationalism by a close nation. It is quite impossible today. Abstractly it may be true that national cultures benefit from criticism by resident strangers; actually the criticism is resented. It is possible to buy the position of a 'subject' for a few shillings in an office of naturalization. It is a mistake to think that one thereby buys admission into the family of a nation.

The mood of the Twentieth Century—more socialist, more full of sense of society—is not that of the Eighteenth Century. We live in an age of nationalism and citizen armies, not of economic individualism, internationalism among the educated, and standing armies. If a man, rightly or wrongly, is to be pressed to die for his nation—and we have here to assume that 'nation' is more than a mere anthropological fiction—as an enlarged family, not an administrative area on a map maybe ruled out in parallels, he most certainly won't die to defend the persons, wealth and power of those who are only part of that nation by a legal fiction. How foolish to die in torture to defend a mere 'administrative area' called Yorkshire or Nevada, not to speak of Bavaria; or to die to defend somebody *else's* property. The only conclusion of this argument is absolute pacifism.

We may, of course, say with Dean Inge that there are no pure races but only 'sub-species' (and these not equal); and that a 'nation' is a society united by a common error as to its origin. It is a little difficult to ask men to die for a confessed error. The conclusion again is total pacifism. I am sure, however, that Dean Inge would not accept this conclusion—and he may reply that he has stated his alternative, his real basis of community and common action in common culture. Precisely that, for Anglo-Saxony, is ground for the argument of this book. Our concern is identification with the culture to which we here seek to give concreteness and characteristic shape. I observe that the Spens Committee on Education in Britain has reached the same conclusion, on the importance of education in the tradition of our culture.

There is indeed one consideration worth keeping in mind. Messias was to come, and some say that Messias was to be not a person but a people, the people chosen of God and rejected of men. Christ comes again in those most persecuted, in His own kinsmen. Professor John Macmurray has expounded a related thesis in his *Clue to History*. Be these speculations as they may, the moral test for the Gentiles of the advance of their civilization is how far they are nauseated and revolt against this persecution—be it of Jews, Kulaks or Ukrainians. We must not be like the Russian Foreign Office official, quoted by W. H. Chamberlin, who, when German Social Democrats protested against the sending of Volga colonists of German extraction to concentration camps, commented: "They are our citizens, aren't they? We can do what we like with them." The revulsion, widespread and intense, against the persecutors of the Jews—still better the willingness to do something practical for the persecuted—is a sign that righteousness is still alive among us, and that some standards of civilization are still maintained. That many good Germans are now harbouring Jews, entitles us to say this of Central as of Western Europe. Whether it can be said of some traditional lands of the pogrom I do not know. The model attitude in this matter is the admirable attitude of the late Pope, Pius XI.

When, however, criticism of the culture of the host-nations

is combined with revolutionary political views that explicitly
threaten the traditional constitution and morality of these nations—when Jewish intelligence and Jewish imagination and
ambition thrust Jews into the forefront of these movements—
then no invocation of reason is strong enough to prevent this
resentment from flaming out in mass persecution. All Jewry is
threatened by this tactless unwisdom. The fault indeed is not
peculiarly Jewish—or even peculiar to some Jews. Many White
Russian *émigrés* have been fully as guilty of unwelcome criticism.

In free Britain, Catholics have never escaped suspicion, as a
community, of divided allegiance. Every Catholic is bom-
barded yearly with abusive pamphlets from fanatical Protestant societies. In free America, persecution of Catholics by
mob violence was the reverse of inconspicuous in this last century. The very fathers of English toleration were prepared to
justify persecuting laws. Not all the loyalty of all the Catholic
Englishmen from Howard of Effingham has served to allay
this fanatical suspicion. The Jews coming from outside England must not presume upon an absence of criticism and a tolerance that the Catholics never received and to this day in
parts of Scotland do not receive. Nor will it avail for Jewry to
answer that, in all reason, it is not responsible for Karl Marx
or for the Jews who follow him. If leading Catholics advocated conspicuously a policy of violent change in Britain, it is
as certain as it is irrational that the whole Catholic community
(although *not* a separate nation but only a church) would in
fact be held responsible. Among Jews I have found some of
the most beautiful and delightful people I know, some of the
most sensitive and most civilized. I almost wish, therefore, for
the sake of Jewry itself, that it were possible—as a New York
Jew remarked to me—to have "a moratorium on all Jews in

politics for twenty years." However, this is not practicable, nor indeed is it a satisfactory or masculine solution.

Let us turn back to the second solution. It is not necessary that a Jewish national home shall have all the apparatus of flags and war offices, national sovereignty and Luxembourg statehood. This may be a good thing or it may not. It is yet not necessary. On the other hand, it is short-sighted to suppose that Jews should not congregate together in *bloc* communities and in given regions, as Welshmen do in Wales or as Quakers did in Pennsylvania, or that somehow they will be more loyal if they deny that they are Jews and slip unseen into great urban centres, there to remain as shopkeepers and small employers. The historical record indicates the precise opposite. In an alien community, on the defensive, the Jew too easily can become a man of a divided loyalty; a man who has lost his orthodoxy, *déraciné;* a prey of any violent messianic politics, sprung from envy and discontent. Living as a free man in his own community according to his own distinctive ways, he can become a man independent, proud of race, a magnificent colonist, with no more divided loyalty than has any Welshman or Canadian or New Zealander. Nor does this part preclude Jewry, as a racial minority, from fufilling what is perhaps its true moral and messianic rôle internationally in civilization, of providing the yeast for sympathy with all minority and oppressed groups and classes.

It should not be left for Signor Mussolini to discover the possibilities of the Jewish colonist, or for him in some Abyssinian colony to hold them as hostages for ransom. I am not able to understand why the vast Soviet Republic has admitted almost none of these Socialist refugees whose case is so pitiful. Soviet scientists, in December 1937, speak of "serving our dear Fatherland"; and it may be that Russia, "the happy Soviet land," where there is, as we know, no unemployment even in the winter-time in Siberia, is more concerned with the worker at home than with the refugee from abroad. A more probable explanation is that the present régime, as is the manner of despotisms, fears the infiltration of new ideas, as much Left as Right. Nor is it for me to explain why the Soviet Siberian Jewish Republic of Biro-bidjan has been left conspicuously unpatronized in large numbers by the enterprising Jewish nation. Be this as it may, the Russian miscalculation is our opportunity, provided that loyal immigrants go not to the areas of over-population and under-employment but to those of under-population and no unemployment. It is for the British Dominions and for the American people not to expend fair words in their sympathies but to do something. The refugees wait, and an empty stomach is more impatient than a democratic legislature.

§ viii

Science and Freedom

The Englishman—far more than the more optimistic American—distrusts an 'intellectual.' The denunciation by Burke, himself no mean philosopher, of "the cold malignancy of the metaphysicians" to this day awakens a responsive chord. This suspicion infects—I think, moved by a sound instinct—all schemes for 'planning' and 'rationalization.'

Like, however, most 'sound instincts' that remain inarticulate and unexplained to the possessors, this instinct also has its aberrations and perversions. It leads to the cult of "muddling through"; of "bearing our learning lightly," unlike a mere German; of heavy humour (I observe that Charles II, but not Cromwell, had humour—and anyhow, Charles had wit); of "gentlemen beat players"; of the happy amateur; and of confidence that "it will all be right on the night." The young gentlemen from the playing-fields of Eton (such as are not leading the Communist cells of Bloomsbury) are very far from shewing an efficiency that will defeat the Russian or the Prussian or the Italian—very far from shewing it, but only shewing jealousy with interference in their preserves, and the interminable English slowness and positive preference for lack of snap as ungentlemanly.

There are occasions when it is possible to have too many gentlemen and too few men. The inefficient at this moment is the traitorous. The cult of the "little man" is carried to the point of sentimentality, without asking "Little man, what now?" Empty-headed applause for the determination of the Cockney not to be made "a bloomin' 'ero" can end in applause of mere slackness, national self-indulgence and laziness, as well as praise of a phlegm that symptomizes "the real stuff." The belief in the magic virtue of unpreparedness, saved by the miracle of the national humour and genius, is a dangerous belief, a very dangerous belief.

It would be well to have a world of brothers, all free-traders. It is not the world we have. In the world as it is, nations are in competition, and the success of that competition will in large part depend upon the technical methods they use and the technical skill of their citizens. Further, if we could replace this intensified trade competition by a World-State, the economic mechanism involved would be so vast that only the nicest design could bring its successful working within the bounds of possibility. Either way the moral is the same. And to prefer rule of thumb to this technical training is like the man who prefers to plow his fields with a hand hoe. I have no doubt that Stone Age man did prefer his own ways. That is why Stone Age man is dead. And the same remarks apply, as in engineering, so in politics.

There are two conclusions I wish to draw. One touches Education. There are two kinds of education, apart from irrelevant information: liberal and technical. Ever since the days when the universities were designed for the training of the clergy as spiritual directors, a liberal education has been intended as an ordering of experience in fit perspective. It has been intended to fit a man to play, with full and harmonious powers, his part as a man; and, as a member of the ruling classes, to undertake with wisdom and liberality his responsibilities. The same canon applies if we are training squires, in the Eighteenth Century, or civil servants, in the Nineteenth Century. In a democracy, in the Twentieth Century, every soul is entitled to initiation into such an education of the man and the citizen. Understanding of the actual community—and not only second-hand in bookishness—is the necessary background of citizenship. Therefore, and *inter alia,* as is recognized alike in Russia and Germany, every child should at some stage or other go through the common, elementary public schools. That should hold good for everyone, from prince to pauper, if paupers are still to be. That alone is the proper education for a prince. The opposite is a training in incapacity to understand. The basis of maximum national pace in production is individual willingness, personal freedom, social collaboration based on genuine mutual understanding. It is not vacuity in the imagination.

Let me add that part of a liberal education is being acquainted with our own public works. Visitors come from abroad to Rome or Moscow to see for themselves what Mussolini is doing in draining marshes or Stalin in providing crèches. Does British or American officialdom attempt to rescue these seekers and judges of our life and democracy from the cheap witticisms of half-trained guides; does it send them on free tours to see our Preventive Medicine Centre at Peckham, our Mothercraft Centres in Chelsea, our new council housing, or the equivalent buildings, symbols of achievement, in New York or Washington? It does not. Neither does it send its own future citizens. Are the photographs of outstanding manual workers, who have taken a skilled part in a job—as in Moscow—posted up by the factory management, even of municipal or national utilities? They are not. Education for democratic citizenship by radio—an education in which I would spare sensitivities in Berlin and Moscow in exact relation to the extent to which our own were spared: not one jot more—is a thing still of the future.

Technical education is a matter of private profit. It is something more. Its acquisition is a duty owed in return to the society that has liberally educated us, a duty to acquire that skill by which our society may take its place unashamed in the front rank of the nations' progress. Without that progress the mass of men can never escape slavery, or machines replace what Aristotle held to be the necessary servile toil. Without that progress our country becomes backward by comparison, and our level of living, not absolutely advancing, will relatively fall. To them that have will be given. Energy and good workmanship are not all. Trained brains are required behind them. Schooling must be given, enough and apt to train these brains.

Let us be clear that the economic future—to some extent for America with its highly paid workers; far more for Britain with its pitiful dependence under the present system upon the erstwhile big-dividend-earning export trade—is a black one, unless steps are taken to change the grain of our economic system and by adjusted pressures to straighten its mal-growth. We persist in a Gold Economy that presupposes an international trade, in decline if not in abeyance; we reject the organization of an Economy of Goods for our own workers; and then we marvel at the soaring unemployment figures.

Even in the United States, the message of the last Great Depression was symmetrical production for the worker, not asymmetrical speculative production for gold-amassing. The devastation of war itself is not as bitter as the slow, impersonal, relentless devastation due to a change (against which precaution has not been taken) in the economic system from free trade to closed economy and from skilled trade to Oriental rivalry which empties our wharves, closes our warehouses, shuts our factories and throws our workers on the slag-heap. Nor can any political revolution or violence or courage or hope save them from that slow devastation. In part, as the Socialist, Blatchford, long ago pointed out in a passage quoted elsewhere,[1] we must accept the implications of the 'closed economy' and look after our own workers first. In part, we must make it our aim to establish the largest free-trade area, immediately feasible, as our own through Anglo-Saxon (or North Atlantic) federation.

The jealousy between academic and business man, the first marching under the banner of 'scholarship' and the second of 'common-sense'—a jealousy more marked in Britain than elsewhere—is an unmitigated disadvantage to British trade, in which there are far too many dull brains and arterio-sclerotic minds. In America there is a fortunately increasing tendency to insist on the college graduate in the higher ranks of business. In Britain Lord Nuffield has been left too much alone in his gallant endeavour to fill, by his College, this perilous gap in the national defences, this lack of really trained, practically trained and appropriately trained minds.

The fault lies with the academic even more than with the business man, and perhaps most of all with the national temperament. I write this letter to you because you, my dear

[1] Cf. p. 302.

Wells, more than any man living (without suspicion of that martinet, bureaucratic preference which affects other great men), have detected this weakness and have endeavoured to educate the Anglo-Saxon peoples out of it. You have had some vision of a kind of new World Platonic Academy of men of true knowledge, a technocratic General Staff in the war against 'the stupids.' At present Dr. Flexner's Institute of Advanced Studies at Princeton, with Einstein and others on its staff, alone approaches the elevation of this noble Olympus. You alone have adequately recognized the need for the due co-ordination of pure science, technical studies and the labour of the social research worker, politician and practical man. You have viewed even politics *sub specie aeternitatis* or at least *sub specie mundana*—under the guise of a world, not only of space, but of time. That is why your 'blue prints' have an elegance that delights the mind like the poem of some Confucian philosopher.

Now let us do things. . . . Let us have a Social Science Research Council in Britain as in America, where, in our New Atlantis and in this Solomon's House, the most skilful minds can study long-range problems and stake—without whit of governmental, totalitarian pressure—their reputations on their conclusions. That is the real guarantee of advance out of the quagmires of social superstition and the murk of political witchcraft. Intellectual co-operation, instead of being a flashing sword, has become a poor, starved thing of contempt such as Bernard Shaw exhibits to us in *Geneva*. The issue is nothing less than our whole attitude to government: whether it is to be an exercise of domination by a masterly will or whether it is to be co-ordination shaped by the guidance of social physicians, studying the political physiology of our body politic by research and reason.

As Professor Bernal, whose remarks here are not necessarily

qualified by his Marxism, says in his stimulating book, *The Social Function of Science* (1939):

"Unless the scientist is conscious both of the internal structure of science and its relation to society, much of his efforts to improve the status of science and to see that its gifts are given to humanity will be doomed to frustration. On the other hand, neither politicians nor the forces behind them can by themselves either fully realize or know how to realize the latent possibilities of science."

Let us have a new Economic Research Advisory Council, an elaboration of that which Mr. Roosevelt has in his National Resources Board, not some ill-jointed framework, hastily hammered together by a busy Premier and his reluctant civil servants after a breakfast or two. I refer to that of which I know, since MacDonald's decision as Premier was based, *inter alia,* upon memoranda submitted by my own chief of that time. Let us have such a Council or staff answerable on the facts, not policy.

Let the experts' job be to aid our democracy in working—challenged for ignorant incompetence by the dictators—not by pantopragmatic interference, but by finding the radical truth —no business of a paid administrator—digesting it and making it available to politician, trader and business man if and as wanted. We cannot settle these grave, vital issues of population growth and distribution, or of the economics of planning, monopoly and private enterprise, or of race-purity in its biological consequences, by guess-work or by political heat— the Blacks for this and the Reds for that—or by little memoranda of over-worked and under-instructed political secretaries. If we are to defeat organized totalitarianism we must substitute *centralized voluntary advice*—surely democratic enough—responsible and skilled advice on nutrition, preventive medicine, population migration, transport, reconstruction of industry by areas, and the like, for centralized and *involuntary coercion into the disciplined front.* I see no other way of avoiding the dilemma: how neither to sacrifice the Expert State in the modern world to chaos nor the Free State to slavery.

The core of the Anglo-Saxon Tradition is the belief that science, research, experiment, initiative, flourish best when there is rational freedom. Hence from this wise, fertile freedom springs progress, concrete progress for the common man. But, if science is not to be permitted to bear its fruits in applied knowledge utilized by our rulers and captains, applied in terms of nutrition, health, cheap goods, cheap electricity, cheap, good clothes and like triumphs of invention that obliterate class-difference, then it will not be surprising if the unemployed, the miserable, the discontented, the common man, turn from trouble or monotony to the great public works, the vast buildings and motor roads, the absence of unemployment if bought at the cost of authoritarian regimentation, the fine marchings and songs and bands of youth of the totalitarian dictatorships. It is in human nature. And if initiative or scientific development doesn't matter, then the chief prop of argument, from the point of view of civilization, for our free, democratic system is knocked away.

I do not wish this to be interpreted as some preference for 'cosmopolitan,' 'machine' civilization against 'country.' On the contrary, country life—and not only 'electrification and decentralization'—is the root of health. I am under no illusion that the countryman today is fond of the country—he is not— or that the nature of the true peasant where he is found, beneath all the curious customs and romantic fal-de-lals, is not suspicious, dark, obstinate and cruel. But the return of the townsman to the country is entirely to the good. Civilization is 'civic,' but of the small *civitas,* the canton. I would further add that when we once habituate ourselves to think in terms of Anglo-Saxony and Commonwealth, not Washington and Whitehall, we shall again be a country of vast countryside, a land of countrymen more than ever Italy or Germany. But this means that we have got to think, in our mind's core, of Canadians as we now think of Vermonters or Yorkshiremen, and of Americans and British as we now think of Scotsmen and Californians.

The responsible skilled advice that I have advocated, the requisite minimum of planning, looks to the organization of community industry for community good. The route to reconcile this with personal freedom I have indicated. It, moreover, lies in encouraging a rationally free tradition as the kernel of our social morality. But, in practice, what bearing have all these planning, or what some people call 'technocratic,' schemes upon Socialism as a political system and upon the need for popular, classless or worker control of the plansters? What meaning are we to attach to the phrase, Organized Democracy?

§ ix

What of Socialism?

If Socialism is opposed to freedom, then I am opposed to it. If Socialism is the completion of freedom, then I am in favour of it. Everything will depend upon what we mean by our words. Realities, not words, must be the basis of the policy of our new world.

There are three aspects of Socialism. First, it is a movement of the wage-workers to maintain and improve the standard of living of the mass—one of the chief objective tests in history of progress—against exploitation. By exploitation I mean the tendency of a few to rule the economic world for their own private and speculative advantage and, as a simple matter of self-interest, to pass on their gains to heirs who are under no compulsion to make a return to society. I mean in effect the cutting of 'labour costs' before cutting profits. It is a movement that, under Marxist influence with its doctrine of class war, may be purely proletarian—although Marx and Lenin were not themselves of proletarian extraction—and for the private profit of the proletarian who has no savings. It is 'his turn' now. Or it may include within its purview all those who work in society and for society, whether by hand or brain, the salary-earner and the man who receives the wage of ability. In this sense there is nobody who would not wish to be a 'worker' or who would prefer to be a 'non-worker.' The days have gone by when Elizabethan Sir Thomas Smith defined a "gentleman" as "one who did no work."

Secondly, in another aspect stressed by the Fabians, Socialism is the political and economic correlative of a machine technology and of large-scale production. Industrial centralization becomes the only method to secure technical efficiency whether in production or marketing. That centralization means either public control or giant monopolies or trusts geared for private profit. Such monopolies may be indifferent in the short run whether the machine designed to produce wealth may not, by its very efficiency, produce unemployment and poverty.

It may be true that centralization is far from a universal rule; and that, beyond a certain point, *de*centralization may make for industrial efficiency. However, the heyday of the private business is over, and as Berle and Means have shewn in their admirable book, *The Modern Corporation and Private Property,* the captain of industry is not now also necessarily the capitalist but may be merely the manager and hirer of capital. He may, indeed will, welcome outside aid in checking the avarice of the absentee real capitalist, the aggregate of shareholders big and little, not excluding the old ladies who live in Streatham and the Bronx, the dustman and the waiter who have shares in Woolworth & Co. We have again the abuse of the absentee landlord. These dividend-drawers can store their profits over a rainy day and can collectively leave the dismissed workers to charity. Private 'wealth' takes precedence of commonwealth.

Thirdly, the Socialist movement may be regarded as the fourth and final phase in the movement towards democracy and the fight for liberty. The Seventeenth Century saw the achievement of personal liberty in Britain, freedom from arbitrary arrest, *Habeas Corpus*. The Eighteenth Century, from the days of Locke and Bishop Hoadly, saw the fight for religious liberty, toleration, culminating in Catholic Emancipation in the next century. The Nineteenth Century saw the fight for political liberty, the franchise, culminating in Universal Suffrage in the following century. The Twentieth Century sees the fight to make political liberty real in economic liberty, that is, to assure a minimum of security and independence. As Mr. Justice Holmes said, there can be no freedom of contract without equality of status. It is necessary to have a guarantee lest the rich man hold the poor, if not in law at his mercy like one of Stephen's barons, yet actually at his mercy by threat of starvation, and this irrespective of industriousness and good citizenship. Indeed, not malice but mismanagement or that international crisis of which the economic consequences are clearly a national responsibility is today major cause of this misery. The debased Darwinianism—"devil take the hindmost"—of the employer of the last century, whose conduct made Liberalism to stink, is at least partly a thing of the past.

I do not know that Count Coudenhove-Kalergi, in his book, *The Totalitarian State Against Man,* has advanced the cause of democracy by binding it up with capitalist individualism. What is wanted is property for all—small man individualism, if it is blessed with a social sense and not mere avaricious 'shopkeepery.' I do not believe that 'capitalism-as-a-system' is much more than a word. Certainly it is not universally applicable any more than, for that matter, 'public-ownership-as-a system.' Everything depends upon the where and the how. I am still less sure that Count Coudenhove-Kalergi is helpful in implying that equality excludes liberty. It is an ancient argument; and it is at least equally correct to say that equality, such equality of environment and status as gives substantial equality of opportunity, is the pre-condition of active liberty in the rational development of the person. There is much talk today —very rightly—about recognizing the intimate connections between economic and political liberty. The question is: For whom? few or many? As Lincoln said, there is a 'wolf's code' of liberty. Examination of the Anglo-Saxon Tradition shews clearly that by equality has been meant the assertion of a 'common human nature,' common clay, fraternity. It has been basically and through and through a concept of religion and community. I fail to see how any man may be free in a society divided into halves, of one of which he is not permitted to be a member. He is not free of his own community which becomes no community to him. The issue is the ancient curse of *stasis* and of divergence of class interest exacerbated into class war. Where the manufacturer sees 'hands,' the statesman must see citizens. There must be no quarter for snobbery that impedes national co-operation, nor for inequalities, non-functional and with no justification in social service.

Socialism as the trade unionism that presses to raise the general level of liberty, not least through the wages of free individuals, is not today a Party issue in Britain, whatever it may be in America. The battle is not finished, but the conclusion is now foregone. The only issue here is how to produce goods cheap enough for the common consumer in a fashion fair to the trade union producer. The only threat is from a totalitarianism that swallows up the unions.

Socialism as planning is another matter. I fail indeed to see how the problem in Britain of the Special or Distressed Areas is to be dealt with save by national planning, or, for that matter, how the health of the nation, teeth and eyes, are adequately to be cared for by private enterprise. I say this without prejudice in favour of compulsion as against voluntary methods, when efficient.

It was observed long ago that nations may be 'grained' for peace, or, as in Sparta, deliberately for war. The two involve quite different social and material systems. Today, efficient 'graining' of the growth of society for war means more than it did in the freer, happier age of diminutive Sparta. Professor J. B. S. Haldane, the well-known biologist, assures us that "London will need about 1000 miles of 7-foot tunnel," at a cost that, when the whole country is adequately tunnelled, will amount in total to £400,000,000 or £600,000,000. The actual Government scheme at present amounts to a mere £20,000,-000. These sums, inevitably taken in large part from the human necessities of the social services as a consequence of plans for, it may be, defending the Russian or Polish Ukraine for its Russian or Polish benefactors, it is estimated will enable Man, in these culminating days of civilization, to return to the exact models of the primaeval caves from which he emerged as an ape. Incidentally, in the event of war and plague, a sanitary system excellent in a society designed for peace would be a menace for a society engaged 'to the limit' in war. At least it may be agreed, in order that this new, violent zeal for organizing society for war with more than Spanish ferocity may be retained within some limits, that national planning to divide between what of civilization we shall and what we shall not sacrifice is a requirement in the interests of liberty itself.

Even, however, in this field of planning, Socialism is not limited to Party Socialists. Conservative politicians, such as Mr. Harold Macmillan and others in Britain, have maintained the necessity of nationalization and rationalization of vital industries, or at least of their public control through public trusts. Coal, and other fuel, transport, milk-distribution, and even bread-making, have been suggested by these Conservatives as appropriate fields. Conservative Governments have sponsored in Britain an Act, in 1926, which nationalizes the bulk transmission of electricity under the Control Electricity Board, while adopting Socialist Party proposals in connection with London Transport. In the United States the Roosevelt Administration has dealt experimentally with electricity through perhaps the most significant of all the President's schemes, the Tennessee Valley Authority, which, although local, comprises an area four-fifths of the surface of England. Those who agree with Mr. Macmillan in his *The Middle Way,* and with the advocates of a Four-Year Plan, believe that the economies rendered possible by these measures of public control will not only ensure the provision of adequate nutrition in milk, dairy goods and bread, but will render feasible the provision of a national minimum wage, which is itself becoming recognized as a moral imperative.

On the other hand, as touching Socialism understood in doctrinaire fashion as simply and solely "public ownership of production, distribution and exchange," Party Socialists, such as Mr. Douglas Jay, explain that they desire *neither* the equalization of all wages *nor* the "nationalization of everything." They distrust the State Leviathan—alike when sporting itself as Fascism or as Marx-Leninism. They hold that the explanation of evil class divisions that have no justification in social function or social service is to be found in the private inheritance of wealth.

Allowing for the legitimate interest of every parent in the well-being and advancement of his own children, provided that these children will themselves in turn make good—allowing for the good and moral sense for the family—these writers demand the abolition of inherited wealth through taxation in the third generation. They hold it to be intolerable that in England and Wales 6 per cent. of the population hold 80 per cent. of the property (in 1924–30), and 2 per cent. hold 40 per cent. of the property, while in the United States 0.1 per cent. of families at the top of the economic scale receive about as much as 42 per cent. of the families at the bottom. Six out of seven persons in America and nine out of ten in England have manual worker incomes (i.e. below $2500 income in America, or below £100 property in England). These are not the bases of social stability, unless men can be convinced that the glittering prizes are the rewards of ability along roads open to all, or of good luck, as in the Derby Race, that has no respect for vested privilege. Mr. J. Maynard Keynes, indeed, despite support for Sir Stafford Cripps, holds that "there is too little organized sympathy designed to make the private property system work better"—that Capitalism, like Christianity, has failed because it has not been tried sympathetically. The conscientious stewardship, however, of great wealth displayed by a Nuffield or a Rockefeller jr., cannot be counted on as a general phenomenon.

Unequal wealth spells unequal power. An unequal power that disdains social responsibility is an affront to democracy. A political liberty not implemented by a minimum of economic security, a liberty to starve, is also contrary to its nature—it is a reduction to absurdity of democracy, as Carlyle shewed long ago. The high income must carry its specific social responsibility, as it did under feudalism. More—it must be socially warranted. The tragedy of Commercialism lay in the divorce between private wealth and public duty, a point well elaborated by Morris Cohen. The low wage must be within the limits of dignity and decency as a co-citizen. It is, however, not the wage alone, but this issue of dignity and decency, that we have to stress, and stress again. We must not and cannot rest until the common man, the citizen even of the humblest occupation, carries his head high as proud to be member of a community, not only rich and luxurious and 'advanced,' but held together by a common sense of self-respect and earnestly and patiently concerned for *him* as one of its citizens, and for *his* self-respect. All else is a humiliation, however many rich thrusters and shovers there may be. The core of a country's civilization is the self-respect of the humble—nothing else. That civilization alone has succeeded, broad-based, where this can be said to be true.

Political power, says Locke, is ordained, "only for the public good." The object of the State is to increase and maintain the material well-being of the citizen; to provide the conditions of his reasonable happiness; and the facilities of liberty wherein to achieve the conditions of his personal dignity.

The delimitation of that spiritual well-being and the regimentation of liberty with a view to that delimitation is not the province of the State; and the claim to it has the quality of tyranny. It is a function of voluntary society.

In all forms of State, then, be they Communist, Fascist, bourgeois or democratic, we have to keep our eyes fixed upon this measurable issue: Is the standard of living of the common man actually improved? If men would keep their eyes fixed upon this, there would be less enthusiasm for wars and revolutions. Revolution is splendid for the feelings; but its concrete advantages compared with less spectacular reform are often precisely *nil*. Britain is not worse off than France, despite the French Revolution; rather it is better off. If indeed mere ma-

terial standards are sacrificed to increased individual liberties
and facilities of personal moral choice, they may be, as temporary expedients, condoned, just as men cheerfully tolerate
privation in war-time. If both private liberty and public standard of living are sacrificed to the ambitions and glory of the
governors, that society is suspect. Nor is the matter greatly
improved if the mass is led itself to place first the glory of the
tribe in war at the expense of liberty, personal values and material civilization. Here the issue between Fascism and Humanism is precise and clear-cut.

"Say not, O ye Kings, that war is the path to glory. True
glory is not to be found apart from human kindness. Whoso
puts his own glory before the dictates of humanity is a monster
of pride, not a man." (Fenélon.)

The standard of living must be maintained by private property for all—if not three acres and a cow or car, then the
equivalent in rights to social services. The aristocrat can dis-
pense with private property, as Plato shewed; the common
man loses his soul's liberty when he loses his plot and becomes
wage-slave of State or master. The level must be raised by
sharing the wealth which the community has co-operatively
produced. The questions, however, of standard of living and
of unemployment are inextricably joined. It is, indeed, possible
to raise indefinitely the trade union standard of living for the
employed if one is reckless about the consequence in increase
of unemployed. That is no satisfactory method. It is possible,
as in Russia and in Germany, to solve the problem of unemployment if one has no ambition to set a high standard of
living for employed or unemployed by international compari-
sons. The problem is to raise the average standard of all citizens.

The elimination of waste through inefficiency by public control is one route. The danger is bureaucracy. The elimination of excessive profit, by public control or charter companies in the field of public utilities, is another. There is, however, the danger that foreign competition, even with these new margins of advantage, may bring the level of living down to the common one of Europe and competing Asia, if not of Africa. The Far Eastern danger is not remote—a danger from areas unconcerned with the standard of their citizens.

Free trade reduces the price for the consumer; but free imports *without* free migration of labour internationally lowers the upper limits of economic costs in a marketable article, including labour costs. And cheap labour abroad reduces that limit for the export article. With the increase of machinery and of machines to make machines, the advantage of the fine craftsman and of the intelligent engineer, in Britain or North America, is lost as against the human being who can work long hours on low wages and fill his stomach with rice in the more favoured climate of Japan. Apart, moreover, from national aptitude in production, some countries have an advantage in their variety of production; nor will the most industrial country benefit by the elimination of the countryside for the sake of industrial profit.

Great Britain and, subsequently, the United States, have grown capitalistically fat and proud as the salesmen of an international world and in the easy pioneer, cream-skimming days of the last century. The United States has only an 8 per cent. export trade. But I fear to think what must be the economic situation of the discontented workers of Britain as, piece by piece, the export market shuts down in this new world *unless* there is intelligent and ruthlessly efficient national organization for competition abroad or national or-

ganization for the internal market—*our own workers' market*
—of the great natural wealth at home, and in the Commonwealth and in Anglo-Saxony, if not in wider areas. I personally should say that revolution is quite certain—probably ultimately Fascist in character.

Some people see the answer to this problem of the maintenance of local standards of living against the average levelling
tendencies of economic law, in monetary control. Mr. G. D. H.
Cole has gone so far as to propose two systems of money, one
for domestic currency and the other for foreign exchange.
More to the point is it that economic power should be placed
under political control and the primary field of production
of wealth made co-terminous with the field of social regulation. The ultimate consequence of this is the desirability of
world economic regulation, through the International Labour
Office, within the frontiers of a World-Confederation. Thus
concern for cheap world production and concern for world
citizen welfare would come under a common authority. That
is the true free-trade goal.

The immediate consequence is different. The producer must
be induced to regard his job as one having a social aspect and
responsibility. He must be induced to produce primarily, and
as basically necessary, for the benefit of the citizen. He must
produce primarily, if his type of goods fits him for it, for
the workers' home market, not for the cosmopolite gentry
of the luxury foreign market. Producers as a body must *neither*
produce cheap by sweating labour *nor* produce expensively
to meet the tastes of a foreign market in which the home
worker cannot be a purchaser. Good wages are of no benefit
unless there are appropriate goods available, nor are cheap
goods enough on sweated wages. Both are unhealthy economies. That alone is healthy where there is sympathy between the position of the worker as buyer and the worker

as earner under a common public authority. The ideal public authority is the World-State. It does not exist—and if it did, the standard at the moment might not be any too high for the aristocrat among proletarians (so denominated by Lenin himself), the Anglo-Saxon worker.

The Communist ideal is to establish a world economy and to abase the standard of privileged bourgeois-fed workers in parasitic countries, such as Britain and America with their dollar-empires, to the common level and even to the appalling, primitive Russo-Asiatic level. That is the economic meaning of Marxist fraternity. Lenin explained the danger that there might be a successful bourgeois policy in lands that could pay their workers from the profits of the 'free trade' exploitation of a world. Engels rejoiced over the approaching bankruptcy of free trade. In Russia the workers were taught the meaning of equality through starvation in common.

However, our task is not to level all the workers *down* to a present average or Russian monotony, but to level all workers group by group *up* as technologically improved production permits. For the moment we must suffer jealousy of the better-paid nations by the worse, by the proletarian or bankrupt countries—and by the peoples of the East where human life was ever cheap and hope for the civilized living of the common man at a discount. What is needed is a Ministry of Commerce, Technology and Production, to guide and stimulate the recognition of the connection between invention, production and desirable social conditions for the citizen body.

The task is to win vantage-points in the progress of civilization and—unlike previous epochs of history—to keep them. Russia is naturally a country almost, if not quite, self-sufficient. It has been maintained, not unchallenged, by a writer in *The Times* that agricultural and timber production is in 1938 actually lower than in Czarist days. Nevertheless, these great resources of natural wealth remain there to be opened up by Russian comrades. The citizens of the United States are nearly in the same fortunate position.

The British Commonwealth, although not so self-sufficient, has yet more variety. We are fully entitled, in comparative terms, to place it in the blessed ranks of the naturally self-sufficient nations. Its defect is that British subjects have obstinately refused, not only to organize it economically with system, but even to contemplate seriously its organization. An apathy native to these subjects, the British islanders, and an opiate and hallucinatory belief in muddle as a substitute for the self-sacrifice of such organization, seem to have proved insurmountable.

Germany is infinitely less self-sufficient by any gifts of nature, but by super-human efforts of the *Volksgenossen,* the 'companions,' she has fitted herself to carry on war for long periods on a self-sufficient, or almost self-sufficient basis. German organization, however, only deserves a moment's attention so long as Anglo-Saxony remains unorganized. Germany, exposed in Central Europe and obeying an elementary law of politics, organized under threat. Under threat Anglo-Saxony also will organize. Adolf Hitler will be the unwilling parent of this unexpected new world, this immense Anglo-Saxony.

A British Commonwealth organized for free trade, but organized as in effect self-sufficient, can confront, granted maritime power, the would-be self-sufficient economies of Germany and Italy with impunity. We may have to adopt some prudent measure of the Russian—or New Zealand—type of economy, in order to defeat the Germans and Italians at their own economic game. Britain can give earnest of its desire to move on towards free trade and the removal of restrictions by the inclusion of small countries—as Lionel Curtis suggests in *Civitas Dei*—who might desire this position within its cus-

toms union; as well as by intimate trade treaties with the
United States. Personally I plump for nothing less than the
confederation of the whole—I see no other means of killing
internecine jealousy as treason. *L'Union fait la force.* We have
long *talked* of it in international terms. Let us now *do* it in
Anglo-Saxon terms—make this New Commonwealth. If such
confederation, owing to national jealousies, is not possible in
the narrower sphere, we may as well write it off as moonshine
in the wider.

The inclusion, however, within this *bloc,* of areas not culturally similar or assimilable because private financial interests are involved and "there is money in it," may ultimately
be a source of weakness and not of strength.

A Commonwealth so organized can by slow changes modify
its economy to produce, on a large scale and cheap, for the
home market; can provide high wages for its workers who
will buy in this home market; and can raise and maintain
its standard of living so that the worker is both free and secure. The development of this huge area will, as has been
shewn, provide enough to solve, especially in the technical
and engineering, steel and allied fields (as well as by public
works), the unemployment problem—and this while maintaining or raising the standard and not, as in Germany (which
has *no* such natural advantages), by depressing wages. The
weakness of the policy is that it demands a moral resolution
that we have lost, and thanks to which the Empire will collapse and the Commonwealth will Balkanize itself within a
generation into a half-score of third-class nations. The serious
call is, then, also an insistent call. "Something will be done."
Something *must* be done.

§ x

The Task

To do these things we must have faith. It may be that the orthodox religions of the past served a purpose in decanting from politics that excess of fanaticism, that 'enthusiasm' which made Party life impossible. Our generation, for good or evil, has returned to the ages of faith. A political system that obstructs emotion will not only produce no results but it will dam up resentment against itself. The conquering religions of today are political religions—Marxism, Fascism. They have their 'Book' and their Prophets.

How then of us? Christian culture is indubitably on the defensive. Let us not too easily abuse that name or prostitute it for this or that—cry *"Unser Gott."* Humanism is also on the defensive—Hellas and Judaea. How shall we descend from 'ideals' and schemes to the field of practical intentions? How shall we ascend from petty Party wranglings to the level of a resolution that shall not only maintain order and give purpose in our own house, but command respect among the practised ideals of the world? In the first place, we neither want schoolma'ams' text-books on democracy nor robust fellows' playing-fields for amusement. Neither Lenin nor Hitler won that way. This anise and cummin can be weighed out after. First we want faith.

We fight not to be entangled in other men's errors. We fight to build freedom in at least one area of this world. Democratic liberty is not enough . . . nor even Liberal Socialism. We need free community—and if we do not desire to see here in these Anglo-Saxon lands the régime of a Stalin, however cracked up as 'fuller democracy,' or the régime of Hitler, the Nordic visionary, then we must here and now be prepared to labour with sincerity of soul for that community, that sensed, felt community, not as a name, be it England or Vermont or British Empire or Anglo-Saxon 'culture,' but as a community of actual human beings. That labour involves a core of those like-minded who share common ideals, the traditional ideals in which their people have found characteristic happiness and which can give discipline and dignity to themselves. *Unless there is an emotion for this free community of ours more powerful than that aroused in the Marxist for class war, or in the Hitlerian for his race, then these and not we will shape this world's future*—unless, I repeat, there is an emotion shaped by unbending will.

In his important book, *The Totalitarian State Against Man*,[1] Count Coudenhove-Kalergi wrote:

"In this revolution of collectivism against humanism, three great powers have refused to capitulate—precisely those who for a century have carried high the banner of liberalism: England, the United States and France. All three are fully determined to maintain the great human traditions to which they owe their existence, their liberty and their civilization. . . . Comparison, then, is to the advantage of the democracies. One can, consequently, hardly speak of the world victory of the Totalitarian State. Beyond a doubt we assist today at a crisis of liberty. But the issue of this crisis is still pending. . . . Three great world powers now maintain the liberal tradition. Three have repudiated it. A new Sparta and Athens stand face to face: the Totalitarian State over against the Complete Man."

The will for community does not mean that we should go off to obey any orders of State that are orders of governments which, in turn, are composed of politicians and officials, very fallible men, representative only in some very partial sense—

---

[1] The English translation and edition, 1939 (Muller), has now been permitted to become out of print. The French edition, *L'Homme et L'État Totalitaire* (Plon), is available.

since how shall they represent that which as yet knows not its own mind? It does not mean some slick loyalty and refusal to criticize the limits of Party vision.

What is meant is that we have ourselves to rediscover our tradition and to make it articulate; to find in that tradition, as we may, those values that are the best guarantee of human progress—freedom, experiment, sense of community and—as Pericles said—the bravery to guard them. Every nation and people must so rediscover its own spiritual origins in time of trouble.

Freedom is not negative and thin, but freedom to choose our community. Community is the resolution to supersede class by recovery of that which is humanly deeper and more original; to abolish, not function but class, by removing those actual and unnecessary divergences of interest that are the springs of class war; to establish classlessness by replacing class consciousness by operative and vigorous public sense; to carry through this replacement as a matter of practical religion; and to fan the willingness of men to recognize, without envy, inequality of function and also of talent. All that is not an easy but a highly disciplined task—a discipline in the name of freedom. It is the only method by which Marxism and National Socialism will be met on a level, while freedom is yet retained. Those who believe these things must gather together, whether the future be one of peace or defeat or victory. They may have patience, in the midst of bustle of politicians and of pointings here and there, since, whether in peace, defeat or victory, this core of faith will be needed as a stay. Those who will not unite, it is the lesson of politics, are always defeated. Good wishing is not enough.

This mood of service and moral rearmament—to use the word to which has recently been given new currency: I will not reject it—has its complement in a campaign for self-respect. By neither term do I mean anything amiably pleasant, a moral glucose; but the ascetic rigor rather of your own scientific utopias. That any man, because left without aid from his fellows, should have to live in a fashion in which decency of living is almost impossible—I refer to housing and health— is a disgrace to his fellow-citizens. If we can afford war we must also afford peace. That any should choose to live ill when he does not have to is no less a scandal. We live too much upon our easy past. There must be no flinching in turning this people into a healthier, more athletic, better technically qualified, self-respecting folk, so for peace as for war, but so for peace more than for war.

In this campaign that is immediate—which can be effective, unless within these months the Western World chooses either Stalinism or Hitlerism as its historic, ideological ally—in this campaign we can despise no support from any, manual worker, professional worker, Christian, rationalist, who shares our intention. Examining all, we shall not choose all; but we shall demand, of each of our own, patriotism expressed in deeds, classless living, putting commonwealth first, and that which transcends patriotism, a sincerity for the cause of humanity as our conscience is our judge. Such a sincerity involves, indeed, respect for the claims of small nations; respect for the claims of the great German nation that has received less than justice in the past; but above all, respect for ourselves, self-respect. There are times for relaxation and times for discipline, of which discipline we have heretofore been capable. In Anglo-Saxony, as a bearer of liberty and equality, I see no hope save in the revival today of the relentless spirit once shown by the Commonwealth men—now, before the night comes and the trenches and the new tunnels and burrowings are occupied. Peace is indeed possible, but only by craven submission or by that instant and just spirit that sees higher than tradesmen's chafferings and poisoned sectional suspicions, and that conducts life, of man and of nation, as in the sight of its Maker, before Whom Caesars and Czars and tyrants pass and fall like leaves before the autumn wind. It involves the vision alike of men and of nation as part of a wider plan, transcending nation and class, of eternal justice that does not fail, rational justice to the enemy and rational justice to ourselves. I decline to think our task is easy. I believe it can be done.

GEORGE CATLIN.

II

THE NOTES OF THE ANGLO-SAXON TRADITION

"We are of the same humours and inclinations as our predecessors were: you shall find us all alike, much at one, we and our sons."

ROBERT BURTON.

CHAPTER I

Humanism

THE theme of this book is that there is a Grand Tradition of human values, certain values constituting the very norms of civilization, agreed upon by men of insight throughout the centuries. In the current of that tradition a very specific stream is noticeable, common in general to the Anglo-Saxon peoples but not nationalistically limited to them, and influencing thought and political manners well beyond their bounds, which stream takes its rise in the Sixteenth Century and has continued, as detectably consistent and unbroken, to this day. That Anglo-Saxon Tradition has certain definite characteristics or notes: humanism or respect for personality, liberty, experimentalism, tolerance, accommodation in social method, federalism, democracy and certain qualities of moralism and of public spirit.

Men today fight in bloody conflict about ideas. Ideas are more real, more influential in operation, than individual men. The master ideas of our age are Race, Class and Tradition. Unless the last is strong we fall prisoners, first in mind and then, as conscript soldiers, in body too, to these armed doctrines of Race and Class and to these marching ideologies. These ideologies are neither experimental nor tolerant. If we desire not to be drawn into the fatal dilemma, the 'either-or,' of Black and Red, we must rediscover our own spiritual tradition, not in order to be doctrinaires of either hue but in order that we may preserve our own intellectual self-respect in being neither—yes, and our own confidence in ourselves. Our truth and tradition is not limited to ourselves. Historically its influence has been far wider. Native in growth, it is, at least so far as we can see, potentially universal in application. Liberalism is not an affair of one country. The humanist origins of this tradition link it to the great European tradition of Catholicism and of France. It is yet distinctive.

Anglo-Saxony, like Hellas of old, is not held together by race or nationality. It is this common tradition which is its root and stock—this agreed way of life and values. As this tradition is not closely limited, so our confederation is not exclusive and leads out to wider plans of human federation. Nevertheless it has centre somewhere, and that in the most powerful group in the world. With that fact go concurrent responsibilities. If Anglo-Saxony is to be the first essay in actual world unity, it is necessary to keep present to the mind that its ultimate vocation is the constitution of a World-Federation—if one likes the phrase: of 'One Big Government'—which can only find basis in a wider Humanism. And if our business here and now is with ourselves, with building democratic faith in at least our own homelands first, we have nevertheless to bear in mind the fountain of the Grand Tradition of human civilization from which our own tradition takes origin.

To these origins, then, in a gospel of common humanity first let us turn.

.　　.　　.　　.　　.　　.

"In passing by the side of Mount Thai, Confucius came on a woman who was weeping bitterly by a grave. The Master pressed forward and drove quickly to her; then he sent Tze-lu to question her. 'Your wailing,' he said, 'is that of one who has suffered sorrow on sorrow.' She replied, 'That is so. Once my husband's father was killed here by a tiger. My husband was also killed, and now my son has died in the same way.' The Master said, 'Why do you not leave the place?' The answer was, 'There is no oppressive government here.' The Master then said, 'Remember this, my children: oppressive government here is more terrible than tigers.' "

At the dawn of letters, in the days when Cyrus the Persian was entering Babylon, and the Yangtse flowed through reed-swamps that marked the limits of Chinese civilization, Confucius in Shantung enunciated the first principles of Humanism. They have not been seriously changed from that day to this; there is a continuous tradition. Clad by Confucius in a teaching of good-manners, they are these: that what matters first is neither state nor government nor administrative convenience but man; and that man matters as a sentient and as a moral being. Man, the individual, Confucius held, against the anarchists, to be shapen by his society. Civilization, and not merely the simple life, was good, and its institutions a matter of moral concern. But what was good and moral was determined, not by the convenience of the rulers but by *the consensus of the sages*. What mattered was not the whim of the moment; what mattered was the Tradition.

.   .   .   .   .   .

Fertilized by Minoan civilization, at the crossing between Asia, Europe and African Egypt, Hellas developed a culture of her own that has been a glory through the ages. The cruelty, however, of the antique world, which shews itself to this day in the barbarous tortures and exquisite punishments of the East, also was displayed in the human sacrifices, against which priestly Delphi made no protest, until the Fifth Century in Greece. So, also, the same insensitiveness was shewn in the triumphs with captives in chains—although no longer impaled as in the days of Assyrian Essarhaddon—and the gladiatorial shows of ancient Rome.

Hellas marked a departure from the ancient world in the readiness of the Greeks, seafaring men, to criticize custom. While the Latins were still slaying their priests at Nemi and other peoples eating theirs, and the Carthaginians were passing their children through the fire to Moloch, the Greeks were asking questions. If the local customs were cruel, at least they were not too sacred to be criticized. Men were escaping from the unreasoning rule of "the silent ones," the ancestors, and were *appealing from custom to reason* as guide. It is, however, admittedly not given to every man to decide what is rational; he can only discover it when taught. Of the character of the rational good, Plato writes that those will know it and are competent to rule who are sensitive to its tones as the great masters of music are sensitive to music:

"those who . . . have contemplated the mood of nature which is said to exist in the stars, and have gone through the previous training, and seen the connection of *music* with these things, and harmonized them all with laws and institutions . . . able to give a reason of all things that have reason" (*Laws,* xii, 967).

With the coming of Christianity *respect for the individual* entered into the world, and imaginative compassion for men as such, as neither bond nor free, Jew nor Gentile, but equally children of the One God Almighty, the Father of Lights, in whom is neither change nor shadow of turning. The oligarchic creed that men are so far of a different clay that imaginative sympathy need not actively be extended to other classes is condemned, by Pope Gregory the Great, as an insolent belief sprung from the fount of worldly pride. No man may so far presume to assign what other men may be 'worth,' or to limit gifts and diversities of talents that are distributed by a free and inscrutable grace. *Deposuit potentes de sede et exaltavit humiles*—"He hath put down the mighty from their seat," the Neroes and Attilas, "and exalted the humble."

The value of the human being was vindicated by discovering in him something more than the individual and merely
animal. *What was discovered was the person.* He was, further, more than mere individual in terms that transcended any
local, accidental group—he was more in terms of his humanity, and of a humanity that had significance in the universal
scheme and discovered its value there. No human being was
merely a member—what Aristotle, the slave-owner, had called
"an animate instrument"—of human society at a given minute,
far less of any particular human society, even Caesar's. Each
was under obligation to render unto Caesar the things that
were Caesar's and to God those that were God's.

In later centuries it came to be asserted that it was for the
visible Church, as concerned with eternal and not secular
affairs, and therefore higher than kingdoms—being a free
society of baptism and not of the sword, grace not coercion—
to decide what appertained to God and what to Caesar. Calvin
in no wise denied this theory, nor did the Free Churches
later. The judgement of the Catholic Church was guided in
turn by the consensus of the Fathers, although chiefly Revelation (even if in need of interpretation) was posited. Those
princes who talked of an absolute sovereignty or power are
damned by the continuator of St. Thomas Aquinas as like
Nicanor, "that tyrant puffed with pride."

The Schoolmen, however, did not appeal only to the Bible
and Revelation, or even to the interpretations of the Church
Fathers. The famous, if not entirely helpful, canon of St.
Vincent of Lerins laid down that this was to be accepted as
Catholic which was received always, in all places and by all
men. (As a definition of what was 'natural' it had more force.)
St. Thomas, as is well known, appealed with unprecedented
frequency to 'the Philosopher,' Aristotle. Three centuries later
we are told by the Italian theologians at the Council of Trent,.

as characteristic: "School Divinity which, in all difficulties, useth Reason." The Scholastic Philosophy and Theology was one of the most elaborate constructions of logic that the mind of man has wrought and, granted its presuppositions in Christian Revelation on ultimate values, a triumph of the appeal to reason. Its defect was a dogmatism sprung of a confident identification of itself with final wisdom, especially in faith and morals.

Nevertheless, no survey of European civilization can afford to underestimate the part played, not least today, by Catholic culture. There is an admirable *Catholic Humanism* that is not only the mother of the rest but that has distinctive characteristics in its respect for tradition and for the values enshrined by tradition. It is expressed not only by a Catholic such as Erasmus, who was first a humanist, but also by a humanist such as Thomas More, who was first a Catholic. Through Fénelon and Massillon it shaped perhaps especially the culture of France, although its influence is obvious on the mind of Spain and of Italy. It is, indeed, the very key of any intelligible interpretation of the French mind.

. . . . . .

We are now in a position to say what we mean by Humanism. The Humanism of the Renaissance was a rebirth of culture, although in a new form from that of the antique world. It was not a new growth. It was characterized by an admiration for the individual and his will, even exaggerated. In its aberrations it spelled the glorification of tyrants, leaders such as Caesar Borgia, men of 'universal talents,' and men more than life-size in their monstrous activities. The greater humanists, however, from Dante onwards, never doubted the vulgarity of these displays which ended with the hangman and the assassin—*non heroico more:* "not in the heroic style."

The natural right of one man to exercise ruthless power by fist-law was contrary to that *rational natural law* that sanctioned the rights of others. Such men as Ezzelino di Romano, in their pursuit of power, lacked the glimmer of a moral sense: they justified the need for hell. Of the dislike of the Florentines for the tyrants, Jacob Burckhardt, the German historian of the Renaissance, says:

"The deepest ground of dislike has not been stated; Florence was then the scene of the richest development of human individuality, while for the despots no other individuality could be suffered to live and thrive but their own and that of their nearest dependents; the control of the individual was rigorously carried out, even to the establishment of a system of passports."

(Burckhardt wrote in the last century, or he would have recognized an anti-climax in his censure on 'cards of identity.') Against the personal ambitions and convenience of the power-lusting rulers, men claimed the right to say what they liked, without being spied upon, as the core of liberty. However, where there was despotism and its vengeances, the conspirators followed like the vultures, and the spies like the little birds.

At a later stage the despots of hill-cities faded into insignificance as the game of war and power developed between the rulers of the new centralized and national states, the Kings of France and Spain and England. Towards these ambitions for victory or for glory in Fields of Cloth of Gold the later humanists adopted the attitude of *internationalism* and of pacifism. They looked back upon the united *respublica christiana,* "the Christian Commonwealth," itself the heir of the world-empire of Rome, and regarded themselves as *clerici,* clerks, owing a primary obligation to civilization and to catholic, international learning. The pacifism of Erasmus is borne out by the declaration of John Colet: "Better the worst peace than the best war." To these characteristics of Humanism and to the challenge to them we shall have occasion to recur. If they were errors, it cannot be said that they were of a kind to which most Europeans, in the centuries of the Wars of Religion, were unduly tempted to succumb.

The Renaissance had two aspects. On the one side, it was a breach with the immediate past; a laudation of the anarchic individual endowed with *virtù,* i.e. talent, but bereft of scruple; and a releasing of forces co-operating with the Reformation to destroy the dominance of Catholic thought and custom, with its ascetic standards. On the other side, and peculiarly when under Catholic influence, it paid homage to an *idea of civilization as a total of human values* and of achievements sometimes forgotten but never to be rejected, a legacy from the golden past preserved by Byzantium and again unlocked and displayed by scholars.

Further, in a fashion characteristic of scholars and shared with the Schoolmen who went before, the humanists of the Renaissance, even when most guilty of licence in conduct, also paid homage to reason and to *the idea of the rational* as a check upon anarchy. This was, after all, a classic and not a romantic period; and the models, although often ill-understood by men of the late Middle Ages, enjoyed the virtues of measure, grandeur, and tranquillity. It is not until the days of the baroque that the more violent spirit dared to discard its models and to declare itself. 'Rational,' however, was understood in a different sense from the logic and the sense for order which, under the tutelage of Aristotle, had been its characteristic in the universities of the Middle Ages. We shall have occasion later to discuss the *experimentalism* and respect for facts, mother of natural science, which take their rise at this time. As Professor Alfred North Whitehead says, in his *Science and the Modern World:*

"Science has never shaken off the impress of its origin in the historical revolt of the later Renaissance. What reasoning it has wanted, has been borrowed from mathematics, which is a surviving relic of Greek rationalism, following the deductive method. . . . The world required centuries of contemplation of irreducible and stubborn facts. It is difficult for men to do more than one thing at a time, and that was the sort of thing they had to do after the rationalistic orgy of the Middle Ages."

In brief, the respect of the humanists for reason, in its most characteristic historical expression in the Renaissance, was rather respect for *the rational judgement,* emancipated from bondage to custom and dogma, even logical dogma, than for logic and metaphysic.

At the present time, on the continent of Europe, movements denominated 'anti-Europa' are rife. Writers such as Evola, in his *Revolt against the Modern World* (Milan, 1934), while lauding a 'Ghibelline' or German-Italian culture, puts himself into opposition to most of those tendencies, especially to individualism, that spring from the Renaissance. Friedrich Sieburg, in *Germany, my Country,* writes:

"Anyone who is concerned for the preservation in our own or future days of the Great German cultural heritage, should be careful not to scare away our present-day youth by lauding the Hellenic German. The latter ideal touched its apogee at the end of the classical century, in an age which sacrificed the most burning German realities to the Moloch of culture, and evaded painful disputes over the national form by setting up a universal human ideal. . . . The reaction which soon followed was so much the more violent, and Germany now flung herself on the realm of interests which was now no less idealized than it had once been disdained. The notion of the Hellenic German indicates the precise point at which Humanism as a cultural principle has ceased to be adequate to present-day Germany."

The trouble with these writers, in their criticism of 'Europeanism' and Humanism, in their denial of this Grand Tradition that we have described, is that—apart from their condemnation of the international outlook, and also their condemnation of an excessive egoism rightly detected in the Renaissance, but surely not there alone—they confuse the mood of Humanism with the mood of its subsequent French reinterpretation in a fashion characteristically logical and abstract. From this distortion of Humanism into abstract Rationalism the Anglo-Saxon Tradition, with its stress on experiment, compromise and judgement, has from its origins been free. The notes of Humanism there were the notes of belief in reason, in its richest sense of belief in an intelligible universe and a humanity capable of direction by reason; the note of personality or respect for the sentient, choosing and moral individual as representative of that which has end in itself; and the note of humanity as respect for human beings, as such, apart from nation or tribe—with which notes are historically conjoined that of rational quest and experiment.

The Anglo-Saxon Tradition, as something significantly distinct in philosophy, letters, politics and customary attitude to life, as "outlook on the world," takes its rise in the Sixteenth Century out of the common European culture of Catholic Christendom. In the case of that great humanist, Thomas More, once Chancellor of England and now canonized saint, the separation had not yet taken place. Alike the Catholicism of More and the Platonism of his *Utopia* (characteristically enough written first in Latin) are representative of a time when Christendom was one and when humanists regarded themselves as international clerks, scholars who belonged not to a king but to civilization. The appeal of St. Thomas More to a law more august than that of England, and his execution on the issue of the royal supremacy, were the signals for the end of that age. Henceforth the outstanding English writers (if representative—as the Jesuits such as Cardinal Allen and Parsons were not), have ceased to be primarily good Europeans.

The most characteristic institution of the new epoch was the Anglican Church, with its Calvinist Thirty-Nine Articles and its Catholic liturgy. It was a moderate and reasonable institution in which the national genius for identifying reasonableness with readiness to compromise, rather than with logical intransigence, displayed itself. Its view received classical expression in the writings of Richard Hooker (1554–1600), "the judicious Hooker." If we are to say that the characteristics of the Anglo-Saxon Tradition, as distinct from general European culture, receive their earliest expression in any single writer rather than another—and if we agree with Whitehead, at least as touching these times, that

"the mentality of an epoch springs from the view of the world which is, in fact, dominant in the educated sections of the communities in question"—

then Richard Hooker rather than Shakespeare or Spenser is probably the character whom it is appropriate to select. It is relevant that he was a Protestant divine and hence peculiarly a representative of that fusion of the cultures of Hellas and of Judaea (perhaps too much that of the Old Testament) which Matthew Arnold insisted made up the composition of the English mind. He represents the average, raised to the level of educated articulateness.

One notices in Hooker's *Laws of Ecclesiastical Polity,* first, that stress on reason rather than appeal to mere customary authority which is characteristic throughout of the Grand Tradition. Luther and the Protestant reformers had supplanted the authority of the Church by that of the Bible. Many had carried this so far as to regard scholastic philosophy with contempt and to insist upon implicit obedience to a theology which they urged sprang directly and self-evidently from the Sacred Book. That great dogmatist Calvin wrote, in his *Institutes of the Christian Religion:*

"Let it be considered, then, as an undeniable truth, that they who have been inwardly taught by the Spirit, feel an entire acquiescence in the Scripture, and that it is self-authenticated, carrying with it its own evidence, and *ought not to be made the subject of demonstration and arguments from reason;* but it obtains the credit which it deserves with us by the testimony of the Spirit. . . . I know what is objected by some clamorous men, who would ostentatiously display the force of their understanding in opposing divine truth. For they inquire, Who has assured us that Moses and the prophets actually wrote these books which bear their names? They even dare to question whether such a man as Moses ever existed. But if any man should call in question the existence of Plato or Aristotle, or Cicero, who would deny that such madness ought to receive corporal punishment? . . . Persons who, abandoning the scripture, imagine to themselves some other way of approaching to God, must be considered as not so much misled by error as actuated by frenzy."

The Scriptures, then, were self-evident and needed no interpreter, and were an interpreter needed (owing to the perverse obstinacy of men stirred by Satan), then the ill-tempered Calvin was its true interpreter. He knew that Moses himself wrote the record of Moses' own death and burial. And he knew that Servetus, the Unitarian, was wrong and, therefore, by personal intervention had him burned at the stake.

Against this let us set the words of Hooker and we shall readily see how distinctive is the mood, although Hooker confesses that he is writing in an "age full of tongue and weak of brain." They are words which not only the Calvinists and

Puritans of the past, but our Marxists of today with their Book and the Goebbels-followers with their Prophet may digest with advantage.

"These men at the first were only pitied in their error, and not much withstood by any; the great humility, zeal and devotion, which appeared to be in them, was in all men's opinion a pledge of their harmless meaning . . . let any man of a contrary opinion open his mouth to persuade them, they close up their ears, his reasons they weigh not, all is answered with rehearsal of the words of John, 'We are of God; he that knoweth God heareth us: as for the rest, ye are of the world; for this world's pomp and vanity it is that ye speak, and the world, where ye are, heareth you' . . . taking it as meant, that in case the Church do devise any new order, she ought therein to follow the direction of Scripture only, and not any starlight of man's reason. . . . *These men . . . which at the first thought judgement and justice itself to be merciless cruelty, accounted at the length their own hands sanctified with being embrued in Christian blood. . . .* There will come a time when three words uttered with charity and meekness shall receive a far more blessed reward than three thousand volumes written with disdainful sharpness of wit."

Hooker himself, as we shall see, was far from committed to toleration if as a consequence fanatics "gathered strength, much more than was safe for the state of the commonwealth wherein they lived." "We are too patient . . . the spit-venom of their poisoned hearts breaketh out to the annoyance of others." Nevertheless, the principle which he argues must be defended, if need be by force, was itself a principle closely kin to toleration. *"Zeal needeth both ways a sober guide."*

"An earnest desire to draw all things under the determination of bare and naked Scripture hath caused here much pains to be taken in abating the estimation and credit of man. . . . *the name of the light of nature is made hateful with men; the 'star of reason and learning' and all other such like helps, beginneth no otherwise to be thought of than if it were an unlucky comet.*

. . . By these and the like disputes an opinion hath spread itself very far in the world, as if the way to be ripe in faith were to be raw in wit and judgement. . . . Where understanding therefore needeth, in those things Reason is the director of men's Will by discovering in action what is good. *For the Laws of well-doing are the dictates of right Reason.*"

Is, then, Hooker purely a scholastic or a rationalist, a man of remorseless logic like Calvin, but substituting Intellect for Jehovah as his God? Very far from it. The stress is on judgement. Syllogisms cannot rise higher than their sources in major premises of ultimate values. "Herein that (saying) of Theophrastus is true, 'They that seek a reason of all things do utterly overthrow Reason.' In every kind of knowledge some such grounds there are, as that being proposed the mind doth presently embrace them as free from all possibility of errors." Whatever, yet, may be the case with mathematical axioms, the apprehension of absolute values in morals may be incomplete and unclear. "Think ye are men, deem it not impossible for you to err; sift unpartially your own hearts, whether it be force of reason or vehemency of affections, which hath bred and doth still feed these opinions in you."

There is *a law of nature which is a law of reason,* with which law human nature must accord—although Hooker is ready enough to encourage the opinion of St. Gregory Nazianzen, Doctor of the Church, that "God is not a God of sedition and confusion but of order and peace." St. Augustine, we are told, is right in saying that "to refuse the conduct of the light of nature is not folly alone but accompanied by great impiety." How then—if not by Scripture without need of interpretation, and if not by self-evidence beyond error—are we to discover this rule of nature and of reason?

"If the natural strength of man's art may *by experience and study* attain unto such ripeness in the knowledge of things

human, that men in this respect may presume to build somewhat upon their judgement; what reason have we to think but
that . . . men shall have just cause, when anything pertinent unto
faith and religion is doubted of, the more willingly to incline
their minds *towards that which the sentence of so grave, wise,
and learned in that faculty shall judge most sound. For the controversy is of the weight of such men's judgements.* . . . Laws
of Reason have these marks to be known by. Such as keep them
resemble most lively in their voluntary actions that very manner
of working which Nature herself doth necessarily observe in the
course of the whole world. The works of Nature are all behove-
ful, beautiful, without superfluity or defect; even so theirs, if
they be framed according to that which the Law of Reason teach-
eth. Secondly, those Laws are investigable by Reason . . . in
such fashion they are investigable, that the knowledge of them
is general, *the world hath always been acquainted with them;*
according to that which one in Sophocles [*Antigone*] observeth
concerning a breach of this Law, *'It is no child of today's or
yesterday's birth, but hath been no man knoweth how long
sithence."* [1]

In summary, then, we discover that the notes of Humanism
are the appeal to reason, against mere brute dogma believed
because the mass sentiment of some united society wills it to
be believed; the raising to self-consciousness of the individual
and the stress on personality and choice, including moral
choice of community; preference for experiment and experience rather than for *a priori* metaphysical systems; attachment
to learning and scholarship; belief in a tradition from ancient

[1] I heard it not from Heaven, nor came it forth
From Justice where she reigns with Gods below.
They too have published to mankind a law.
Nor thought I thy commandment of such might
That one who is mortal thus could overbear
The infallible, unwritten Laws of Heaven.
Not now or yesterday they have their being,
But everlastingly, and none can tell
The hour that saw their birth.

Antigone, 449–457.

times, expressing deeper truths of human nature, which although it might be broken by barbarism may not have its value destroyed; and the attachment of importance to the judgement of the learned throughout the ages concerning what that tradition may be.

Over against Humanism is to be set alike the barbarian tribalism, with its crude authority of the local social organism caked in custom, and the wild lawless freedom—without rule of reason, arbitrary, power-asserting—of the Middle Ages. Over against it also must be set a more doughty antagonist, as over against Hellas is set the wisdom of Egypt. It is a mighty dogmatic ideology, materialized in a social system, coercive, persecuting and relying (as the Renaissance Popes at their best realized and sought to correct) upon the fanaticism of ignorance for its mob support. It yet boasts itself as being morality because it is the expression of the common, undisrupted, homogeneous culture and willed way-of-thinking of a united society, with massive strength because of this compulsive, uncriticized unity—strength often issuing in abuse of power. This antagonist was not Catholicism, nor was Humanism in opposition to Catholic learning; but it was the Inquisition's misbegotten child. It was Catholicism in a particular mood as militant orthodoxy sustained by clericalism, from the abuses of which the Protestant Revolt resulted.

Richard Hooker wrote his *Laws of Ecclesiastical Polity* "to teach men a reason why just and reasonable laws are of so great force, of so great *use* in the world." The English tradition which takes its distinctive rise in him has here, at the beginning, the authentic characteristics of Humanism, as of Utility. Hellas and Christendom are its parent-lands. It is indeed Anglican and insular. It lacks the earlier internationalism and pacifism, despite Hooker's insistence on a "Law of Nations." "We covet (if it might be) to have a kind of society and fellowship even with all mankind." It is narrower than the majestic breadth of Catholicism; but it is free from some of the dangerous and irrelevant infallibilities of that system and the bonds retightened at Trent. At least the Anglican tradition is a legitimate child, in the indubitable lineage of the Grand Tradition of humanity as displayed in the record of human thought on Society and Morals.

We have supposed a consensus of the great sages, the masters, authors of the Tradition. We have asserted that the extent of this consensus, not the divergence, is remarkable. It gives meaning to the Stoic term 'citizen of the world.' On it Hooker, by good right of spiritual inheritance, quotes Sophocles. It gives meaning to the term 'good European.' As the Anglo-Saxon civilization develops it acquires new and distinguishing characteristics—different, for example, from the Catholic and the French. But it is a reassurance in proclaiming our judgement, as a people, on values and on decency and manners in civilization, that we should know, at the start, of the authentic Humanism—of the validity by the least insular test—of that which we seek to study, to display, to glorify and to vindicate. It has the Note of Reason; the Note of Personality; and the Note of Humanity. It also speaks a common language with the great masters upon ultimate values, upon the beautiful and good.

CHAPTER II

Freedom

§ i

"ZEAL, shaking loosely the slack reins, drives over the heads of scarlet prelates, and such as are insolent to maintain traditions, bruising their stiff necks under his flaming wheels." In John Milton (1608–74) the English Tradition through his very denial of a tradition differentiates itself and writes new chapters into the testament handed down.

Milton indeed displays too often that protesting mood of bad temper of which Luther set the fashion, exculpating himself on the ground that he "could not write a dull style." For Milton an opponent is a "cursing Shimei, a hurler of stones." There is a "tart rhetoric in the Church's cause," "a sanctified bitterness against the enemies of truth," in denouncing "the Prelates, her spiritual adulterers . . . the internuntios or the go-betweens of this trim devis'd mummery," and their weak arguments vapoured out "with quips and snapping adagies." It is "unlike a Christian to be a cold neuter in the cause of the church." To be brief, Milton when roused had a foul mouth such as that of which Hooker complains. His excuse is a mood in himself, and his fellows, of exasperation such as inspired Foxe's *Book of Martyrs*. The consequence of this mood (compared with which the dissipated Charles II shines with reasonableness and tolerance) was not only the persecution in England of Papist and Prelatist, but the Puritan temper that exposed to bitter persecutions the Quakers in New England.

Nevertheless, as others before him and since, Milton laid down in his indignation principles that were better than the practice he countenanced, and that grew into our tradition. Even the compulsion, as Secretary of State, to write to "the Most Eminent Lord," Cardinal Mazarin, on behalf of his "Eminence's most Affectionate Oliver, Protector of the Commonwealth," may have had the sobering influence of practical compromise.

Be this as it may, Milton claims for himself, in speech and writing, what his editor calls "the protestant licence to the utmost, arraying text against text." Especially is this true in his *Doctrine and Discipline of Divorce,* where he appeals to reason against custom in the name of "the good of man and the plain exigence of charity." He does not doubt there to be "a regenerate reason"; nor that it is but "the fault of a perverse opinion," where a practice is "continued in despite of *reason and nature." Magna est veritas et praevalebit.*[1] The right to discover and pursue that truth—not perhaps without noise and factious, uncharitable denunciation—he claims:

"Give me the liberty to know, to alter, and to argue freely, according to conscience, above all liberties."

Thus he sought that the land should enfranchise "herself from the impertinent yoke of prelaty, under whose inquisitorious and tyrannical duncery no free and splendid wit can flourish." Against the loud denunciation of Milton it is well to set the satire of the Catholic Dryden, with his flaying of Shaftesbury, the founder of the Protestant Whigs, under the title of Achitophel.

What then is the heart of the matter? Freedom to speak,

[1] "Mighty is truth and it will prevail."

freedom to write, freedom not to be spied upon. Civil liberty is not absence of grievances and a swinish ignorant contentment or slavish timidity about voicing their grievances. "But when complaints are freely heard, deeply considered and speedily reformed, then is the utmost bound of civil liberty attained that wise men look for." What then of some central authority which shall choose for men; and what of the social organic unity of the State? Milton himself had explained that reason is but "liberty of choosing." Shall each then choose his own way, or must there not be, as Hobbes said, a "publique conscience," and that resident in the mind of Leviathan? How far must not men subordinate their variety and private inquiries and searchings for truth to the values of homogeneity, unity and the moral custom of their people?

"I fear yet this iron yoke of outward conformity hath left a slavish print upon our necks; the ghost of a linen decency yet haunts us. We stumble and are impatient at the least dividing of one visible congregation from another, though it be not in fundamentals; and through our frowardness to suppress, and our backwardness to recover any enthralled piece of truth out of the gripe of custom, we care [mind] not to keep truth separated from truth which is the fiercest rent and discussion of all. We do not see that, while we still affect by all means a rigid external formality, we may as soon fall again into a gross conforming stupidity, a stark and dead congealment of wood and hay and stubble, forced and frozen together, which is more to the sudden degenerating of a Church than many subdichotomies of petty schisms."

Was Milton right? Had not the massive uniformity of the Catholic Church for so many centuries prevailed and survived against the subdivisions of the sects following their free choices and own imaginings? And would not this be an hundred times more true if State, even Hobbes' State, stepped into the shoes of Church? What, again, of Plato's Commonwealth, in which Milton rightly and by name discovers his perfect antagonist? Would this lead to "a sudden degenerating?"

Milton meets this charge by an appeal to organic sentiment, in lieu of mechanical conformity—indeed to a pride fantastic, overweening, arrogant, even if hastily cloaked with Puritan humility. It is well to recall, consider and digest this appeal.

"What does (God) then but reveal Himself to His servants, and as His manner is, first to His Englishmen? I say, as His manner is, first to us, though we mark not the method of His counsels, and are unworthy. Behold now this vast City: a city of refuge, the mansion house of liberty, encompassed and surrounded with His protection; the shop of war hath not then more anvils and hammers working to fashion out the plates and instruments of armed Justice in defence of beleaguered Truth than there be pens and heads there. . . . Methinks I see in my mind a noble and puissant nation rousing herself like a strong man after sleep and shaking her invincible locks. . . . Lords and Commons of England, consider what Nation it is whereof ye are, and whereof ye are the governors . . . our English, the language of men, ever famous and foremost in the achievements of liberty."

Not Mussolini, not Hitler, has spoken in stronger terms; nor Kipling sung of it. The boasting is, nevertheless, not empty provincial pride but is exposed to an empiric test, satisfying enough to any humanist. It is the test of spiritual vitality and the test of progress.

"I have sat among their learned men, for that honour I had, and been counted happy to be born in such a place of philosophic freedom, as they supposed England was, while themselves did nothing but bemoan the servile condition into which learning among them was brought; that this was it which had damped the glory of Italian wits; that nothing had been there written now these many years but flattery and fustian . . ."

That also the present writer can say of Italy, remembering the words of men of letters, and of Germany and also of

Russia—save that in Germany those who spoke were aristocrats, with world-famous, sounding names, and in Russia common folk talking of tyranny. And if Milton sometimes used a language of insular pride, later satirized by Daniel Defoe in his *The True-born Englishman,* at least Milton had some evidence to support his statements of principle.

It is not the case, be it noted, that the empiric tradition was limited to the Anglo-Saxon world with its pioneering background in the experiences told of by Hakluyt and Raleigh and its philosophy in the pages of Francis Bacon. Vesalius and Paracelsus were not of this nation. Before Caxton was Gutenberg; before Drake was Cabot. The glorious dawn in Italian civilization reaching noon with Leonardo da Vinci had continued in full daylight to shine on Galileo and Torricelli. But the climate of the times increasingly became adverse, as a matter of historical record, to the flourishing of such men. A new and suspicious dogmatic moralism rendered more deadly by jealous institutions and by a paternal but suffocating conservativism of government suppressed the hopes and rewards of originality and declined to admit the chances of error for the sake of the advantages of trial. In Germany religious fanaticism and more material calculations of ambition released bands of low marauders who devastated the land and its civilization, in civil war and *stasis,* in the name of principle and of high professions.

§ ii

In Oliver Cromwell (1599–1658) we see this same admixture of confidence in the power of the nation, and stress upon it, with a genuine belief in personal liberty of thought and speech and choice. In Cromwell it becomes a mixture of the spirit of discipline with that of humility that is of vital relevance for our own days. How shall we have *both* discipline *and* freedom? Let us turn back to the figure of the great English dictator, so singularly dissimilar from most dictators, a figure as English hero less grand than Abraham Lincoln but yet so grand that we may still learn from study of it.

Who does not know the revealing answer to the Presbyterian divines? "I beseech you, in the bowels of Christ, think it possible that you may be mistaken." Himself before his death declaring, after agony of doubt, "the Lord hath filled me with as much assurance of His pardon and His love as my soul can hold," Cromwell was yet no man to make his assurance a foundation for the compulsion of the conscience of others. Liberty of conscience was 'a fundamental,' just as that Parliaments should not make themselves perpetual was 'a fundamental.'

"What we gain in a free way is better than twice so much in a forced, and will be more truly ours and our posterities . . . That which you have by force I look upon as nothing."

Cromwell has the stain on his shield of Drogheda. No purpose is served by palliating it, although it is often forgotten that not only Irish, but Sir Arthur Ashton and the Protestant English with him were among those murdered. It is no palliation of the massacre, this worse than the German 30th of June, that "this bitterness will save much blood through the goodness of God." It is the old excuse for vile conduct, made worse by talk of God's "righteous justice" which "brought a just judgement upon them." The Old Testament often did the Puritans [1] small good. Oliver was sometimes little better than

[1] The word 'Puritan' defies precise definition, as something living and changing, as much as does 'humanist,' 'romantic' or even 'liberal.' Here it is used generally as what I may call a 'Left-Wing Protestant,' a notion to be grasped rather in terms of an historic tendency persisting through and beyond the Reformation than as the upholding of a logical doctrine. Professor J. W. Allen, however, has provided a learned and interesting discussion of this term in his *English Political Thought, 1603–1660*, vol. I.

his generation in its bigotries. This atrocity, however, is no reason for doubting the sincerity, the freedom from hypocrisy —and, if there were self-deception, how few of us are free from it—of the last prayer, one of the great monuments of the English language.

"Lord, though I am a miserable and wretched creature, I am in covenant with Thee through grace, and I may, I will, come to Thee for Thy people. Thou hast made use of me, though very unworthy, a mean instrument to do them some good and Thee service; and many of them have set too high a value upon me, though others wish and would be glad of my death. Lord, however Thou dost dispose of me, continue and go on to do good for them. Give them consistency of judgement, one heart, and mutual love, and go on to deliver them, and with the work of reformation, and make the name of Christ glorious in the world. Teach those who look too much on Thy instruments to depend more upon Thyself. Pardon such as desire to trample upon the dust of a poor worm, for they are Thy people too. And pardon the folly of this short prayer, even for Jesus Christ's sake, and give me a good night if it be Thy pleasure."

Such was the last testament of the great Lord Protector, and so he passed. He had not only made England again respected on the four seas. He cared for New England. But, above all, he identified the English name with an idea that combined strength with liberty and a practice that conjoined Admiral Blake with Milton. May his spirit be with us now.

There were not lacking those who were disgruntled with his authority, and these not only 'prelatists'—men such as those Levellers who denounced him as "that landscape of iniquity, that sink of sin, and that compendium of baseness." The Left-Wing Puritan was not an easy man to rule, and it can be urged that Cromwell interfered with personal liberty in practice as much as Laud. If the Protectorate upheld the banner of liberty abroad, in Savoy and Jewry, it denied liberty at home to prelatist and papist: its principles changed colour when they reached home shores. The rulers of Germany and Russia today would allege that they also permit liberty of witness when there is no danger that this witness will sink to the whisper of conspiracy.

What differed, then, three centuries ago, was the ruler's mood—Oliver's willingness to permit criticism and even to suffer his admonishers to enlarge on his faults. This is more impressive than the mere fact that, as Maidston says, "he was naturally compassionate towards objects in distress even to an effeminate measure." So were Robespierre and Lenin. The point is that he was prepared to be reasoned with, and that he could understand that there was also the other man's point of view.

> "For he no duty by his height excused,
>   Nor, though a prince, to be a man refused."

The mood of the dictatorship was one that advanced, rather than retarded, the cause of personal liberty and freedom from arrest 'for reason of state' which won through to victory in *Habeas Corpus* and the British Bill of Rights of 1689. Its mood, at least, would not have been disowned by Pym and Hampden.

This achievement of temper, as a matter of sober moral restraint, is the more remarkable since the Puritans, as iconoclasts and Bible-crusaders, had every temptation to be fanatics of the Old Testament mould, taking Samuel hewing Agag in pieces as their moral model. The Presbyterians of John Calvin's fold were indeed temperamental persecutors; and the *mot* is not unjust that accuses the Puritans, pilgrims to America, of "leaving a land where they were persecuted for a land where they might persecute." Persecute in fact they did. The record is damning. Nevertheless the individualism of Protestantism, the Independency of Brownism, introduced an inner contradiction and a doubt even into persecution. Roger Williams the Baptist, although he did not love the Quakers and, with the virulent invective of the day, could call George Fox "a filthy sow," yet expressed his true belief and his sense of achievement when he declared from Rhode Island, in a letter to Sir Francis Vane, "We have drunk of the cup of as great liberties as any people we can hear of under heaven."

§ iii

This belief in liberty of expression, liberty of writing, liberty from spying, liberty from arrest for reason of state, by *lettres de cachet* or otherwise, is no mere Parliamentarian eccentricity. It is unnecessary here to search in the obscure ambiguous records of mediaeval baronial liberties, from King John's and Cardinal Langton's day, where right was read as right*s* and the issue was ever a matter of detail, having its legality and precedent. It is sufficient to turn back to Hooker, in whose pages we find the clear exposition of the theme that the basis of government is consent, albeit that those gathered together are no mere chance aggregate but a natural society of social creatures, finding, as Aristotle said, their fit life in such a polity. The judicious Hooker perfectly combines the classic theories of Social Organism and of Social Contract, as does later Burke.

"Of this point therefore we are to note, that sith men naturally have no full and perfect power to command whole politic multitudes of men, therefore utterly without our consent we could in such sort be at no man's commandment living. And to be commanded *we do consent,* when that society whereof we are part hath at any time before consented, without revoking the same after by the like universal agreement. Wherefore as any man's deed past is good so long as himself continueth; so the act of a public society done five hundred years sithence standeth as theirs who presently are of the same societies, because corporations are immortal; *we were then alive in our predecessors, and they in their successors do live still. Laws therefore human, of what kind soever, are available by consent. . . . Laws they are not therefore which public approbation hath not made so. . . .* Now if men had not naturally this desire to be happy, how were it possible that all men should have it? All men have. Therefore this desire in man is natural."

Liberty guarded by consent. Consent, because government was (as St. Thomas had said) not for the sake of the governors but of the governed. What mattered was their happiness. But liberty is to be understood in the context of the tradition of the generations. And happiness is to be sought not without recollection of the reality of original sin: "those Laws of Reason . . . are not sufficient . . . now that man and his offspring are grown thus corrupt and sinful."

Such Whig leaders as Algernon Sidney (1622–83) and Russell knew that their foundation lay in this consent which they understood how to combine with national pride. Their liberty and their country's were made to march together. Sidney, in his *Discourses,* writes:

"As liberty solely consists in an independency upon the will of another, and by the name of slave we understand a man who can neither dispose of his person nor goods, but enjoys all at the will of his master, there is no such thing in nature as a slave, if those men or nations are not slaves, who have no other title to what they enjoy, than the grace of the prince, which he may revoke whenever he pleases. . . . It has been hitherto believed in the world, that the Assyrians, Medes, Arabs, Egyptians, Turks, and others like them, lived in slavery, because their princes were masters of their lives and goods: whereas the Grecians, Italians, Gauls, Germans, Spaniards, and Carthaginians, as long as they had any strength, virtue or courage amongst them, were esteemed free nations, because they abhorred such a subjection. They were, and would be, governed only by laws of their own making: 'potentiora erant legum quam hominum imperia.' " [1]

The executed Sidney was a scoundrel, but there is no doubt that to the men who built up the England of the Eighteenth Century he, not either Charles, was a blessed martyr. His companion in conspiracy, Rumbold, supplied inspiration to Jefferson. The Whig and the Liberal tradition were in the making. Meanwhile another victim, the noble Montrose, in Scotland, had already developed his theory of government as a matter of balance—of checks and balances—a theory of which we shall hear more.

Whiggery, indeed, was more than tinged with oligarchy. For all his talk of independency, Sidney was an oligarch as much as any baron who confronted King John. So too were the Parliament men, but in a different manner. For Harrington, author of *Oceana,* power should rest with the yeoman farmer. For the Puritans oligarchy should be one of grace and election, whereas for the Whigs it was the case that manors maketh man. For the Puritan divine, Richard Baxter, author of *The Saints' Everlasting Rest,* the unregenerate blaspheming masses, not elect, are the "God-damn-me's." Oliver Cromwell is clear that "it's not what they want; it's what's good for them —that's what matters." Milton does not hesitate to scold the idolatrous mob when, like the Israelites of old, it backslides. There could be such an evil as "a licentious and unbridled democracy." "If there be a king, which the *inconsiderate multitude* are now so mad upon, mark how far short we are likely to come of all those happinesses which *in a free state* we shall immediately be possessed of." Therefore Milton wrote, in order

"to stay these ruinous proceedings, justly and timely fearing to what a precipice of destruction the deluge of this epic madness

---

[1] "More potent were the rules of laws than of men."

would hurry us, through the general defection of a misguided and abused multitude."

§ iv

The notions, however, of "the free state" and that "to be commanded we do consent" persisted; nor could all the sophistry of that keen, extravagant mind, Thomas Hobbes, dislodge them. It was the triumph of the philosopher, John Locke (1632–1704), that he inscribed these watchwords on the banners of the heavy men of property and of acres, the Whig lords.

Reason succeeded to grace; common-sense to god-fearing indignation. A new mood supervened with the new century. Alexander Pope followed John Milton. John Locke's doctrine of contract, his riddling criticism of the Bible-quoting loyalism of Filmer, were the stir of the times. He justified the conscience of the English Revolution to itself and set quiet the men who felt some shame at forcing the abdication of their liege lord.

"It is evident that absolute monarchy, which by some men [Hobbes] is counted for the only government in the world, is indeed inconsistent with civil society, and so can be no form of civil government at all . . . wherever any persons are who have not such an [common, contracted] authority to appeal to, and decide any difference between them then, those persons are still in the state of Nature. And so is every absolute prince in respect of those who are under his dominion. . . . No man in civil society can be exempted from the laws of it. . . . *Wherever law ends, tyranny begins,* if the law be transgressed to another's harm."

But King James II, Locke argues, strove to establish an absolute monarchy, free from the obligation of mutual contract implied in any social authority that had a moral claim to allegiance.

What, then, is liberty or civil freedom?

"Freedom of men under government is to have *a standing rule to live by,* common to everyone of that society, and made by the legislative power erected on it. A liberty to follow my own will in all things where that rule prescribes not, not to be subject to the inconstant, uncertain, unknown *arbitrary will* of another man, as freedom of nature is to be under *no other restraint but the law of Nature. This freedom from absolute, arbitrary power* is so necessary to, and closely joined with, a man's preservation, that he cannot part with it but by what forfeits his preservation and life together."

Here, then, is the essential combination—freedom, but freedom under law prescribed irrespective of persons, or groups, not arbitrary privilege. Here follow, as corollaries, the right to personal freedom from arbitrary imprisonment and the right to be brought to trial by due process of law. These rights are 'natural' in this sense, that they flow direct from the fount of the social order itself—of any social order entitled to respect and constituting a source of political obligation.

The Fight for Personal Liberty was the first of the four great fights in the battle for democracy—for Personal Liberty, Religious Liberty, Political Liberty and Economic Liberty; and Locke established its appropriate formula, re-established the Aristotelian formula: "Above all men is the law." It is the maxim inscribed over the entrance of Harvard Law School. It is a variant of that written below the pediment of the building of the Supreme Court at Washington: "Equal Justice under Law." It connects with that 'Spirit of the Common Law' which, as Dean Pound, of Harvard, and so many others have demonstrated, including Lord Haldane, so connects and distinguishes by a common heritage the Anglo-Saxon peoples.

The Law, however, is the work of legislators, politicians and partisans. What if what Bentham called 'Judge & Co.' have a bias also, a class bias? That no individual shall be victimized by being prosecuted under some process directed especially against himself, and not common to all in his position, may be an advance. But has Locke reflected whether 'the Law' is equally effective as a safeguard when whole classes are affected, or whether positive law may not be the instrument of sectional animus and class war? Superficially, it appears that he had not. The Civil War had been fought, by the Parliamentarians, in chief about taxes and men's pockets. Hampden and his Ship Money had been the tinder and spark. Naturally enough then—but dangerously enough also—Locke, the Whig spokesman, defines the end of government: "the great and chief end, therefore, of men uniting into commonwealth, and putting themselves under government, is the preservation of their property"—the preservation of their *property against taxes*—against the King's exactions ostensibly for 'his' Navy.

What are the implications of this? Whatever the Whig lords might think, the implication for Locke seems to have been the natural and sacred right of property *for all*—or, at least, for all who had "admixed their labour" (the Marxist phrase is his) in converting the bounties of Nature or otherwise manufacturing them. His private bias is shewn in his generous recommendations before the Council of Trade for dealing with the unemployed. But, in fact, Locke gives his answer to our question: an answer reminiscent of Hooker and of the Schoolmen before him.

"I will not dispute now whether princes are exempt from the laws of their country, but this I am sure, they owe subjection to *the laws of God and Nature*. Nobody, no power can exempt them from the obligations of that eternal law. . . . God, who hath given the world to men in common, hath also given them *reason* to make use of it to the best *advantage* of life and convenience. . . . *The end of government is the good of mankind.*"

It is the opposite contention to that of Halifax (1633–95)

that "to govern men it is often necessary to treat them scurvily." Here, then, we have the heart of the matter. Liberty is freedom of expression and action subject to law. Positive law itself is subject to that Natural Law which is the law of God and reason. And reason dictates those measures that are 'convenient'—the Utilitarian thesis—for the good of mankind, men being considered as equal in their *prima facie* claim on these benefits. How equal?

"I cannot be supposed to understand all kinds of 'equality.' Age or virtue may give men a just precedency. Excellency of parts and merit may place others above the common level."

Locke turns for support to Hooker. When he speaks of "men being . . . by nature all free, equal and independent," he implies such an equality as "makes it the foundation of that obligation to mutual love [fraternity] amongst men on which he builds the duties they owe one another." And for Hooker, enlarging the Golden Rule, these men are "weak, being of one and the same nature." Equality, then, is this: nothing else but assertion of a common clay. Hooker is asserting what Pope Gregory the Great laid down in the early days: that the doctrine of inequality springs *ex fonte superbiae,* "from the fount of pride." And "He hath put down the mighty from their seat." Hooker and Locke are asserting what Pope Pius XI asserted: that all men are of one common human race.

Locke then does not assert liberty. He denies liberty, in Nietzsche's sense of liberty without equality. He asserts *liberty under law;* and that law a rational law *resting on the premise of equality, not an equality that ignores diversity of function, but an equality resting on sense of community* with the humble, and on the Puritan sense of how precarious, in the eyes of God, is the salvation of the most confident and proud.

That god-fearing equality is indeed far more than Puritan; it is the traditional belief of Christianity and of Catholicism in all times of religious aliveness. True liberty is such civil freedom to act as allows, conditions being equal, like freedom to those of like clay. Later examination will shew that Jefferson and Lincoln made the same distinctive assumptions as Hooker and Locke about liberty, and the same distinctive assumptions about equality.

§ v

There is, however, a significance to liberty, more negative but more aggressive than mere liberty of choice in conduct under law, that runs like a skein through all these arguments. It is seen authentic in Algernon Sidney and in Locke's political works. It is intimately connected with the major battle of all, that for personal freedom from arbitrary arrest. *It is liberty from political despotism,* even if urged in the name of the security or good of the State, but urged without appeal— an authority that, possessing powers, sees no reason to give reasons. It is Personal Liberty as against Reason of State. On the contrary, powers should be divided and, as George Washington was to say: "the concentration of powers in one hand is the essence of tyranny." Tolerable for some this awe-inspiring concentration might be, when it was, as with the great Frederick's Prussia, efficient and enlightened, even heroic. Even thus it involves making the common man the mere corpuscle, cog or instrument of some Social Organism, State or Nation; and not making the social institution the means for the assessable good of individual, choosing, sentient men, present or future. The system, however, becomes entirely intolerable when it lapses—and there is no constitutional means to prevent its lapsing—into stupidity and unimaginative repression.

The process is from the efficient Augustus, *pater patriae,*
to the sombre tyrant Tiberius; from Tiberius to the mad Caligula; and from Caligula to Nero, both tyrant and mad. So
great a drama, however—the theatre of a world-empire ruled
by sadistic autocrats from their luxury palaces on high Capri
—need not be supposed. Lesser despots provided the problem
of the Eighteenth Century, when Whiggery continued the
campaign of the Commonwealth men. A Louis XV. Or a
Frederick William III of Prussia on the throne of Frederick.
Or a conscientious George III with his clouded mind. The invective of Milton was requickened, more shrill and flash, in
Byron. The Devil is made to speak of "old, blind, mad, help-
less, weak, poor worm," George III:

> " 'Tis true, he was a tool from first to last
>   (I have the workmen safe); but as a tool
> So let him be consumed. From out the past
>   Of ages, since mankind have known the rule
> Of monarchs—from the bloody rolls amass'd
>   Of sin and slaughter—from the Caesar's school,
> Take the worst pupil; and produce a reign
> More drench'd with gore, more cumber'd with the slain.

> "He ever warr'd with freedom and the free:
>   Nations as men, home subjects, foreign foes,
> So that they utter'd the word 'Liberty!'
>   Found George the Third their first opponent. Whose
> History was ever stain'd as his will be
>   With national and individual woes?
> I grant his household abstinence: I grant
> His neutral virtues, which most monarchs want;

> "I know he was a constant consort; own
>   He was a decent sire, and middling lord.
> All this is much, and most upon a theme;
>   As temperance, if at Apicius' board,

Is more than at an anchorite's supper shown.
  I grant him all the kindest can accord;
And this was well for him, but not for those
Millions who found him what oppression chose.

"The New World shook him off; the Old yet groans
  Beneath what he and his prepared, if not
Completed: he leaves heirs on many thrones
  To all his vices, without what begot
Compassion for him—his tame virtues; drones
  Who sleep, or despots, who have now forgot
A lesson which shall be re-taught them, wake
Upon the thrones of earth; but let them quake."

CHAPTER III

Experiment [1]

§ i

"The understanding must also be cautioned against *the intemperance of systems,* so far as regards its giving or withholding its assent; for such intemperance appears to fix and perpetuate idols, so as to leave no means of removing them. . . . Let such, therefore, be our precautions in contemplation, that we may ward off and expel the idols of the den, which mostly owe their birth either to some predominant pursuit, or, secondly, to an excess in synthesis and analysis, or, thirdly, to a party zeal in favour of certain ages, or, fourthly, to the extent and narrowness of the subject."

So Francis Bacon, Lord Verulam, "the deep and judicious Verulam," attacks Aristotle—or, rather, through him, the presumptuous academics in their universities—in the jewelled phrases of his *Novum Organum,* because these systematizers suffocated experiment, in order *"that everything should be certain and decided."* Aristotle "drags experiment along as a captive constrained to accommodate herself to his decisions. . . . The Aristotelian philosophy, after destroying other systems

---

[1] The common reader is advised to omit, for the moment, this chapter and the next, which are philosophical, and discuss issues impossible to omit but necessarily technical. He must not blame me if he ventures. The student will realize that they are indeed the heart of the whole matter. . . . The *clerc* and student nowadays are unimportant persons, without the wealth of the ladies' lunch clubs, but even the student must be allowed his occasional luxuries and licenced hours for thought, when he is let out to run, unchaperoned even by a teacher of *belles lettres* or by a publicity expert and sales manager.

(as the Ottomans do their brethren) by its disputatious confutations, decided upon everything." It is a small matter that Bacon, seeing Aristotle reflected in the mirrors of the know-all superiority of vested academics, with lectures checking all "out of the common track"—not indeed the Church Schoolmen; for it is of the modern times that Bacon says, their whole bent was rather upon "fulness than weight"—should misunderstand that great man, as Hobbes was to do after; should mistake Aristotle for a conjurer with words and *a-priorities;* and should attack as an enemy one who indeed fought on his own side. What emerges clear is what Bacon affirmed and what he suspected.

He stood, in that great Age of Discovery, in an age of enlarged spatial horizons, of Drake, Frobisher, Raleigh and Hakluyt, descrying new horizons not geographic and, in his *Magna Instauratio,* his "Great Instauration," had mapped out, on "our small globe," "the Coast of the New Intellectual World." He had summoned to follow him adventurers in ideas. An Aristotelian without knowing it—striking against the cramping system—elaborating his inductive method, Bacon is the collaborator with Locke, and his grandfather in ideas. Not without precedent in Friar Roger Bacon, in the Fourteenth Century—odd coincidence of names—Francis Bacon, together with Locke, reshapes and moulds the set of the Anglo-Saxon Tradition in philosophy and science, a set and character permanent, distinctive and, in its effect, distinguished.

The avoidance of intellectual presumptuousnesses masquerading as ideals; the importance of the modest, questioning work of experiment—there is the kernel of it. Concern for the objective; concern also for results for humanity here and now; stress on reason, but also stress on what has been happily called the quality of being 'judgematical' as the fine quality of reason, rather than syllogistic logic—these are its qualities.

"The foundations of experience (*our sole resource*) have hitherto failed completely or have been very weak; nor has a store and collection of particular facts, capable of informing the mind or in any way satisfactory, been either sought after or amassed. On the contrary, learned, but idle and indolent, men have received some mere reports of experience, traditions as it were of dreams [myths], as establishing or confirming their philosophy, and have not hesitated to allow them the weight of legitimate evidence. . . . The human understanding, from its peculiar nature, easily supposes a greater degree of order and equality in things than it really finds; and although many things in nature be *sui generis* and most irregular, will yet invent parallels and conjugates and relatives, where no such thing is. . . . The human understanding resembles not a dry light, but admits a tincture of the will and passions, which generate their own system accordingly; for man always believes more readily that which he prefers. He, therefore, rejects difficulties for want of patience in investigation; sobriety, bcause it limits his hope; the depths of nature, from superstition; *the light of experiment, from arrogance and pride,* lest his mind should appear to be occupied with common and varying objects. . . ."

It is important to the understanding of this especial philosophy to note that Bacon reckoned the sceptics as being along with the presumptuous dogmatists in error, the one by defect and the other by excess. There is *no* denial by Bacon of the objectivity of truth; that which it is sought to know is knowable by reason and may *progressively* be known, nor would experiment have meaning were this not so. Experiment is dependent upon belief in reason; or, alternatively, is futile. Bacon's whole attack is precisely against "sciences which may be called 'sciences as one would,'" disturbed by "an infusion of the will and affections." "These factions therefore must be abjured, and care must be taken that the intellect be not hurried by them into assent." "*Those who have handled sciences have been either men of experiment or men of dogmas.*" What is denied is that any man at any time can claim that for him, in what is essential, all is completely known and that he has no reason to be humble in experiment any more. "Nor could we hope to succeed, if we arrogantly searched for the sciences in the narrow cells of the human understanding, and not submissively in the wider world." In all this—in his theory of the human understanding—Locke is at one with Bacon. As we shall later see, when we consider *the implications of toleration in relation to experiment,* the point is important.

The pursuit of truth, however, is not by noise; nor is the understanding of justice. As much as Erasmus—with his dictum, "Where is Luther, there is noise"—Bacon is a good humanist here, as also in his stress upon invention rather than indignation as cure for the world's evils. "Civil reformation seldom is carried on without violence and confusion, whilst inventions are a blessing and a benefit without injury or afflicting any." As we shall see, the maxim is somewhat too slick, but the stress on the peaceful works of civilization, threatened to be unroofed by the ready bluster of the passions, is sound. The authors of inventions, Bacon urges, deserve the honours of gods; men of civic merit merely those of demigods. What are the instances of power in history? What are "the *fasces* (to borrow a term from the insignia of empire)?" The products of "the wit or hands of man. These are such works as are most noble and perfect, and, as it were, the masterpieces in every art"—O excellent Verulam! O great humanist!—"for since *our principal object is to make nature subservient to the state and wants* of man, it becomes us well to note and enumerate the works, which have long since been in the power of man." Liberty, one notes, is construed as physical —Hobbes repeats this—a motion "by which bodies strive to deliver themselves from any unnatural pressure or tension, and to restore themselves to the dimensions suited to their mass."

For the rest, "creation . . . is compelled by our labours (*not assuredly by our disputes or magical ceremonies), at length, to afford mankind in some degree his bread,* that is to say, to supply man's daily wants." The book itself, the *Magna Instauratio,* he had written, with its "new instrument" ("novum organum") of induction from experiment, "as some mark of his sincere and earnest affection to promote the happiness of mankind." Here speaks the true English forerunner of Utilitarianism.

The impetus given by Francis Bacon was to endure among his countrymen. Their mood, like his, increasingly became one that suspected doctrine and welcomed experiment. Unanimity of opinion and conformity in ideology were no tests of truth about fact. As Bacon says, with patent but meaningful irony, "there is no worse augury in intellectual matters than that derived from unanimity, with the exception of divinity and politics, where suffrages are allowed to decide." Bacon is more technocrat than democrat in mood. Human advance depends upon the humility to serve and understand nature through experiment.

There is, Bacon urges, "an opinion, or inveterate conceit, which is both vainglorious and prejudicial, namely, that the dignity of the human mind is lowered by long and frequent intercourse with experiments and particulars, which are the objects of sense, and confined to matter." Himself was protomartyr to his own doctrine. The sometime Lord Chancellor of England, stepping from his coach on a winter day and with his own hands stuffing with snow a fowl accidentally killed, caught cold and died. But he had carried out an early experiment in meat-refrigeration which is one item in our modern prosperity, humble but lucrative, enabling poor men and poor men's children to eat good meat. The Lord Chancellor's secretary, Thomas Hobbes, one of the most brilliant of heretics from that political tradition that we are outlining (and excluded from the Royal Society), was by devious routes through disciples in France the true founder of modern Utilitarianism. But especially a product of Bacon's genius was this Royal Society, of King Charles II's day, which Bacon foresaw and depicted in his vision, in *New Atlantis,* of 'Salomon's House.'

It is noteworthy from whom Bacon receives most violent attack—from the Jewish philosopher Spinoza, one of those great pillars of logical dogmatism against whom the Scottish-German Kant directed his *Critique*—a great man but a thinker after the final, dogmatic style of Marx; and from de Maistre, the ultramontane upholder of a Catholicism of the brand best received by the returned émigrés of Restoration France. The final rebuttal in logic of Spinoza and defence of Bacon had to wait until the days of Bertrand Russell. Bacon's plebeian experimentalism, even if written up in a Paracelsan alchymistic style and "enigmatical folded writing," interfered with the *a-priori* necessitarianism—the grand reduction of ethics to a gnostic geometry—of the one, and with the gentlemanly defence of priestly infallibility by the other. Here, in Bacon, was a man who expounded Humanism in the authentic, curious fashion of Leonardo da Vinci.

§ ii

Such men as Sir William Petty, Seth Ward the astronomer, Sir Christopher Wren, Sir Robert Boyle, in their "Invisible Colledge," later the Royal Society, continued Bacon's work and "Defence of experimental philosophy." As much as he, they recognized the dangers of "the pernicious and inveterate habit of dwelling on abstractions." Boyle was content to prefer being "the father of chemistry" even to being "the uncle of the Earl of Cork." As Sprat, the historian of the Society, said: "they have attempted to free [the knowledge of nature] from the artifice, and humours, and passions of sects: to render it an instrument, whereby mankind may obtain a dominion over things, and not only over one another's judgements." Even the tropes, figures and "ornaments of speaking" are suspect, as "in open defiance against reason; professing not to hold much correspondence with that; but with its slaves, the passions."

The temper of mind spread across from the natural sciences into the social. Petty, led to the study by his observations and John Graunt's on the death-rate, the 'Bills of Mortality,' developed his views in his *Essays in Political Arithmetick* (1683–87). That sociological inquiries were within the proper field of the Royal Society was not in doubt, or that these inquiries must be other than philosophic disquisitions on the moral virtues and what society ought to be. On the contrary, this politics was of the kind that could be measured; and that indicated the shape and contours of London's (and mankind's) new problems by precise enumeration of population and figures of deaths and births—in brief, by mass observation. Sprat writes further:

"The very way of *disputing* itself and inferring one thing from another alone is not at all proper for the spreading of knowledge. . . . For if but one link in the whole chain be loose, they wander far away and seldom or never recover their first ground again. It may easily be proved that those very themes on which they built their most subtile webs were not all collected by a sufficient information from the things themselves, which if it can be made out, I hope it will be granted that the Force and Vigour of their wit did *more harm than good*."

Petty, by contrast, outlines the programme of studies appropriate for training men of the type he wished in public life and, in the last, finest sifting, in his 'Colledge.' The subjects, *inter alia,* should be: "Of opticks, visions and scenes. Of Magneticks. Of ships and sailing. Of Housing. Of Land carriages.

. . . Analysis of the People. Principall salts. Chymicall operations," etc.

§ iii

It is in this spirit that we enter the Eighteenth Century, with its early, grand expression in the philosophy of the 'judgematical' Locke, who took the sting in great part out of the bite of Original Sin and the all-obsessing fear of Hell by demonstrating that man's mind, when he entered the world, was as a sheet of parchment, clean for the reception of sense-impressions, and not figured with 'innate ideas' or—by implication—stained by the heritable sin, unblottable save by the waters of grace, of our first forefather, Adam. The extent of Locke's work here, deriving at one remove from the principles of his philosophy and emancipating the human spirit, will not be comprehended and assessed until one reflects upon the cloud of god-fear, stretching from John Calvin and such Puritans as Prynne on into the Eighteenth Century, and shadowing with madness such gentle souls as Cowper.

In 1689 John Locke, philosopher and apologist of the Glorious Revolution that made the Monarchy an instrument of the Legislature, completed his *Essay concerning Human Understanding*. It is a vulgar opinion that his theory of knowledge and morals and his political principles, grounded on acquaintance with exile and civil war, are unconnected, if not contradictory—the anti-dogmatism of the one discontinuous with the natural rights doctrine of the other. Anyone who will with care re-examine the evidence, however, will find small reason for holding an opinion so discreditable to Locke where that thoroughness in thought is concerned which, with vision, constitutes the substance of philosophy.

Northern Europe in the Seventeenth Century lay under the harsh hand of Calvin and Calvin's Jewish God, the God of the Torah and the rabbins. Even Catholicism, under Jansenist influence, was returning to the austerities of Augustine's theology of Predestination. The shadow of the Almighty's Wrath, justly directed against the utter corruption of our human nature, darkened the age. Luther and Calvin, agreeing 'in fury premature,' had been at one in this. The minds of men were obsessed by thought of original sin even if it did not drive all, as it drove poor William Cowper, to insanity.

As. Dr. Samuel Johnson, no lover of the presbytery, put it: "Men are evidently and confessedly so corrupt, that all the laws of heaven and earth are insufficient to restrain them from these crimes"; and placed himself among those liable to be damned, "sent to hell, Sir, and punished everlastingly."

The Enlightenment, cis-Alpine child of Florence and of Venice, dissipated this gloom for men who discarded superstition, emerging from 'the gothic night' of theological prejudice. Not unworthily, on the frontispieces of a thousand books, it found its symbol in a rising sun, the glorious dawn of Reason's Illumination. Men, then, had a faith and a reason for faith, and a sure ground of intellectual certainty beneath the footsteps of their adventuring minds. Optimism ruled in this generous time. Marmontel discovers, in man, "ce fonds de rectitude et de bonté morale, qui est la base de la virtu." D'Holbach declares that "the morality suitable to man should be founded on *the nature of man.*" Not the fear of inscrutable Deity but the hope of rational man becomes the guide in the civil polity and the moral world.

The philosopher, however, who first contributed to the removal of the hereditary curse on man that stunned and abashed his powers (the curse on Adam and the curse on Babel) was Locke, with his attack, remote but relevant, on inherited, innate ideas, and his resolved insistence that "men, barely by the use of their *natural faculties,* may attain to all the knowledge they have."

It was not a mistaken instinct that led the Rev. Dr. Whewell to feel uneasy about Locke's argument that man's soul, new-born, is one unvaried blank, till it received the impressions of external data of experience. "Yet has this blank," says Whewell (using a metaphor "more apt and beautiful") "been already touched by a celestial hand, and when plunged in the colours surrounding it, [the soul] takes not its tinge from accident, but design."

Why this priests' quarrel about new-born children, sped in instant haste to baptism? There is another side, other than Whewell's roseate colouring of the soul (as well as something latitudinarian, Arminian, in Whewell, with his "surrounding" colours, not the dark pigmentation of the seed of Adam)—a soul yet not left, as by Locke, pristine, natural and blank.

It is a side far more significant alike for contemporary theology and for contemporary politics. It is that of the soul blackened by God's original curse blazed forth against fallen Adam and his wench. Its meaning can be told in the words of Hooker, no fanatic of damnation predestined. "Seeing then all flesh is guilty of that which God hath threatened eternally to punish, what possibility is there this way to be saved?" And the answer is: none save by supernatural grace—through faith, the true faith, the one, only *true* faith in its utter bondage of mind and spirit, perchance the one, only true Catholic, or Protestant, faith (or Calvinist, or Brownist, or . . .), through the utter attachment of man's soul to that faith. In all this the orthodox gospel reckoned for so much, that mere acts of humanity were but rags, even rags of offence, heretical pride, "downright treachery, sabotage." (What mattered was to beat the Catholic and the infidel sceptic—the Catholic who held the golden gates of

Heaven with a pontiff's key . . . or, yet fouler sin, the sceptic who made Heaven itself to vanish). In the words of the Thirty-Nine Articles: "Works done before the grace of Christ, and the Inspiration of his Spirit, are not pleasant to God . . . yea rather . . . we doubt not that they"—the works of Solon, Socrates and Plato—"have the nature of sin."

Of which theology there was a strict political corollary. "Laws politic," says Hooker, "ordained for external order and regiment among men, are never framed as they should be, unless presuming the will of man to be cowardly, obstinate, rebellious and averse from all obedience unto the sacred laws of his nature; in a word, unless presuming man to be in regard to his depraved mind little better than a wild beast." Halifax, the politician, a century later draws from the theologian the corollary in the art of rule. "As mankind is made, the keeping it in order is an ill-natured office." This is not only the opinion of Halifax, 'the Trimmer,' and the King's man. In Massachusetts, Cotton Mather protests that the rule of the saints may not be challenged by the unregenerate rabble. Shakespeare's stinking-breathed multitude are for the author of *The Saints' Everlasting Rest,* Richard Baxter, Puritan divine, the sons of Belial, "the God-damn-me's." For John Milton they are "the inconsiderate multitude," mad on kingship, suitable to be ruled by a grand council of those fittest to govern, chief gentry of quality.

This, then, was the issue. Is man by nature corrupt? If so, an elect few, perhaps five righteous men, must govern and should discipline the rest. Democracy is fantastic, unreal poppycock; nay, immoral, as confusing values. And, if theology reinforces sound philosophy and morals, even supplies the argument and reason, then to doubt, or challenge aristocracy, is not only immoral but blasphemy. Here, in Original Sin, is the lynch-pin of irresponsible rule; that is, rule by power from above (such as St. Paul approved and the bishops or presbyters had the ear of), not from below; and the keystone of anti-democracy. How can sound rule issue from corruption? By nature, long long ago, man was simple, good and innocent—until he fell by the temptation of knowledge carnal and spiritual, by fleshly lust of Eve and conscious shame, the intellectual serpent prompting him to seek to know; to be puffed, like that worm of death, with intellectual pride and negation; to disobey; and to rebel. Thus in Adam all sinned and man became a rebel in his corrupt instinct; and power is from above, bearing not the sword in vain to curb an evil race. Dominion is, not *iure naturali,* but by reason of sin.

In Adam all sinned, therefore men are justly accursed and *governed for their good* to rectify accursed impulse. To which argument Locke replies.

"Let anyone reflect upon himself . . . to be the same soul that was in Nestor or Thersites. . . . Can he think [their actions] his own any more than the actions of any other man that ever existed?" But let him once find himself conscious of any of the actions of Nestor, he then finds himself "the same person with Nestor. . . . In this personal identity is founded all the right and justice of reward and punishment. . . . It may be reasonable to think, no one shall be made to answer for what he knows nothing of, but shall receive his doom, his consciousness accusing or excusing him. . . . Supposing a man punished now for what he had done in another life, whereof he could be made to have no consciousness at all, what difference is there between that punishment and being created miserable?"

Thesis one, then, of Locke is: Men, being not of one consciousness with Adam, cannot be rightly held answerable for the supposed sin of Adam; nor should men be counted cursed; since curse depends upon responsibility and responsibility is individual, not racial, and for conscious acts.

"*Individual* and for conscious acts"—*not racial.* But *is* it a matter of such acts? Are the priests right or Locke? Are there not cursed peoples, as Ham was cursed and Judah blessed. And inferior peoples? Is not the curse in the sperm and the germ? Who said that the great life-curses have to do with the house-morality of me or thee? The animals are cursed, though innocent and unwitting, to be our food. And is there not a silly optimism in saying that each man starts life having a mind which is, "as we say, white paper, void of all characters, without any ideas."

Full-fledged notions, indeed, of "elephant, army, drunkenness" . . . "impressed on the original substance of the mind, from the first moment of its existence, by the Creator," these a man will not have, until experience supplies them. But a distinctive cast or character to his mind (or, as Hume oddly says, "impressions"), a soul or formative principle, determining the ideas that attention and experience furnish and itself by heredity determined, a 'style' in his mind, this original sin or gift surely he will have? And what, then, becomes of the case for this universal *optimism* about man?

§ iv

Locke has his reply (by which, it is to be confessed, he somewhat weakens his argument). There are indeed innate *practical* principles. "But these are inclinations of the appetite to good, not impressions of truth on the understanding." In brief, (*a*) there *are* innate natural tendencies, empirically observable bases of psychological claims and—whatever convention might be—of normal 'natural rights,' in brief, a Human Nature; but (*b*) these tendencies *may be overruled,* so far as they blindly deviate from their *neutral* natural origins, *by the understanding or reason.* The understanding, however, is led by no certain recognition of innately impressed truth but only (*c*) by truth *discovered through experience.*

Locke emancipated man by appealing from the theologians' God-implanted ideas to external Nature and to man's natural faculties that discovered Nature. That, behind Nature, lay an "eternal source of all being, original of all power," did not affect the historic impact of Locke's argument upon orthodoxy. Man is, of his own quality, a thinking being, gifted with reason. And his natural liberty is a consequence of that quality. "Wherever thought is wholly wanting, or the power to act or forbear according to the direction of thought, there necessity takes place." Liberty is a natural right to *thinking beings. Significant liberty is rational liberty*—each man having the natural right, as a man, to explore for sound reason. (Only Hobbes, the veteran sceptic, doubts that it exists save by fiction imposed by authority—"right reason is non-existent.") Milton's faith here becomes Locke's considered philosophy.

Thesis two, then, is: Reason, furnished by new individual experience, and not by innate, racial intuition, is able to control the natural inclinations; and in that power of control lies the freedom of man.

Here the intellectualism of Locke—as of the Fellows of the Royal Society—clearly shews itself, and the connection between this optimistic confidence in the individual mind, searching out experience by its 'natural faculties,' and his individualism. In all of which Locke better represents his age than his contemporary, Alexander Pope.

> "Say, where full instinct is the unerring guide,
> What Pope or council can they need beside?
> . . . honest Instinct comes a volunteer,
> Sure never to o'er-shoot, but just to hit
> While still too wide or short is human wit; . . .

In vain thy reason finer webs shall draw,
Entangle justice in her net of law,
And right, too rigid, harden into wrong;
Still for the strong too weak, the weak too strong."

Pope here is a writer of the transition, an Augustan poet anticipating the gospel of the baroque and the romantics, a Catholic, yet appealing to intuition from the authority of Holy Church, her rationalizing Schoolmen and her Councils. Locke speaks to the part of his age, the age still of Bacon and Descartes, of Mandeville and, soon, of Voltaire, an age that built on the instincts without submerging reason before them and, above all, distrusted the habits of the race. Error in man, says Locke, is a degree of madness, due to false association of ideas, and this due to vulgar custom which suffocates criticism, so that a "whole gang of ideas, always inseparable, shew themselves together."

If, however, the distinctive quality of man has its characteristic operation in a power to suspend instant desire and postpone satisfaction, and "in this lies the liberty man has," it further follows that, as Locke puts it: "Government of our Passions is the right Improvement of Liberty." And therein he includes passion for righteousness, unproven by reason— that is, he includes, as he calls it, 'Enthusiasm,' native to converted 'God-damn-me's.' Such, unlike Rousseau, Locke holds in horror. "Enthusiasm is a fault of the mind opposite to brutish sensuality," writes Locke in his *Journal,* "as far in the other extreme exceeding the just measure of reason as thoughts grovelling only in matter, and things of sense, come short of it." So much for "the men of principle" and their scholastic dogmas. His route is the good Confucian, Aristotelian route of the Middle Way.

Thesis three, then, is: That the Emotions should be con-

*trolled by Rational Judgement, and that it is the distinction
and glory of man to be able so to control them.*

Locke here makes the bold claim that the passions of man
may be controlled by his reason, tacking from side to side in
its long progress through a universe of experience, calculating
like a scientist or navigator the probabilities as it goes. The
contention underestimates the religious element in man, for
here, says Locke, "men make a greater allowance to raving,
though indeed it be a more dangerous madness; but men are
apt to think in religion they may, and ought to quit their
reason."

§ v

To follow, on the contrary, the guidance of reason ascend-
ing upon the stairway of experience—here is Locke's creed. In
its distinctive shape, it is displayed in the writings of one of
the greatest of Locke's friends, whose name in Locke's own
days even outshone his own—Sir Isaac Newton. Starting from
experience—and that the humblest, such as his famous falling
apple—Sir Isaac reduced the heavens to an intelligible scheme
with a boldness that rivalled and outdistanced Kepler's own.
It was indeed precisely to this rational intelligibility, confirming the purposes and teleological designs of Providence, and
displayed by Newton, that his age attached importance. Reason stood sure in Newton.

Frankly, the Anglo-Saxon Tradition again came close, with
Newton, to Continental Humanism and to that neat rationalism that finds its expression in the French spirit. Newton, with
his rational clarity, spoke a language that Voltaire could understand, while the great observer, who was also Protestant
pietist, could sympathize with Voltaire in his impatient protest
against *ces impertinences scholastiques.* This granted—that

Newton, while a decoration of the English name, spoke the language of international genius—the point is not one to be exaggerated. It is true that, to the select who read his *Principia Mathematica* and to the many who talked of his discoveries, Newton's chief virtue was, as Professor Maclaurin, of Edinburgh, explained, that he shewed how

"The great mysterious Being, who made and governs the whole system, has set a part of the chain of causes in our view"—

in brief, that Newton was a belated Protestant scholastic, writing his *Summa contra Gentiles*. But there are other elements in Newton.

This presumption of reasonable intelligibility was, as Professor A. N. Whitehead has said, *a condition of the advance of physical science itself* which had to possess faith in some constancy in the 'hang' of phenomena, some possibility of formulae and natural laws. Even if Bacon's warning was forgotten that, "however men may amuse themselves, and admire, or almost adore, the mind, it is certain that, like an irregular glass, it alters the rays of things, by its figure, and different intersections," this *rational faith, so long as it was coupled with belief in experiment*—a posteriori, not only a priori—in itself was healthy and mothered the advancement of learning.

The good Professor Maclaurin, popular expositor in the days when George III was king, in his *Account of Sir I. Newton's Philosophical Discoveries,* rightly seizes on a further point. Sir Isaac Newton's characteristics were his "caution and modesty," not to speak of his very un-French piety.

"Sir Isaac Newton had very early experience of this temper of philosophers, and appears to have been discouraged by it. He had a particular aversion to disputes, and was with difficulty induced to enter any controversy . . . such was often their obstinacy, that truth was able to make little progress, till they were succeeded by younger persons who had not so strongly imbibed their prejudices . . . *those who had been accustomed to imagine themselves possessed of the eternal reasons and primary causes of all things*. . . . He saw that it was necessary to consult nature herself, to attend carefully to her manifest operations, and to extort her secrets from her by well-chosen and repeated experiments."

The Professor amiably compares his hero's success with the failure of the presumptuous "Cosmas Indopleustes of old, misled by an injudicious zeal," who "compiled a system of nature from some expressions in the sacred writings." As for the Cartesian dogmatists—followers of Descartes who himself, soldier of fortune, referred to his philosophy as a 'romance'—

"they set out from the *first cause;* and from their ideas of Him pretend to unfold the whole chain, and to trace a complete scheme of His works. *This is the philosophy that stands in opposition to our author's to this day.* Mr. Leibnitz himself calls spinozism *un Cartesianisme outré;* and it is apparent that his method, and many of his doctrines were derived from this source . . . the pretended clear ideas of Des Cartes, and metaphysical speculations of Mr. Leibnitz, have been received by many for true philosophy; not to mention the extravagancies of Spinoza, and a thousand crude notions that deserve no memory. . . . We may also learn at length, from the bad success of so many fruitless attempts, to be less fond of *perfect and finished schemes* of natural philosophy; to be willing to stop when we find we are not in a position to proceed further; and to leave to posterity to make greater advances, as time and *observation* shall enable them."

The claim that we are here concerned to make—and it is one of the first importance, if correct, for the future of civilization—is that there is *a vital connection between the Anglo-Saxon experimental mood and what is called Newton's "philosophy"; and between this, again, and those advances in the inventions and the physical and natural sciences that have put the Anglo-Saxon peoples in the vanguard.*

Even so, there is an excessive smoothness of reason in Newton, who was, after all, primarily a mathematician, writing towards the end of that great age of mathematics. Newton, rather than Pope or even Addison, is the great Augustan.

This placid confidence finds its nemesis in the work of David Hume (1711–76). He, like Hobbes, was a heretic in our English Tradition, which is perhaps not surprising, since he was a Scotsman, 'a metaphysical Scot.' . . . What it is here of moment to point out is that Hume, in so far as he deviated from this tradition, did so, not in the direction of dogmatism, but of a more radical scepticism, such as Bacon had eschewed —a scepticism, nevertheless, which a careful perusal of the works of Hume will shew may easily be exaggerated. Later, when we come to Lenin's attack upon Hume, we shall perceive the full and basic political importance of this.

The characteristic of the Eighteenth Century had been a belief in Reason happily espoused to Common-sense. The close of the century saw the beginning of a doubt about Reason herself. As Professor Carl Becker has shewn, in his *Heavenly City of the Philosophers* (1932), the very assurance of Progress, which drew its latest, finest picture in Condorcet's *Esquisse d'un Tableau Historique des Progrès de l'Esprit Humain,* was sapped and weakened. Reason turned inwards to examine reason, and discovered—Kant. Examination of the form shewed as residue of analysis—nothing. Or rather, the so-called 'Practical Reason' and its judgements were left, because good morals demanded them. However, by the bankruptcy of this reduction to futility, the Anglo-Saxon Tradition, which had never trusted chiefly to the Pure Reason, was *(unlike German philosophy)* comparatively untouched. From its very supposed intellectual deficiencies, its logical piecemeal and unpresumingness, it drew strength. And in Hume, as in Hobbes, it found the nursing father of its next matured philosophy, Utilitarianism.

§ vi

It is not my intention here, where our concern is with what Maclaurin calls *"the Experimental Philosophy,"* to discuss Utilitarianism at length.[1] In passing, attention may be called to the intimate connection, from Bentham to Sidgwick and Maitland, between Utilitarianism and practical legal reform, as well as to the significance, for science, of the Inductive System in the *Logic* of John Stuart Mill.

About Pragmatism, however, Utilitarianism's later variation, it is necessary to speak more at length. The Seventeenth and Eighteenth Centuries had seen great strides in the development of Mathematics and of Physics. The Nineteenth was to see the same in the fields of Biology and Psychology. Here, in fields more intimate to the life and pride of man himself, even more obstinate prejudices, religious and academic, had, as Darwin found, to be broken down. In psychology, William James (1842–1910) was in the fortunate position of being both philosopher and experimental pioneer. The dedication of William James' book, *Pragmatism* (1907), will be noted:

"To the memory of John Stuart Mill from whom I first learned the pragmatic openness of mind and whom my fancy likes to picture as our leader were he alive today."

I have no desire to tie the modern expression of the Anglo-Saxon Tradition to acceptance of Pragmatism. On the contrary, technically I should regard Bertrand Russell as a better continuator of Locke, as well as a more eminent philosopher, than James. And Russell is a very precise critic of Pragmatism.

[1] But *vide* pp. 184, 242.

He writes:

"Pragmatism, in some of its forms, is a power philosophy. For pragmatism, a belief is 'true' if its consequences are pleasant. Now human beings can make the consequences of a belief pleasant or unpleasant. Belief in the superior merit of a dictator has pleasanter consequences than disbelief, if you live under his government. Wherever there is effective persecution, the official creed is 'true' in the pragmatist sense. The pragmatic philosophy, therefore, gives to those in power a metaphysical omnipotence which a more pedestrian philosophy would deny to them. I do not suggest that most pragmatists admit these consequences of their philosophy; I say only that they are consequences, and that the pragmatists' attack on the common view of truth is an outcome of love of power, though perhaps more of power over inanimate nature than of power over other human beings."

There are several comments to be made on this criticism. It is carefully guarded by the initial phrase, "in some of its forms." It is, moreover, true that Russell and Professor John Dewey, the most eminent exponent today of Pragmatism—or, as it is technically sometimes called, Humanism—march together, not only as educationalists, but in their broad attitude towards empirical philosophy. Both of them are empiricists; nor is there any issue between neo-realism of Russell's type and the pragmatists at this point. Further, "power over inanimate nature" comes as near to the definition of good as power over men comes to the definition of evil.

We can, then, here take William James as expressing a common attitude with common antagonisms, without refining on differences in the exposition of this common tradition. And both expressions of this tradition have the most intimate relations, as providing a favouring mental climate, with the development of natural science. Moreover, it is an ironic, unkind thrust to call James' philosophy not enough 'pedestrian,' which it was its modest boast to be. At least we may say that only against the background of the common tradition, and because he shared the mental temper characteristic of this civilization, could James have written:

"See the exquisite contrast of the types of mind! The pragmatist clings to *facts and concreteness,* observes truth at its work in particular cases, and generalizes. Truth, for him, becomes a class-name for all sorts of definite working-values in experience. For the rationalist [intellectualist] it remains a pure abstraction, to the bare name of which we must defer. When the pragmatist undertakes to shew in detail just *why* we must defer, the rationalist is unable to recognize the concretes from which his own abstraction is taken. He accuses us of denying truth; whereas we have only sought to trace exactly why people follow it and always ought to follow it. *Your typical ultra-abstractionist fairly shudders at concreteness.*"

It is interesting to note that James discusses favourably the philosophers of science, Mach and Ostwald, whereas Lenin, in his *Materialism and Empirio-Criticism,* spends pages precisely in endeavouring to demolish the follies of the former. Just as it was said of Newton and Spinoza that they were "of a philosophy that stands in opposition," each to the other's, so we may say the same of James and Lenin. The mood of James, as of Newton, Locke and Milton, encourages Science; the mood of Lenin, tracing from Hegel, believes that it encourages Science by dogmatic materialism but in fact crushes it under the leaden cope of a neo-theological conformity. The difference is quite fundamental (despite, as we shall see, Professor Sidney Hook's mediating interpretation), and irreconcilable.

Further, it will be noted, James follows Bacon and Locke in affirming the truth of reality, while limiting the power of the instrument that discovers this truth. To put the matter differently, James' pragmatism is a theory of knowledge, not a theory of reality—and in this James is in line with the tradition of Bacon and Locke. James is *not* in the position (as certain kinds of idealists are, such as Fichte, the first Fascist) of denying objective reality, the *fact;* or of denying the significance for us of this *system of facts* we call the natural universe; or the need for humble *impartial* research into 'reality,' as man's highest obligation. Commenting on Mach and speaking sympathetically, James says: "The only literally true thing is reality."

"Pent in, as the pragmatist more than anyone else sees himself to be, between the whole body of funded truths squeezed from the past and *the coercions of the world of sense* about him, who so well as he feels *the immense pressure of objective control* under which our minds perform their operations." (*Pragmatism,* ed. 1911, p. 233.)

There are indeed "solid truths"—what Bacon would have indicated as the matters in which "our logic instructs and informs the understanding in order that it may not, with the small hooks, as it were, of the mind, catch at, and grasp mere abstractions, but rather actually penetrate nature"—but even here, even with the most solid and axiomatic, we must still admit the hypothesis that some new experience, some new discovery of Copernicus or Einstein, may impinge—so that our truth is revealed as merely empiric, inadequate and as what "won't work." It is not for the experience to be conformed to the dogmatic system, but for the system to be reconformed in accordance with the empiric fact. The world is, and should be regarded, if we are to grow, as what John Dewey calls *"an open world," a non-dogmatic world,* not "a closed world"—an "open world," in which the possibility of these new emergent perceptions of fact must always be allowed for. Our experience is never absolute, nor is it at any given time—but only in the infinite recession and succession of the ages—part of total and Absolute, social or cosmic. No man or society or state is entitled to say, "Before time was, I am"; therefore I know.

What James is arguing *against* is "the great assumption of the intellectualists, that is, that truth means essentially an inert static relation. When you've got your true idea of anything, there's an end of the matter. You're in possession; you *know;* you have fulfilled your thinking destiny." What James is arguing *for* is that "however *fixed* these elements of reality may be, we still have a certain freedom in our dealings with them," especially as touching how we will to adjust ourselves to them for our own better living. "On the one hand *will stand reality,* on the other an account of it which it proves impossible to better or alter. If the impossibility prove permanent, the truth of the account will be absolute."

"The essential contrast is that for rationalism [intellectualism] reality is ready made and complete from all eternity, while for pragmatism it is still in the making, and awaits part of its complexion from the future."

Briefly and crudely, the Marxist affirms dogmatically that god-negating Matter (or, if instead of a Marxist, it be an Hegelian or Fichtean, he says 'the Idea') *is;* he affirms that he knows its nature; and he affirms that it 'determines' human conduct; and, lastly, that, thanks to his 'science' or 'system,' he has the key of that predetermination. The Fascist, in so far as he has a philosophy, affirms, in Hitler's words, that what matters is '*our* truth'; and that "Recht ist, was dem deutschen Volke nützt, und Unrecht, was ihm schadet."[1] The will of

---

[1] Quoted by Frank, Minister of Justice, at Leipzig, 2. x. '35. There is a certain ambiguity here about *Recht*. "Law or 'Right' is, what is useful to the German Folk; and Illegality or 'Wrong' what harms it." Of course this sentiment is not peculiar. Far stronger expressions will be found in British writers. Cf. Sir Henry Jones, at Bangor, v. '16. "The State . . . owns us, we belong to it. We derive the very substance of our soul from the organized community in which we live and which we call the State." Before we join with a Free Church divine, who recently denounced a statement such as that of Herr Frank's as "obscene," we need to compare with it statements such as the above by Sir Henry Jones, and others by F. H. Bradley and by Dr. Bernard Bosanquet.

the Ego as god-ignoring National Ego creates its own world; and truth is what aids in that creative act to which 'the facts' must yield. The distinctive Anglo-Saxon EXPERIMENTAL PHILOSOPHY, even in its pragmatic form, affirms that there is an *objective reality;* to that we must submit and we must study it before we can control it. But our knowledge of this reality is so far *incomplete* that we can never dogmatize finally about it, for ourselves or others, although by experiment we may enlarge it, and by successful application we may confirm it.

In his *Retreat from Reason* (1936), Professor Lancelot Hogben wrote, after a criticism of National Socialism and its militaristic "exaltation of barbarism," in milder but sufficiently damning comment on doctrinal Marxism:

"Before Marxists can expect to claim the support of people who value the scientific outlook, they will have to relinquish the luxury of clothing their conclusions in language which is totally unsuitable to scientific discussion. . . . Once you have convinced yourself that the universe is wound up by the Absolute, you can enjoy the advantage of believing that your mistakes are inevitable and that everything will turn out for the best in spite of all the inaptitudes avoided by painstaking study of how we behave like human beings. Besides this you need not have the decency to apologize to those you have abused, when you find that you have been wrong. . . . The attempt to impose an intellectual dictatorship of German dialectics on the empirical foundation of our own social heritage strikes at the foundations of Rationalism. . . . We shall not harmonize the public needs of a progressive society with the private needs of human nature until we have a science of human nature."

Patently, this experimental attitude towards life decisively determines the approaches to politics. Over against the dogmatic attitude, which would be ashamed to confess that it did not possess "the real key" to all problems, few neater instances of the experimental mood will be found than in the following excerpt from a speech by President Franklin Roosevelt outlining an agricultural policy:

"Deep study and the joint counsel of many points of view have produced a measure which offers great promise of good results. I tell you frankly that it is a new and untrod path, but I tell you with equal frankness that an unprecedented condition calls for the trial of new means to rescue agriculture. If a fair administrative trial of it is made and it does not produce the hoped for results, I shall be the first to acknowledge it and advise you."

One further comment upon this school. Three times now we have detected places where what we have attempted to delineate as a distinctive empiric Anglo-Saxon tradition, in philosophy and in science and in politics, seems to cloud and become indistinguishable from what we shall later chalk out as its counter-thesis. This happened in the case of the Puritans when they became confident that they—even a minority—when called of the Lord, were entitled by sanctity and quality to impose their godly minority rule on the unregenerate. It happened, as we saw in passing, in the Augustan age with Pope, with his pre-Rousseauite cynicism about reason and his rash confidence in instinct. And it now happens when incautious phrases of our pragmatists—such as James' "Truth is *made,* just as health, wealth and strength are made, in the course of experience" or his " 'The true,' to put it very briefly, is only the expedient in the way of our thinking, just as 'the right' is only the expedient in the way of our behaving"—seem to imply ideas that go over to the opposite school which Socrates and Plato assailed, in the persons of its earliest forerunners, long ago.

The major difficulty here (as Tennyson indicated) is, not so much truth about Nature, but truth about values. Truth about

Nature, including Human Nature, and the discovery of it have been our concern in this chapter, where we have observed that significant, fertile connection—so vital for civilization and progress—between the Anglo-Saxon mental tradition and the brilliant galaxy of natural scientists who have adorned our civilization. Truth about moral values raises a different issue: whether these may be 'known'; and whether, again, they may be 'made,' turned this way or that like a waxen nose.

CHAPTER IV

Tolerance .

§ i

BACON and Locke between them shaped the Anglo-Saxon Tradition. It is because of their work that we are entitled to speak of such a tradition at all, as distinct from general European Humanism. Newton, indeed, was an international figure. Locke also influenced European thought, through Montesquieu—and this deeply. But Locke is not only a European figure; he is inexplicable save in terms of local origins. To a third aspect of his thought, besides civil liberty and the philosophic bases of scientific experimentalism, we must now turn—to the contribution especially associated with Locke's *Letters for Toleration* (1689-90).

John Locke, the philosopher, has insight enough to detect the radical bases of his own assumptions. He penetrates beneath the contradiction that had beset the Puritans. Revolting against the majestic but stifling authority of Rome, relying upon the plain letter of the Word, panic-stricken by fear of eternal damnation, in trembling working out each his own salvation, obstinately insisting on the priesthood of the laity and the right of each to work out that salvation without interference by guidance of his private conscience and of the Word, the Puritan must needs insist on liberty. Nevertheless the Puritan could not rid himself—not even so liberal a mind as Chillingworth's could rid itself—of the notion that the Word was indeed self-evident; that there *was* some prime authority,

better than that of Rome; that the questing soul yet personally, certainly and finally knew the way of righteousness and
grace. There was a discipline, and the Puritan knew it by direct insight. The quest for certainty was gratified.

Milton might hold that there should be freedom to publish
books, even that of the deplorable Salmasius; and might assert
that truth, *were conditions equal* [important reservation], must
always win. But Milton had no doubt that he, and good men
with him, knew better what conduced to "a free state" than
the superstitious, passion-led multitude, sunk in their sins.
Cromwell might sincerely respect liberty of conscience; but he
lacked no doubt that at times he knew what was good, and
that what was good for the mass, not what they wanted, was
what mattered. There were some called upon by vocation to
guide more casual men:

> "Such as thou hast solemnly elected,
>   With gifts and graces eminently adorned,
>   To some great work, thy glory,
>   And people's safety."

The temptation—a temptation to their moral pride—to decide themselves in junto what was "the people's safety" was
immense; and the Restoration came because the Puritan fell
into this temptation. *The Puritan liberty, their "soul-freedom,"*
was in perpetual inner struggle with their desire to discipline
and do good to others, and to insist in them upon *godly conduct* in accordance with a known and final law. All the
ambiguity—and we must note it—shews itself in Milton's description of that liberty which he distinguishes from the liberty
merely civil, which latter alone would not so stir him but
that he would "love my peace better."

"I saw that a way was opening for the establishment of *real
liberty;* that the foundation was laying for the delivery of man

from the yoke of slavery and *superstition;* that the principles of
Religion, which were the first objects of our care, would exert
a salutary influence on the manners and constitution of the
republic."

By 'slavery,' it is to be feared, Milton did not mean concrete
chattel slavery, but something more spiritual. He knew definitely what 'superstition' was. Astonishingly enough, Milton
and all the Puritans would have agreed with the Popes (for
all Milton's book-freedom) that liberty to err in superstition
is slavery. And equally they both would have been sure that
they knew what was superstition, what true religion. Mariol-
atry was superstition; Bibliolatry was true religion—the canon
of the Church, false; the canon of the Bible, true. The Old
Adam of intolerance was alive in Milton, even when he most
thought it the New Adam of redemption.

However, decades of being in a minority had wrought a
work in Milton of belief in inquiry which centuries of being
in a majority had left unwrought or dulled in the Holy See.
Like Communists and Fascists, most of the Puritans were
men who, in a minority, clamoured against heavy authority
for freedom to proclaim their doctrine; but in the saddle they
could comprehend no other righteousness save their own. Is
not fanaticism right; and is anything achieved save by an
intolerant moral idealism—intolerant, because militant and
disciplined? That is the great issue.

John Locke took the other route. Locke marks a watershed
in human thought, a line determinant in the Anglo-Saxon
Tradition, because he chose Tolerance. Liberty is more than the
right to soul-freedom of the righteous—freedom from the
slavery of what we and ours, 'us' as against 'them,' think to be
superstition. *It is the right to free speech and free belief of
everybody, so far as the State is concerned,* both those in grace
and those reprobate. The 'final law' could only be that of rea-

son. The basic error of the repressors of liberty had been to suppose themselves sole possessors of that reason, under lock and key, *in scrinio pectorum suorum,* as Boniface VIII said—"in the cabinet of their own breasts." Locke analysed the processes of knowledge, how we know that we know, scrutinized the claim to 'innate ideas'; and developed a consistent theory. *Locke's genius gave liberty a philosophy in tolerance and empiricism.* He gave *Religious Liberty.* That was the second great battle for liberty: the second wave in the oncoming tide of freedom. He found aid and comfort in such men as Bishop Hoadly, of Bangor. *Locke's liberty was tolerant liberty for all alike* in their right to express and promote their actual views, not merely what some people know *should* be their ideal views. It may be that Locke, the philosopher of secular experience, was wrong, as against the faith of the Puritans. But there is no doubt at all that he moulded and set the Anglo-Saxon Tradition and, through it, liberalism the world over.

Locke's theme is not new. In explicit exploration into philosophic profundities it does not rival Spinoza's. In practical advocacy it does not anticipate Roger Williams (1600–83), fierce fighter against *The Bloody Tenet of Persecution,* in his early years in Providence. In worldly prudence John Selden (1584–1654), "the Glory of England"—as Grotius called him—long before had given the lead, with his ill-concealed contempt for fanatics, shared by his friend Thomas Hobbes. "Religion," said Selden, "was no more to be left to the clergy than the law to the Chancellor." The State should decide; and the parson should be *"materia prima,* apt for any form the State will put upon him." As for the authority of the catholic Church and the General Councils, the Holy Ghost could not be claimed for them: at the count, when it came to a vote, "the odd man is the Holy Ghost."

" 'Tis a vain thing to talk of an heretic; for a man can think no otherwise than he does think. In the primitive times there were many opinions. One of these being embraced by some prince and received into his Kingdom, the rest were condemned as heresies; and his religion, which was but one of the several opinions, is first said to be orthodox and then to have been continued from the time of the Apostles."

So Selden visited the House of Commons to see the Presbyterians argue, or, as Whitelocke says, as if "to see wild asses fight, as the Persians used to do." No very different view was that of Selden's senior, Robert Burton (1577–1640), in his *Anatomy of Melancholy:*

"It is incredible to relate what factions . . . have been of late for matters of religion [today, let us read 'matters of class and race'] in France and what hurly-burlies all over Europe for these many years. . . . No greater hate, more continuate, bitter faction, wars, persecutions in all ages than for matters of religion. . . . The Turks to this day count no better of us than dogs. . . . The Jews stick together like so many burrs; but as for the rest, whom they call Gentiles, they hate and abhor."

The toleration of books and free writing, against authority whether of State or of Church, had been insisted on long ago, before Milton, by Bacon:

"The punishing of wits enhances their authority and a forbidden writing is thought to be a certain spark of truth that flies up in the faces of those who seek to tread it out."

And, also long before, merchants had grumbled that persecution was not good for trade.

This is Locke's background. And if Selden tended to replace Pope by Prince, and to pave the way for a new intolerance by his declaration that: "Is the Church or the scripture the judge of religion? In truth neither but the State," Milton (more characteristic of the century) had retorted: "The State shall be my governors but not my critics." What hitherto, however, the advocates of toleration in ideas had not done was to provide a reason for their belief, as distinct from the indifference bred of tedium in bitter arguments.

Against claimants to knowledge of absolute truth, the philosophic father of Liberalism puts forward his doctrine of *Probability*. Here is the very nursing cradle of Tolerance. At the birth of Liberalism presided Empiricism and Hope. We have, indeed, Locke claims, a few, simple, sensible intuitions that are certain knowledge. The sky, even a philosopher can say, is blue—the day-time sky, that is—or, more surely, if there are clouds about, 'That: blue.' Upon these intuitions given by the senses we may reason, supplementing direct *evidence* by indirect, of different degrees of probability, replacing bare common-sense by Ptolemy, and Ptolemy by Copernicus.

Reason itself plays no absolute rôle; depends upon its sensual evidence; and is only that faculty which makes deductions and compares probabilities. Whether syllogistic reasoning itself displays a formal truth, absolutely necessary, or is merely concealed tautology (save so far as the data of experience are supplied for inference), Locke does not discuss. But his remarks on the syllogism and mathematics incline against the belief that these are instruments for detecting new, necessary and absolute truths. (To his suggestion of a demonstrated system of Ethics, we will return.) Two drops of water added to two drops of water do not make four drops of water by inherent necessity, but only by definition of words. "If we will but observe," he writes, "the actings of our minds, we shall find we reason best and clearest, when we observe only the connotation of the proof, without reducing our thoughts to any rule of syllogism."

The pragmatic, Baconian argument of Locke—the understanding being, as he says, *"for the conduct of life"*—makes him proof against the sceptical logic of Hume that nettled Kant. It is he himself who anticipates the great formalist, Kant —the critic of pure reason as touching its content if not its form—by declaring that we have no knowledge of things-in-themselves whether of body or spirit, save of ourselves, and, he adds piously, "of God, by demonstration." Of those complex ideas we call moral values we have no absolute knowledge.

The claim to absolute knowledge "concerning faith and morals" is customarily called the doctrine of papal infallibility (although a likeness of it is found, as an inner light, among Protestant sects where every man is his own Pope). It is a theory which, secularized, is in vogue in Chancelleries and palaces as Caesaro-Papalism, Mussolinism, Hitlerism—and Stalinism. Why search for a truth that is locked up in one's own kitchen cupboard?—and, if not, is but an escaped, irrelevant and wanton huzzy? Briefly, no less an issue is at stake than the old one: What is Truth? All our contemporary politics hinges just on that.

Against dogmatist ("I know the Truth and am sure that I am sure") and sceptic ("There is *no* Truth") alike, Locke maintains his more sober theory of the limits of human knowledge.

Thesis four, then, is: Rational judgement is founded on Probability, inferred from such Experience as approximates to impartial perception of sensual facts, and not on Dogmatic Certitude; and that which arrogantly lays claim to Absolute Truth by that act shows itself probably False.

§ ii

The great battle at issue between Marx and Locke is, in essence, a battle about the nature of truth. Let us examine this argument further.

John Locke adhered to what is called, by technicians of philosophy, 'the correspondence theory of truth.' The meaning of the word 'true' is the correspondence of the idea with the fact. The fact, then, determines what is to be called true and, so far, truth has objectivity. It does not respect the person of the knower.

The attainment of that truth is possible and approximation desirable, but, except where there is direct sensual perception, it is not so complete as to give certitude. Knowledge grows with the clarification of experience but judgements grounded on incomplete perception are but probable. For man, who is not an Absolute Knower, there is but relative truth.

Relative truth, however, serves a function for man. "The understanding faculties," says Locke, "are given to man, not barely for speculation, but also for the conduct of his life." That remark, however, is not to be taken for the comfort of those who rest themselves upon intuitive certainties concerning values, not based on observation through the senses. The mark of the adult man is his willingness to look at, and face, facts, and to act in the light of this clear, fearless sight. It is the stamp of maturity. It is the immature, infant mind that wills to be surrounded by a fancy world over which it has day-dreams of power or to be identified with mythological heroes in their power and, with great giants. Man, questing for certainties as beacons, must in fact be contented with few and glimmering ones. "Man would be at a great loss," Locke says, "if he had nothing to direct him but what has the certainty of true knowledge," and not, also, a practical judgement that operates in "the twilight of probability."

Here is a classic statement, as touching the theory of truth and reality, of the English philosophical tradition founded by Locke, although anticipated (as we have already noted) by Bacon and not unforeshadowed even in the remote days of the *magister subtilis,* the pragmatic Duns. As John Dewey, in his book of this title, has so recently warned us, we must be on our guard against the primitive *Quest for Certainty,* the fruitful mother of myths, superior to the evidence we have gathered from experience.

The undogmatic metaphysic of Locke is integral with his theory of knowledge. Unlike Fichte and Hegel, it makes no claim to closed and systematic certainty. It maintains an *open world,* in which constructive truth is reached by approximation. It makes the common-sense assumption—the dualistic assumption—of the reality alike of external nature and of the perceiving mind; but it places its stress on the basis of knowledge in *sensa,* sense data, and does not, in its argument, preclude the possible reality of a monistic world of *sensibilia,* the total capable of being sensed. It does not preclude the theme of 'Neutral Monists,' such as Mach and Bertrand Russell, that sense-data are the ultimate constituents of mind and matter alike. Upon these technical issues we cannot here enter. It avoids, and anticipates the obsolescence of, the dilemma of idealism or materialism and does not engage in this philosophic fight of kites and crows. It does not cumber us with enthusiastic, unprovable faiths; but refers us to the slowly assimilable evidence of our senses and to the deductions to be made therefrom by logic. It thus leads us to explore, by the instrument of reason, this evidence, ordered (for convenience sake) under the hypothetical schematism of experimental science, and to reduce all to natural law as our navigators' chart.

What we may know—adds Locke, using an emphasis odd and unexpected—with a certainty comparable to mathematics, are those conclusions that follow, in a political science, from hypothesis and definition, as that, where there is no right of property there can be no theft and that "no government" (by definition) "allows absolute liberty." Locke's references, in the

Essay on the Human Understanding, the Bible of our Anglo-Saxon philosophy—references, be it confessed, much too obscure and dubious—to a demonstrable science of Ethics, upon which he is congratulated by Leibniz, must be understood in the light of such dicta as these. Hume and Bentham follow here, and amplify. Here is a feather in the cap for those who would rule politics after the style of the medical man rather than of the medicine man.

The calm contemplation of human action, and the drawing of deductions by comparison and analysis, which is political science, is interfered with by interested censors who dislike, as treasonable, unpatriotic, reactionary or revolutionary, what does not conform to their own propaganda for action and their own political theology.

"Whilst the parties of men cram their tenets down all men's throats whom they can get into their power, without permitting them to examine their truth or falsehood, and will not let truth have fair play in the world, nor men the liberty to search after it; what improvements can be expected of this kind? What greater light can be hoped for in the moral science? The subject part of mankind in most places might instead thereof with Egyptian bondage expect Egyptian darkness, were not the candle of the Lord set up by Himself in men's minds [that is, Reason], which it is impossible for the breath or power of man wholly to extinguish."

Locke's *Letters for Toleration,* as also his political doctrine of popular consent, flow naturally, as an application, from his metaphysic of knowledge. In these letters he writes: "You may say the magistrate is obliged by the law of nature to use force to promote the true religion; must he stand still and do nothing until he certainly knows which is the true religion? If so, the commission is lost, and he can never do his duty, for to the certain knowledge of the true religion he can, in this world, never arrive." In the age of Addison (1672–1719) and Pope (1688–1744), Locke turns his irony upon the enthusiasts, graceless zealots, men "who are *sure because they are sure.*" "He that would seriously set upon the search of truth ought in the first place to prepare his mind for the love of it." That is, by suspension of judgement and reliance on probable evidence.

Thesis five, then, is: Human judgement being of its nature approximate, unclear, but probable, it is unjust that any man, prince, president or pope, who desires freedom to announce his own necessarily fallible conclusions should refuse like toleration to his neighbour (unless that neighbour has freely chosen to receive him as infallible).

This maxim is the weapon used by Voltaire in his warfare on dogma and its children, the tyranny of the mind and fanaticism, infamous in practice. In England—and China— Voltaire found his pattern states . . . and in Locke his philosophic mentor. "Locke seul a développé *l'entendement humain,* dans un livre où il n'y que des vérités; et, ce qui rend l'ouvrage parfait, toutes ces vérités sont claires."

The philosophy of Locke is as grey and sombre as the English skies. In the night heavens, however, of a dark and disturbed age of civil wars it disclosed in those skies the great stars of eternal truths. They still rise on our horizon. Locke insisted indeed that men saw those truths remotely, apprehending them through the earthly haze of probability—but that such truths existed he never denied, to which the human mind could, as to the best in music, progressively approximate, "probably as a taste of what intellectual creatures are capable of." It was reserved for the next generation, of the Abbé de Saint Pierre (1658–1743) to call this approximation "progress."

Among those enduring truths, apprehended although not comprehended, might be ranked the goodness of justice and of liberty, derived from consideration of the rational nature of man and of God and even capable of demonstration—little although Whigs might plumb their full meaning.

The desire for freedom was, for Locke, an ineradicable impulse of our nature—and here Pavlov, the physiologist, later was to confirm him. Bacon, it is interesting to note, defined freedom in purely physical terms. Its denial is felt misery. Its affirmation is a physiological claim, a need of health, a 'natural right' of man, as much as nutrition or excretion, which stands in no necessary need of control by rational moral law as an "inordinate desire." So the child cries and the animal struggles to release bound limbs. This desire is a reasonable impulse, peculiar in its loftier manifestations of *choice* to intelligent beings and, hence, its exercise is the especial prerogative of the human race. To the brute creation the very impulse to freedom is itself a matter of necessity. Choice, independence of judgement, is man's alone. "We are born free," says Locke, "as we are born rational."

Moreover, since none had the right to usurp to himself knowledge of absolute truth, none could be excluded from a claim to approximate to it. *The right to toleration of opinion followed from Locke's theory of truth and probability:* and Milton's demand to speak freely now trod on the ground of a philosophic proof.

§ iii

Jeremy Bentham (1748–1832), patriarch of the utilitarians, adopted the same maxims of toleration. The moral man submitted his judgements to the arbitrament of reason and the test of "the greatest happiness of the greatest number." Most men, however, including professed philosophers, were guided by "the principles of sympathy and antipathy"; and thrust their antipathies down other men's throats.

"The fairest and openest of them all is that sort of man who speaks out and says, I am of the number of the Elect: now God Himself takes care to inform the Elect what is right; and that with so good effect, and let them strive ever so, they cannot help not only knowing it, but practising it. If, therefore, a man wants to know what is right and what is wrong, he has nothing to do but to come to me."

It is, however, in the work of the leader of the utilitarians of the second generation, John Stuart Mill (1806–73), that we get the most satisfactory exposition of "the Liberty of Thought and Discussion."

John Stuart Mill uses appeals, and makes assumptions, that we have found recurrent in English thought since Hooker and Bacon: the appeal to utility; the appeal to the happiness of mankind as the object of government; the appeal, especially interesting, to the desirability of *variety*. This last raises again the issue, long before discussed, in Hellenic civilization, between Pericles and Plato.

There must, argues Mill, be liberty of thought if there is to be progress, since no man can be sure that it may not be the *minority* opinion that contains the truth. Again, the basis for toleration is found in scepticism about rash confidence that the truth has been discovered—in 'probabilism.' "Even in actual philosophy there is always some other explanation possible of the same facts." And—Mill rightly notes—it is precisely the good men, like Marcus Aurelius and Decius and Torquemada and Pius V, not to speak of Lenin and Hitler, who are likely to persecute because they feel secure in their own consciences. It is the good men who are dangrous to mind-freedom.

"First, if any opinion is compelled to silence, that opinion may, for aught we can certainly know, be true. To deny this is to assume our own infallibility.

"Secondly, though the silenced opinion be an error, it may, and very commonly does, contain a portion of truth; and since the general or prevailing opinion on any subject is rarely or never the whole truth, it is only by the collision of adverse opinions that the remainder of the truth has any chance of being supplied.

"Thirdly, even if the received opinion be not only true, but the whole truth; unless it is suffered to be, and actually is, vigorously and earnestly contested, it will, by most of those who receive it, be held in the manner of a prejudice, with little comprehension or feeling of its rational grounds. And not only this, but, fourthly, the meaning of the doctrine itself will be in danger of being lost, or enfeebled, and deprived of its vital effect on the character and conduct; the dogma becoming a mere formal profession. . . .

"The price paid for this sort of intellectual pacification, is the sacrifice of the entire moral courage of the human mind."

The discussion of universal education, and, later, the effect of that education, gave a reality to the issue of liberty of thought such as it had not possessed before, since the days of the dominance of Catholic ideology. For the first time it became again possible for some authority—the State—to instil into the minds of children ideas and principles of conduct such as authority might believe good, and to do this uniformly throughout the country.

Hitherto much of the Whig and Liberal discussion lacks reality, in its bearing upon modern times, because only the thought, fully matured, of the adult individual is visualized as in conflict with the coercive authority of the State. The issue so posed, it is patent that, in Selden's words, "a man can think no otherwise than he does think"; and no sovereign authority can compel the thought of the mind. But the issue is falsely posed. The whole theme of Robert Owen's *New View of Society* (1813–16) had been the importance of 'perfecting' men's minds and character by the right environment, including the right education. The Platonic stress on education, as more than mere schooling, has come into its own again.

Shall we, then, abstain from giving dogmatic education, dogmatic moral education, because we are not *certain* of the truth, or because our *assumed certainty* may check the discovery of fresh truth? James Fitzjames Stephen, in his incisive *Liberty, Equality, Fraternity* (1873), argued that the practical work of government, and maintenance of order, could not be held up until we have arrived at absolute truth, at which *ex hypothesi* we never could arrive. As a practical matter, therefore, it was necessary to arrive at certain common-sense moral judgements and to proceed *as if* these were final. Mill himself had foreseen the point when he noted how Dr. Johnson, 'dictionary Johnson,' had argued that "the persecutors of Christianity were in the right; that persecution is an ordeal through which truth ought to pass." Mill refers to his own Victorian Age as one described as "destitute of faith but terrified at scepticism"; points out that what is 'useful' socially is itself legitimate matter for discussion; and concludes by asserting that persecution, far from being mere 'ordeal,' may be successful. If "the truth will prevail," it is necessary yet to note Milton's condition that it must have a free and open field.

Mill is quite frank and bold about the consequences of his own argument. The *dogmatic* teaching of Christianity in the schools is injurious. "I believe that this narrow theory [of Christianity as a complete rule for our guidance] is becoming a grave practical evil, detracting greatly from the value of the moral training and instruction, which so many well-meaning persons are now at length exciting themselves to promote." Indeed this attitude (Mr. Mill of the East India Company ob-

serves) is disastrous for government in Hindu India. Moreover, "if the arguments of the present chapter are of any validity, there ought to exist the fullest liberty of professing and
discussing, as a matter of ethical conviction, any doctrine,
however immoral it may be considered." Mill instances the
question of Tyrannicide. Others will occur to the reader—
let us say, James's unhappy dictum that the good is the expedient, or issues of sexual pathology. The implication of Mill's
argument is that no such instruction shall be given as shall
actually extinguish all debate on these issues. Instruction—
ideology—shall not be totalitarian, whether in the name of
Christianity or any other belief. It is, he holds, undesirable as a
practical matter, since it retards progress by checking the exploration for new truth.

"The beliefs which we have most warrant for, have no safeguard to rest on, but a standing invitation to the whole world
to prove them unfounded."

J. S. Mill, however, backs up this argument, from the conditions favourable to discovery and progress, with another
taken from the nature of what he [? dogmatically] holds to
be a desirable civilization. This second argument is outlined
in the chapter, in the essay *On Liberty* (1859), entitled 'Of
Individuality, as one of the Elements of Well-Being.' Initiative, *my* initiative, is the mainspring of social progress. The
utility of initiative alone constitutes a bridge between the
(superficially contradictory) individualism of Mill's Essay
On Liberty and the majoritarian and socialistic principles involved in Mill's *Utilitarianism*. It is always the minority that
initiates: such initiation is the warranty of progress for the
good of the majority. And, if this leads to *variety* in the social

scene, variety (as Pericles had said) is a good thing.[1] It is here, too, that Mill turns for support to the great humanists of the German *Aufklärung* or *Éclaircissement,* Goethe, Schiller, and the rest, and quotes Wilhelm von Humboldt:

"The end of man, or that which is prescribed by the eternal or immutable dictates of reason, and not suggested by vague and transient desires, is *the highest and most harmonious develop-ment of his powers to a complete and consistent whole.*"

§ iv

Bertrand Russell, in *Power* (1938), criticizes Mill—citing, rather unfortunately, this precise instance of Tyrannicide— on the ground that he held that "men were to be free in so far as their actions did not injure others, but when others were involved they might, if expedient, be restrained by the action of the State . . . but in fact almost any opinion worth either advocating or combating is sure to affect someone adversely." J. S. Mill, in fact, makes the customary lawyer's distinction, about freedom of speech and writing, expressed by Mr. Justice Holmes, reiterating the decision in *Schenck* v. *United States* (249 U.S. 47, 52). It is whether there is "a clear and present danger." This is the test whether advocacy is academic dis-cussion of theory or practical incitement to crime. That the

[1] These famous words are perhaps worth re-stating:
"Our constitution is named a democracy, because it is in the hands not of the few but of the many. But our laws secure equal justice for all in their private disputes, and our public opinion welcomes and honours talent in every branch of achievement, not for any sectional reason but on grounds of excellence alone. And as we give free play to all in our public life, so we carry the same spirit into our daily relations with one another. We have no black looks or angry words for our neighbour if he enjoys himself in his own way, and we abstain from the little acts of churlishness which, though they leave no mark, yet cause annoyance to whoso notes them. Open and friendly in our private intercourse, in our public acts we keep strictly within the control of law. . . ."

courts should decide on the criminality of literature only *after* publication had been laid down and agreed since Blackstone's day: there must be "no previous restraints on publications."

Russell continues by admitting the ardent reformer to be a man who usually neither gives nor asks toleration. Governments' attitudes are dictated by danger to their own stability, whereas the common citizen "takes very little interest in freedom of propaganda except in those circumstances in which it seems to government most dangerous, namely, when it threatens the existence of governments or right to choose the government." The former instances "are pre-revolutionary situations, and to say that, where they exist, governments should tolerate adverse propaganda, is to say, in effect, that they ought to abdicate."

"What, to the philosopher, can be the uses of propaganda? He cannot say, like the propagandist: 'Pin-factories exist to manufacture pins, and opinion-factories to manufacture opinions. If the opinions manufactured are as like as two pins, what of that, provided they are good opinions? And if the large-scale production rendered possible by monopoly is cheaper than competing small-scale production, there is the same reason for monopoly in the one case as in the other. Nay, more: a competing opinion-factory does not usually, like a competing pin-factory, manufacture other opinions which may be just as good: it manufactures opinions designed to damage those of my factory, and therefore immensely increases the work required to keep people supplied with my produce. Competing factories, therefore, must be forbidden.' This, I say, the philosopher [i.e. Russell] cannot adopt as his view. He must contend that any useful purpose which is to be served by propaganda must be *not* that of causing an almost-certainly erroneous opinion to be dogmatically believed, but, on the contrary, that of promoting judgement, rational doubt, and the power of weighing opposing considerations; and this purpose can only be served if there is competition among propagandas."

Mr. H. G. Wells has put the same case, in *The Anatomy of Frustration* (1936), against the devoted propagandist, the idealist without a doubt who feels that by intolerance he does good and fights the evil, the man who essentially is *a soldier of thought, not a thinker,* in words that deserve quotation:

"Energetic men . . . perceived the attractiveness of the suggestions of the formulae, and they wanted to exploit that attractiveness with an uncomplicated directness. . . . To qualify or criticize was enfeeblement of effort, sabotage, downright treachery. It would mean having to reconsider, instead of getting on."

Russell concludes his chapter, on 'Competition,' by a phrase which condenses into a few words the entire difficulty, and to which we shall return. *"When a community is in fundamental agreement as to its form of government, free discussion is possible. . . .* A stable governmental framework is essential to intellectual freedom; but unfortunately it may also be the chief engine of tyranny."

Freedom, however, let us add, is even possible with those who disagree on fundamentals when they only ask to be left alone; do not seek to dragoon others by physical compulsion or by such moral compulsion as becomes its effective equivalent; and content themselves with non-violent non-co-operation. On this a speech of Lord Hugh Cecil (who will not be accused of partiality to radicalism), in 1917, on the subject of conscientious objectors, is relevant:

"The conscientious objector does what the rebel does not. He appeals to a higher law altogether than the law of the State. The Jacobites of 1745 and the supporters of King George II were essentially aiming at objects on the same plane as one may say, and justified their objects by arguments of the same sort, with a different termination. Neither appealed to a different standard of morals or a different standard of expediency from the other; but it is the very essence of the conscientious objector's position that he says the State has, up to a certain point, undoubted authority over him, but that in this respect he is bound to obey a higher law than the law of the State—a religious law or a moral law which prohibits him from obeying the law of the State. 'I only ask,' he says, 'leave to obey it in my own person, and because I feel the burden of it upon me. I am bound, as I conceive, to obey this higher law. I am bound, therefore, to disobey the lower law of the State, not because I am seditious or rebellious, or because I want to impose my opinions upon anyone else in the world, but because every individual is responsible here and hereafter for what he does by his own act and by his own will, whether the State commands him or whether it does not.' . . .

"We ought to maintain that the State must conform to this higher law. And so we say as against the Germans. But shall we even retain to ourselves that self-respect which is essential in maintaining a great moral cause if we do not act up to our own principles for which we are fighting in the face of Europe, if we do not say to ourselves and in our own country when people are acting conscientiously that their conscience must not be forced, and when they obey their conscience that they must not be punished and disabled for so obeying, because that is the allegiance we owe to the higher law we obey, and because so we must act as citizens of the true city of the new Jerusalem which is the mother of us all?

"It is in the belief in that higher region of allegiance which imposes upon us something more than the State can ask from us, and which gives us something that the State can never give, that we should vindicate the great cause that we have in hand. . . .

"I hope therefore that this Amendment will be rejected. I hope it first of all because it is a retrospective law, and so contrary to all sound principles of legislation. I hope it still more because it appears to enforce the law of the State as superior to the moral law; and I am certain that if we give countenance to that way of thinking, we run the danger of becoming, as I fear that the Germans have some of them become, idolaters of the State, so that it is, indeed, the abomination that maketh desolate, a blood-stained idol, the Moloch of our time.'

§ v

Let us summarize the argument and, first, the objections.

The bankruptcy of the Enlightenment, objectors can say, lies exposed in the words of Locke. 'Facts,' of the more vital order, are not something static and external to ourselves, even in their primary substance. Happiness is an actual experience and, hence, 'a fact.' It is a fact having more significance and meaning for us than observations of sticks and stones; and these merit and hold our unharnessed and alighting attention because related to this our central fact. But it is a fact dependent for its nature upon our own attitude and creative activity. Whether we are heroic is not an issue of 'yes' or 'no,' but of whether we will to be heroic and affirm 'yes' creatively, as makers and poets. The other is an attitude possible only for the irreligious mind. As Señor Ortega y Gasset says, in *The Modern Theme,* "Rationalism, for the sake of retaining truth [static truth, that is] renounces life."

Locke's great predecessor, René Descartes (1596–1650), in his *Meditations,* wrote: "Whence then come my errors? They come simply from the fact that the will, being so much greater in volume and extent than the understanding, I do not confine the former to the limits of the latter but extend it to things I do not understand." It is Descartes who is the especial object of Ortega's attack. The will, responding to the stimulus of a living world that transcends logic, and of which the 'facts' are plastic to creative power, answers to the guidance of a more *real* truth than does, says Ortega, the analytic intelligence—which systematizes its ideas, representing still, dead 'facts,' and suspends its slow judgement until analysis has dissected to death each living system, probing for a fallacy.

The vitalist and anti-rationalist truth moves from the inside creatively out to conquer experience. Nor does it do this, as the idealist may suppose, by conforming the world in contemplation to ideas, but by the will reshaping the world of sensible experience in accord with its own willed attitude, attending to the meaning of this enriching or menacing experience and turning an unseeing eye to that experience which is, for it, without meaning or power. As even Locke himself said, the substance is found in the *power*. Cartesian 'truth'—saving for its thin assertion of the irreducible, featureless 'I' of its creator on a wet day in a hostelry in the Netherlands; an 'I' clad in a few innate ideas—stands over against us, objective. And still more is this true of the more explicit Lockian theory of truth—a 'truth' that, as it were, moves from the outside in.

Locke ignores, the objector can say, that there is a truth-for-us as well as truth-over-there; and assumes that there is only a neuter and emasculated truth such as prompts no man to action. As Aristotle phrased it: "Intellect moves nothing" [but adds: "All men by nature desire to know"; and therewith begins his *Metaphysics*]. Where human evils have to be remedied by human effort, and some men have the intelligence to grasp the nature of the evil and the remedy, it is insufferable that they should be asked barely "to study facts," and to appeal only to the halting judgements of their fellows, in which consensus of the halt even the lamest arguer might have his say, instead of appealing, by ear and eye, to the emotions and passions of these followers and themselves *making* those facts. Nor is it clear why those who have grasped truth, and who are skilled in that presentation which moves men to the realization of what are known to be values, should be limited in giving publicity to this truth, by any obligation to check or govern those passions and emotions that lead to holy wrath and righteousness.

Nor, again, is it clear that the 'falsehood-for-us' that contradicts this truth should be tolerated, especially when it is a practical impediment to change, a weapon for the national or class traitor, and a source of division, friction and weakness in the community, preventing the majority from building *their* community as they will and choose and have vision, even on the ruins of the liquidated minority and their pretended rights! What matters is, not to trace the course of that pure reason that Hume found ended in scepticism, but to discover the truth-for-us, that is, the order of ideas that increases our power. *Truth is meaningful* as having a virtue; that virtue is power; and power is virtue. *Per virtutem et potentiam idem intelligo* (Spinoza).[1] That which triumphs *is* virtue and truth. Such is the position anti-Locke—the position of those who, confident to suppress discussion, hold it proper to tell lies for the better advancement of 'the truth.' In every case, it will be noted, their community, their "us," for the good of which they present "their truth," may be discovered to be something less than humanity, for whose welfare alone is made the moral law of Nature and of God. Their position is anti-Humanist.

In the case of Russell, he himself indicates the weak point in his own armour. Free discussion, he says, is only possible where a community is in fundamental agreement. It would seem to follow that where disagreement is so deep-set that no mere discussion can transcend it, that difference—in the interest of free and healthy development itself—must be liquidated. A certain homogeneity of community life is the presupposition of intellectual freedom, and even of compromise itself. It will be noted that whereas we may consider many of the attacks on Locke's position, in the name of a 'dynamic concept' of society, to be meaningless claptrap, the difficulty raised by Russell still remains. The development of Locke's

[1] "By virtue and power I understand the same thing."

own tradition, to be successful, implies a *general acceptance* of a libertarian régime. Where this acceptance does not obtain, such a régime must defend itself against the advocates of intolerance and *may have in self-defence to be intolerant.* Humanism, then, itself involves, for its defence, *this* measure of anti-Humanism.

This may appear to be a paradox. Historically, however, there is no doubt that it was the accepted position. In the heyday of Liberalism, in the Victorian Age in Britain, intolerance became the name for some inexplicable falling away from intellectual grace. It was indeed still present, but lurked obscure in what Herbert Spencer called "the murky waters of ecclesiasticism." It was indeed inexplicable, since the compelling cause had disappeared. But Milton had no doubt whatsoever that the Commonwealth was entitled in its own defence to take punitive action—in brief, to persecute both Anglican 'prelatists' and Roman 'papists.' Locke, as touching Catholics, had the same view. For two centuries in 'free' England there was no question of the full toleration of Catholics. Still later does such tolerance by public opinion come in the United States. And, although Milton might doubt whether an oligarchy of spiritual aristocrats were not better than a dictatorship, that oligarchy or dictatorship Milton was prepared to defend. The dictator himself, Cromwell, was more tolerant than his admiring Secretary, Milton. Winking at the law and its penalties, he allowed prelatical incumbents to stay in their benefices. But he remained a stern persecutor of Papists. It may be said that these men, with their 'foreign' allegiance (so has the 'Christian Republic' fallen . . .), constituted a menace to the State. The point is that it was held that *religion of itself—their* religion which refused to divide, as Calvin refused, politics and morals; *their* ideology—made them a menace to the State.

Locke, tolerant in other respects, remains constant to this rule. It is immaterial whether born Englishmen, bearing some spiritual allegiance, in a voluntary society or Church, to a Head who was in Heaven but whose Vicegerent was in Rome, *were* necessarily disloyal bcause this Vicegerent might declare that the Divine Head disagreed with George I or George II. The point is that not only the bulk of the population, but the Whig leaders and philosophers, thought the risk too great. It follows, it is to be feared, that the Fascists and Marx-Leninists of today would receive no lenient treatment from the Fathers of English Tolerance were they now alive—the concentration camp or the Siberian labour-gang would be their portion. The toleration of the intolerant, however honest—and the less to be tolerated the more honest—may be good in itself; but it is no part of the historical tradition of Anglo-Saxon Liberalism.

What of Mill? Should homosexuality and incest be discussed in every school because some people may conscientiously believe that their vigorous moral prohibition is deplorable? But Mill, it may be said, would not advocate it in schools. Is this, however, to give the moral reformers an equal chance in exploring truth?—since the mind of man is determined, as the Jesuits knew, in his early years. But Mill makes two great exceptions to his rule of liberty of discussion —two very utilitarian reservations—namely (a) those not mentally adult, and (b) the backward races [who determines which these be?]. Mill here yields to Plato most of his case. The theme of Mill's *Utilitarianism* prevails over the 'variety' theme of his *On Liberty*. The more adult will *guide* the less adult in seeking for the greatest happiness of the greatest number.

Mill, indeed, is concerned to defend the 'under-dog' and, in *The Subjection of Women* (1869), the under-sex. But, throughout, his real concern is to defend minorities and, especially, a minority that may prove an aristocracy of talent. He is no Marxist to wish the 'under-dog' to become the 'over-dog.' He does not even wish his aristocracy to rule as self-appointed guardians of the interests of others—although here, as we have seen, inconsistency begins to creep in—but only to be free from constraint by their inferiors. Mill would probably reply that being 'more adult' is something self-evident and gives natural authority; whereas what is an aristocracy of talent, gifts or virtue, is not self-evident, and the rule, therefore, must be one of liberty. The problem is not so simple and the answer far from entirely satisfactory.

§ vi

With what residue are we left? First, with the mood that inspired even Cromwell himself, the disbelief in personal infallibility, the willingness to reason together, the patent belief that even if force has to be used it is yet a "necessary evil" (Paine's famous phrase about all government) and that

"What we gain in a free way is better than twice so much in a forced, and will be more truly ours and our posterities."

Secondly, with the philosophic reasoning, tracing from Bacon and Locke through Mill to James and Russell, which provides ground and defence for this modesty and for any thought-out doctrine of toleration, namely, that *from the nature of the human understanding* comprehension of truth can never rise higher than a cumulative probability and can never rise to a certainty so complete that we are morally entitled—and, if entitled, also morally obliged—to thrust it down the throats of our neighbours as *the* system. The approximation to complete truth must be *inductive* from ever-enlarging experience. As Russell says (here truly following Locke), the philosopher "will not allow that any [creed] is free from falsehood, or that, if by chance it were, this fortunate fact could be discovered by the faculties of the human mind." A moral humility is recommended which places in the forefront of its mind the truth of human fallibility, the impossibility of final satisfaction in the quest for certainty. Especially is this true as touching values which must be judgements of direct intuition confirmed by tradition and not matters of proof. This assertion of tolerance is the fruit of an entire philosophy which admits second place to none—neither to Hegel nor to Marx—but claims prerogative dignity in profundity and in the enunciation of permanent truth. It is the philosophy of *an open world,* not of *a closed system*.

Thirdly, this philosophic thesis of tolerance, against dogmatic materialism and dogmatic mystic totalitarianism, is put forward as practically advantageous in world-history as especially favouring a mental climate in which spiritual liberty, the discovery of new truth, scientific advance, invention and material progress thrive.

Fourthly, variety in living and thinking, and liberty, are themselves part of a tradition of living. That tradition itself, in accordance with Mill's own admission, may—and must— be *taught*. (Perhaps, as the Spens Commission in Britain has recently recommended, be taught in schools.)

Further, this liberty itself involves a manner of life which may be attacked by hostile ideologies and hostile, rival régimes, and which must be defended, even to the point of excluding or repressing that which destroys fundamental agreement in the community. The Anglo-Saxon Tradition of Tolerance is not an opinion but a competing faith. Those who oppose it by their own aggressive propaganda are its enemies. The method by which preferably they should be dealt with is by education. But the time factor cannot be ignored. Education

may need to be supplemented by the resolution of a people
to conduct its own social experiment of individual freedom
without free interference by those who totally challenge that
freedom. It may prevent that interference by self-defence
against coercive action; but it condemns its own civilization,
and reflects on the strength of its own tradition, if every discussion of other ideas is, in panic fright, construed as constituting "proximate danger."

CHAPTER V

Democracy; Accommodation; Federalism

§ i

"MEN being . . . by nature all free, equal, and independent, no one can be put out of this estate and subjected to the political power of another without his own consent."

These words of Locke are almost verbally repeated in the more famous words of the Declaration of Independence, whose draughtsman was Thomas Jefferson (1743-1826). In typical Anglo-Saxon fashion this Declaration sought to submit "Facts . . . to a candid world"; and indicted George III for exercising "an unwarrantable jurisdiction" by his breach of pre-existent law and custom, of the accepted constitution of the Commonwealth and of the law of Nature. "A Prince, whose character is thus marked by every act which may define a Tyrant, is unfit to be the ruler of a free people." In its exhortation, however, it used words—Locke's words—which it was easy for Bentham to riddle in his *Fragment on Government* (1776) and *Anarchical Fallacies* (1791):

"Natural rights is simple nonsense: natural and imprescriptible rights, rhetorical nonsense—nonsense upon stilts. . . . Are all men born free. . . . No, not a single man, not a single man that ever was, or is, or will be."

The words, however, about men being "created equal," whether used by Jefferson or by Locke, are not such "nonsense upon stilts" as might be supposed. The subsequent reference to the demand for "Life, Liberty and the pursuit of Happiness," if not called by Bentham an "inalienable Right" would be called by him the demands of a patent instinct. When Bentham asserts, as the basis of his "greatest happiness of the greatest number" principle, that each is "to count for one," he is himself asserting a natural right although one unanalysed as such by him.

Locke and Jefferson are indeed at pains to explain their meaning. Locke, as we have seen, like Hobbes, asserts that there exists among men, "promiscuously born to all the same advantages of Nature," a certain rough natural equality. He calls in Hooker to provide the basic argument that "being of one and the same nature"—and that frail—is the ground of all mutual moral obligation. As, later, the great lawyer, Blackstone, says: "It is the sense of their weakness and imperfection that keeps mankind together." It is, on the other side, the argument from human personality, and from the duty of using other men only as persons, later enunciated by Immanuel Kant. As Locke says, "There cannot be supposed any such subordination among us that may authorize us to destroy one another *as if we were made for one another's uses,* as the inferior ranks of creatures are for ours." There is no other rule "than that of reason and common equity." The same sentiment is Jefferson's when he writes, quoting the Roundhead Rumbold:

"The general spread of the light of science has already laid open to every view the palpable truth that *the mass of mankind has not been born with saddles on their backs,* nor a favoured few booted and spurred, ready to ride them legitimately, by the grace of God."

Jefferson, however, significantly explains and expands his position when he comes to discuss Education. In his proposals for elementary education in Virginia he writes:

"Of the boys there sent in one year, trial is to be made at the grammar school for one or two years, and *the best genius of the whole selected, and continued six years, and the residue dismissed. By this means twenty of the best geniuses will be raked from the rubbish annually,* and be instructed at the public expense."

Locke earlier explained himself in the same sense, already quoted:

"I cannot be supposed to understand [mean] all sorts of 'equality.' Age or virtue may give men a just precedency. Excellency of parts of merit may place others above the common level."

The Anglo-Saxon theory, then, of human equality involves no doctrine at all of strict biological equality or of equality of talents, or any social or educational structure resting upon this supposition. The thesis of President Jackson that, in politics, any man is competent for any job, is no necessary assumption. The degree of equality and competence in these matters is empiric.

By equality is meant here that there is such a thing as a human race, not a multiplicity of races, and a human nature, itself basis of a Natural Law; and that this race is, as one, united by common bonds that have the strength of mutual obligations. As Hooker says, the Laws of Nature "do bind men absolutely, *even as they are men.*" Whether indeed, as according to the myth of descent from Adam, all men are indeed of one race is an issue of biological fact. The assumptions here are essentially those of the Christian religion.

Further, by equality is meant—and the teaching is traditional Christian and, indeed, Stoic teaching—that no men are born entitled to dominion over others; that dominion and subjection are not, in this sense, natural but must be justified in each case by the common good. It is a denial of some abstract, intangible, untestable superiority. The foe is irrational privilege; pretension to superiority without justification in function. The issue is again empiric.

Moreover, in assessing this common good, each man is to be treated as a moral personality and not merely as an instrument for the advantage of another. The final ground for human equality the representative writers agree in discovering in the fact that man, as such, is a rational—and therefore moral, choosing—being. He is the subject of laws of conscience, eternal and natural, above all positive law and custom. And these laws bind him to respect an equal right and duty in his fellows. Every man has a right to his own moral judgement, but *only as a rational being* and as part of his thinking powers. *Freedom is subject to law, the law of nature and reason:* there is no right to irrational anarchy.

§ ii

The recognition of the freedom proper to the rational being is the contribution of Humanism to Democracy. The contributions derivative from the principles of Experiment and Tolerance are not less relevant.

Looking back over the faith and the work of the Victorian Age, and its harvestings in the Great War and the Marxist Revolution, from the perspective of the decade of the Peace of Versailles, John Morley of Blackburn, in the final edition of his *On Compromise*, wrote:

"A painful interrogatory may be thought to emerge. Has not your school—the Darwins, Spencers, Renans, and the rest—held the civilized world, both old and new alike, European and transatlantic, in the hollow of its hand for two long generations past? Is it quite clear that their influence has been so much more potent than the gospels of the warring churches? Is the modern principle of justification by Success and the fiat of the God of Battle, so great an improvement on the savage and sanguinary struggles that once tore the world over justification by Faith and Grace? *Circumspice!* Is not diplomacy, unkindly called by Voltaire the field of lies, as able as it ever was to dupe governments and governed alike by grand abstract catchwords, veiling obscure and inexplicable purposes and turning the whole world over with blood and tears to a strange Witches' Sabbath?"

Consideration, however, of our achievements, rather than of the disappointments arising from the victories here and there of the fanatical school, the school of No Compromises—consideration, again, of the American scene and of achievement there—may lead to a more robust judgement.

In a recent broadcast address, entitled *Foundations of Democracy,* Professor (now United States Congressman and erstwhile State Senator in Illinois) T. V. Smith, of Chicago, said:

"Americanism as a way of life is a large faith in, and a smaller practice of, what we of ourselves do so well know: friendliness, humility, humour. . . . Intolerance is a vice we Americans cannot afford. We had to learn friendliness not only with friends but, as it were, with enemies. We had to learn, and did learn, to stomach opposition without suppressing opponents. . . . We forget our Americanism when we forget that this, our preference for friendliness, is the secret of our success in subduing a continent to the life of man. . . . That's what gentility of the ballot means, as contrasted with the coercion of bullies. Whoever knows for certain that he's not God is glad to welcome the aid of other men in determining what's politically right. Voting as such an aid reduces the risks of ignorance. . . . It's a clever device, this balloting business—and profound. It helps us to 'split the difference' as we used to say in Texas, and to achieve on a large national scale the *golden mean of compromise.* We Americans literally think it more important thus to settle issues between us than it is to settle them absolutely right. . . . This is so *because we admit that God alone knows what is absolutely right. We men do know what's friendly and decent.* So in decency to one another we've agreed to call right whatever nobody kicks over the traces about. How profoundly we differ from some others in this regard! Now come Fascists to share God's prerogative and Communists to monopolize it. This leaves many of us plain American citizens (with only revolutionists and immigrants for ancestors) hardly knowing which way to turn. So we just turn back in all friendliness to one another, and we covenant once more to take stock with ourselves and to abide by whatever we can agree upon, whether any of us are fully satisfied with it or not. That's the democratic principle and that's the decent thing to do."

The characteristic note that sounds from this discussion is the note of Accommodation. It is not an operatic or a tragic note. But it is a note that is important if decent human values are not to be reversed. It is intimately connected with Jefferson's idea of equality and, as T. V. Smith makes clear, it is a necessary prelude to the note of Democracy as understood in Anglo-Saxony (*not* the Rousseauite Democracy of worship of the infallible, sovereign, majority will *qui est toujours droite*).

Clearly there will not be Accommodation without recognition of such a measure of equality that one man will respect without impatience another man's judgement. There must be that measure of community—so that the common workman who fights for a country, and without whom the country cannot be defended, will also be listened to in his grievances as a citizen by those who govern the country.

As T. V. Smith continues, in his distinguished book, *The American Philosophy of Equality* (1927), as he leads up to a plea for what he calls "functional equality" ("in terms of *co-operative* practice equality of treatment . . . the large, abstract claim of equality has served to inhibit real, concrete equalities"):

"The chief consequences that may be urged as justifying equality of treatment are fairly comprehended under the term 'co-operation.' It will hardly be thought to demand argument that men work together better when they regard themselves as substantially equal. Indeed, in so far as inequality is confessed and paraded, co-operative activity is certainly inhibited. Activity may go on: one working for another, or another directing the one. But neither true co-operation nor maximum efficiency nor happy contentment exists."

It was de Tocqueville who commented on this sequence of thought and habit in the Democratic Way of Life as practised in English-speaking America:

"The more I advanced in the study of American society, the more I perceived that this equality of condition is the fundamental fact from which all others seem to be derived and the central point at which all my observations constantly terminated." (*Democracy in America,* i. Introduction.)

It has been the peculiar characteristic of British constitutional history, as of so much of American social life, that this principle of Co-operation and Accommodation has seeped so deeply into the very fibre and has dyed to its hue the very habits of authentic thought.

The greatest and distinctive triumphs of the English political tradition have been in terms of this tactic of Accommodation—the almost bloodless Glorious Revolution of 1688–89; the Great Reform Bill of 1832; the bloodless Emancipation of the Slaves in the British Dominions (not less complete than in an America disunited and torn by Civil War); the union of South Africa; the accommodation with Ireland; all the work of reform from the legal reform inspired by Bentham's distinctively Anglo-Saxon philosophy to the social reform of the Health and Unemployment Insurance Acts. The significance of the origins of British Socialism in Robert Owen's Co-operative Movement is markworthy.

The most outstanding admitted catastrophe was also the most outstanding instance of departure from this policy—

the criminal obstinacy of Lord North and the Germanic George III. The Marxist theme of inevitable war and inevitable class war found its examples in the infamous 'Peterloo Massacre' of 1819, with its death of eleven men, and in the physical-force section of Chartism which led that movement to fruitless anti-climax after the successful fruit of the opposite policy—with its ruse even of a financial scare as 'pressure' on Government credit—had been gathered in by the Reform Bill. To find a break, that was not also a mistake, in social Accommodation, one must look back to those Civil War years that, nevertheless, ended in the lassitude of the Restoration. England declined to brook a tyranny, even of the Saints. And here too the empiricism, experimentalism, if not opportunism, of Cromwell's own policy will be noted.

§ iii

Intimately connected with the notes of Tolerance and Accommodation in domestic affairs is the note of Federalism in its connection with the Anglo-Saxon view of Democracy.

It is no accident that the totalitarian view of society tends so often to Caesarism and centralization (despite the partial exception of Russia), and that the democratic view of society tends to Federalism and devolution (despite the partial exception of France). The lines here cannot be drawn too closely, but enough remains to be significant. And what does remain is of high significance when the issue is that of sketching the outlines of the World-State of the future (of the immediate future, if war supervenes) and of determining the position of small states in this present. Half the practical force of the democratic case in contemporary Europe rests upon this inner logical association between that theme of Accommodation between organized communities in a wider whole which is Federation and the theme of Democracy. It will make a great difference whether the World-State of the future is founded upon the principles of Mazzini or upon those of Bonaparte. Our task is to give political sanction and coercive force to the moral imperative of Kant's "cosmopolitical institution" and of Mazzini's "federation of man."

Kant and Mazzini were not (unless indeed we count Kant's Scottish ancestry!) Anglo-Saxons, and nowhere in this book have I suggested that "the right philosophy" is something limited to a chosen people—I have suggested the precise contrary. Nevertheless, this federalist trend has been so marked in Anglo-Saxon lands that it has tended to lapse into the excess and weakness of individualist separativism. In the United States, at the beginning, no more could be achieved than Confederatism. In the British Commonwealth all we have is a lax Confederacy. Did Anglo-Saxon Re-Union come, almost certainly in the first stage it would not go beyond a confederatism similar to that contemplated in the Articles of Confederation of the United States. Experience would have to achieve closer unity. The work of the *Federalist* and the work of Lincoln were to insist that, if Federalism were the basis of the Constitution, nevertheless Federalism also meant the effective preservation of the Union.

Just as the principle of Accommodation is the negation of that Hobbesian psychology of "my interest" as dominant motive, taken over by the Classical Economists and reapplied by Marx, so the principle of Federalism is the negation of that— logically connected—Hobbesian doctrine of giant sovereign power, that "mortal god," modelled on Roman Caesar, "lord and god," which sovereignty the Founding Fathers of the American Constitution were at such pains to deny or destroy by division and balance of powers. As Professor A. H. Smith writes:

"Since the Declaration of Independence . . . it is universally held that neither a legislature nor any other agency of government is a complete expression of the sovereignty of the people. . . . The people of the United States are a greater sovereign than the people of any particular State, and they claim the right, through their judicial organs, to determine all cases of conflict between the various agencies of government."

Federalism links with Democracy because, in either case, the assumption is made that no man or body of men is so superior to the rest as to be entitled to ignore the diversity of human life and the vitality of variety; and to impose on all, thanks to knowledge of "the Doctrine," the strait-jacket of a uniform plan for living even if the jacket be tailored as the very cassock of a Jesuit saint, let alone of a red-shirted commissar or black-shirted gauleiter. Any man who chooses may put on cassock or shirt so long as he conducts himself friendly with his neighbours, but if any will force him into it willy-nilly, then others will force that man also to mind his place.

§ iv

Abraham Lincoln (1809–65) makes clear, with singular force, what are the assumptions of this line of thought. Lincoln had to deal with men such as Senator Douglas and Choate, who were frank to maintain that the opening words of the Declaration were "a string of glittering generalities." These men had none of the doubts of Jefferson, who "trembled for his country when he remembered that God is just." Lincoln states his position:

"I think the authors of that notable instrument intended to include *all* men, but they did not intend to declare all men equal *in all respects.* . . . Its authors meant it to be as, thank God, it is now proving itself, a stumbling-block to all those who in after times might seek to turn a few people back into the hateful paths of despotism. . . . I go for all sharing the privileges of the government who assist in bearing its burdens. . . . I doubt not that the people of Nebraska are and will continue to be as good as the average of people elsewhere. What I do say is that *no man is good enough to govern another man without that other's consent.* I say this is the leading principle—the sheet-anchor of American republicanism." (1854.)

In Independence Hall, Philadelphia, in 1861, he reverted to the same theme of the Declaration:

"It was not the mere matter of separation of the colonies from the motherland, but that sentiment in the Declaration of Independence which gave liberty not alone to the people of this country, but hope to all the world, for all future time. It was they which gave promise that in due time *the weights would be lifted from the shoulders of all men,* and that all should be given an equal chance. This is the sentiment embodied in the Declaration of Independence."

And in his Message to Congress, of that same year:

"This is essentially a people's contest. On the side of the Union it is a struggle for maintaining in the world that form and substance of government whose leading object is to elevate the condition of men—to lift artificial weights from all shoulders, to clear the paths of laudable pursuit for all, to afford all an unfettered start and a fair chance in the race of life . . . that ballots are the rightful and peaceful successors of bullets; and that when ballots have fairly and constitutionally decided, there can be no successful appeal back to bullets . . . such will be a great lesson of peace; teaching men that *what they cannot take by an election, neither can they take by a war;* teaching all the folly of being the beginners of a war" . . . [1863] "they who take such an appeal [from ballot to bullet] are sure to lose their case and pay the cost."

In this connection it is not irrelevant to quote again the speech in which a great English Liberal, John Bright, stated the issue of liberty in relation to the American Civil War and the institution of property in human beings called negro slavery. It was made, significantly enough, to the London Trades Unions' convention, in 1863. No difference of viewpoint divides him from Lincoln:

"You wish the freedom of your country. You wish it for yourselves. You strive for it in many ways. Do not then give the hand of fellowship to the worst foes of freedom that the world has ever seen, and do not, I beseech you, bring down a curse upon your cause which no after-penitence can ever lift from it. You will not do this. I have faith in you. Impartial history will tell that, when your statesmen were hostile or coldly neutral, when many of your rich men were corrupt, when your press—which ought to have instructed and defended—was mainly written to betray, the fate of a continent and of its vast population being in peril, you clung to freedom with an unfaltering trust that God in His infinite mercy will yet make it the heritage of all His children."

At the beginning of the great contest that issued in the Civil War, in 1855, Lincoln had not scrupled to write, "the Autocrat of all the Russias will resign his crown and proclaim his subjects free republicans, sooner than will our American masters voluntarily give up their slaves." This statement—which must be interpreted as meaning 'of their own initiative'—makes it the more important to note Lincoln's own methods. The first note is one of strict *constitutionalism,* the opposite of the fanatic mood:

"I am naturally anti-slavery. . . . I cannot remember when I did not so think and feel, and yet I have never understood that the Presidency conferred upon me an unrestricted right to act officially upon this judgement and feeling. . . . I understood, too, that in ordinary civil administration this oath even forbade me to practically indulge my primary abstract judgement on the moral question of slavery. . . . And I aver that, to this day, I have done no official act in mere deference to my abstract feeling and judgement on slavery."

The second is an affirmation of what he means by *conserva-*

tism, an affirmation fully in the tradition of Coke and Cromwell, of Washington and even of Jefferson, in their own Anglo-Saxon way conservatives all:

"What is conservatism? Is it not adherence to the old and tried, against the new and untried? We stick to, contend for, *the identical old policy* on the point in controversy which was adopted by 'our fathers who framed the government under which we live'; while you with one accord reject, and scout, and spit upon that old policy, and insist upon substituting something new."

The recognized and established liberty of America was not the liberty of "the wolf's dictionary"—the liberty to prey upon whatever could be found weak enough to be victimized. Like Edward Coke before him, and Stephen Langton earlier, Lincoln enunciated a tradition in liberty.

Third, Lincoln appreciated the weakness of Democracy when confronted by military and slave-holding systems. He had the genius to recognize the time for *decision,* when those who have taken the sword must learn the lesson and consequence of taking it. Unafraid of being accused of dictatorship, 'King Lincoln'—as the Vallandigham case shews—when exercising his constitutional rights as Commander-in-Chief, exercised the war-powers of the Republic to the full:

"I think that in such a case to silence the agitator [Vallandigham, 'damaging the army,' in time of war] and save the boy [a deserter] is not only constitutional but withal a great mercy . . .

"And this issue embraces more than the fate of these United States. It presents to *the whole family of man* the question whether a *constitutional republic or democracy*—a government of the people by the same people—can or cannot maintain its territorial integrity against its own domestic foes. It presents the question *whether discontented individuals, too few in numbers to control administration according to organic law in any case, can always, upon the pretences made in this case or any other pretences, or arbitrarily without any pretence, break up their govern-*

*ment, and thus practically put an end to free government upon
the earth. It forces us to ask: 'Is there, in all republics, this inherent
and fatal weakness?' 'Must a government, of necessity, be too*
strong for the liberties of its own people, or too weak to maintain
its own existence?'

"So viewing the issue, no choice was left but to call out the war-
power of the government, and so to resist force employed for its
destruction by force for its preservation . . .

"What would you do in my position? Would you drop the war
where it is, or would you prosecute it in future with elder-stalk
squirts charged with rose-water? Would you deal lighter blows
rather than heavier ones? Would you give up the contest, leaving
any available means untried?

"I am in no boastful mood. I shall not do more than I can; but
I shall do all I can to save the government, which is my sworn
duty as well as my personal inclination. I shall do nothing in malice. What I deal with is too vast for malicious dealing."

That was Lincoln's answer to the issue: "whether any government not too strong for the liberties of its people, can be
strong enough to maintain its existence in great emergencies."
That answer, I submit, must be taken in the tradition of
Anglo-Saxon Democracy as definitive.

What did Lincoln set out to conserve? A tradition that
enshrined personal and political liberty in its midst. That
"inestimable jewel . . . that great and free government that
we have enjoyed all our lives . . . that any one of your children may look to come here [to the White House] as my
father's child has." The words at Gettysburg re-echo:

"Fourscore and seven years ago our fathers brought forth upon
this continent a new nation, conceived in liberty, and dedicated to
the proposition that all men are created equal."

That dedication had been preserved in an enlarging and more
prosperous nation. Obedience to Natural Law had been justified by Nature. "No human council hath devised, nor hath

any mortal hand worked out these great things. They are the gracious gifts of the Most High God, who, while dealing with us in anger for our sins, hath nevertheless remembered mercy."

What was this democracy? It was not one that stirred up black against white, or even free-man against slave-owner. It maintained freedom for the Slavery Abolitionist to preach his doctrine within the law. It maintained that, as to what the law might be, the majority constitutionally determined must decide, since "if the minority will not acquiesce, the majority must." It maintained the citizen right of every free man to enter into that majority as one who "assisted in bearing the burdens of government"; and it proposed to extend that freedom to the practical utmost. It asserted, for this purpose, the equality of men, while not denying an inequality of talents that should have like opportunity to find their natural level "in the *race* of life." Lincoln asserted that "no men living are more worthy to be trusted than those who toil up from poverty."

The absolute right of the majority, as full sovereign, over the minority was *not* asserted. The American Constitution, with its balance of powers, did not give that right, nor did Lincoln interpret it to have done so. The tradition was federal, although not confederate, as touching the structure of the Union. As touching the Constitution not Lincoln or Jefferson, nor, for that matter, Hamilton or Jay, questioned that doctrine of the division of powers, enunciated by Locke and hallowed by Montesquieu.

§ v

Herbert Spencer (1820–1903), in his *Man versus the State,* attacked with indignation what he termed the theory of "the divine right of majorities":

"While men have abandoned the old theory respecting the source of State-authority, they have retained a belief in that unlimited extent of State-authority which rightly accompanied the old theory, but does not rightly accompany the new one. Unrestricted powers over subjects, rationally ascribed to the ruling man when he was held to be a deputy-god, is now ascribed to the ruling body, the deputy-godhood of which nobody asserts. . . . The function of Liberalism in the past was that of putting a limit to the powers of Kings. The function of true Liberalism in the future will be that of *putting a limit to the powers of Parliament.*"

It is a mistake to underestimate the influence of Spencer on his contemporaries, especially in America. The Supreme Court of the United States had to be warned by Mr. Justice Holmes that the XIV Amendment to the Constitution did "not enact Mr. Herbert Spencer's *Social Statics.*" Nevertheless, as Spencer himself admits, in the passage cited, "men have retained a belief" very contrary to that of Mr. Spencer. His "Administrative Nihilism," his anarchism, represents just that side of Liberalism that is today, for good or ill, most completely dead. No more than Hobbes or Hume can Spencer be quoted as an authority interpretative of our political tradition. John Stuart Mill is in a quite different category.

John Stuart Mill, nevertheless, is as concerned as Spencer with the dangers of majority sovereignty. He yet did not stay within the limits of Spencer's two significant half-truths: that the Liberal is "one who advocates greater freedom from restraint, especially in political institutions"; and that Socialism, including what Spencer calls Tory Socialism, "involves Slavery." Unlike that brash Philistine, Macaulay, Mill's mind is not solely preoccupied with the defence of the propertied minority. He does not say with Samuel Taylor Coleridge, distorting Locke, that government exists not only for the defence of property, but "it is founded on *unequal* property; the inequality is the essential term in the position"—Cole-

ridge who subsequently went on to make the odd comparison
about throwing the men of property as a "lamb to the wolves."
. . . Mill's famous chapter, in his *Principles of Political Economy,* "On the Probable Futurity of the Labouring Classes,"
acquits him of this. However, he feels that, as he says in *On
Liberty:*

"The 'people' who exercise the power, are not the same people
with those over whom it is exercised. . . . The will of the people,
moreover, practically means, the will of the most numerous or
most active *part* of the people; the majority, or those who succeed
in making themselves accepted as the majority: the people, consequently, *may* desire to oppress a part of their number; and precautions are as much needed against this, as against any other abuse
of power."

"The only government which can fully satisfy all the exigencies of the social state, is one in which the whole people par-
ticipate," he writes in *Representative Government.* Mill does
not conceal from himself that peoples of different character
and different stages of civilization or amid different conditions require different constitutions. Not all peoples are privileged enough to be capable immediately of freedom. This is
not mere arrogance—although it is not untouched by that—
but springs from reflection on the political task:

"It may be laid down as a political truth that by irresponsible
monarchy rather than by representative government can a multitude of insignificant units [cf. Germany] be welded into a people,
with common feelings of cohesion."

Mill comes here very near to the fallacy of praising the
Big State because it is big. He continues, however, by pointing out that systems which may confer immediate benefit may
be vicious and baneful for humanity. "Some of the most fatal

changes in human affairs have been, as to their more manifest immediate effects, beneficial. The establishment of the despotism of the Caesars was a great benefit to the entire generation in which it took place. . . . Yet this was the commencement of a régime by whose gradual operation all the civilization which had been gained, insensibly faded away." There are indeed peoples in whose "eyes the possessors of authority can hardly take too much upon themselves, provided the authority itself is open to general competition." For Mill, however, all this is a false line, although perhaps suited to the life of lesser breeds without the Liberal law. Communism indeed, of Owen's co-operative type (non-Marxian), he will approve; but it must be the voluntary, unselfish Communism of an *élite*. For the rest, he looks for political health to the hopes of the normal self-helping man—each man the best guardian of his own interests:

"The person bestirring himself *with hopeful prospects* to improve his circumstances, is the one who feels goodwill towards all engaged in, or who have succeeded in, the same pursuit."

That individual may indeed, as Mill elsewhere points out, be aided by social legislation and even by compulsory education—compulsory against his parents to protect *his* right. But, for all that, it is the free right of the minority, or of the individual—that ultimate minority—that Mill is concerned to protect. Although Bentham and Mill do not talk in terms of natural rights, they imply them. As much as Spencer, Mill is sure that there is a threat from majority dictatorship:

"It has been said that the dangers incident to a representative democracy are of two kinds: danger of a low grade of intelligence in the representative body, and in the popular opinion which controls it; and danger of class legislation on the part of the numerical majority, these being all composed of the same class. . . . The only quarter in which to look for a supplement of, or completing corrective, to the instincts of a democratic majority, is *the instructed minority:* but, in the ordinary mode of constituting democracy this minority has no organ."

The Founding Fathers of the American Constitution, by imposing that instrument and deciding upon the difficult process of Amendment, had decided that the United States, in substantial part, should be governed from the grave. Does Mill propose that, in addition, the minority shall govern the majority? The answer is twofold. Mill believes that minorities are the pace-makers of progress and he wishes them to be safeguarded. "Nothing is more certain than that improvement in human affairs is wholly the work of the uncontented characters." But he distrusts the minority that wills to dictate to *the other* minorities, and he suspects that most domineering majorities are in fact but the mouthpieces of domineering minorities. Mankind is *always* ruled by minorities—the men of energy. The question is, *how much* ruled? Mill complains that Parliament too seldom looks at social questions "with the eyes of a working man." Nevertheless, he fears the presumptuous sovereignty of a majority, all of one class, led by some small group of 'class-conscious' politicians. He objects to that sovereignty of a majority anyway, even supposing the common interest to be real, not factitious.

His father, James Mill (1773–1836), had declared that, without the representative system, "we seem to be forced upon the extraordinary conclusion that good Government is impossible." John Stuart Mill caps this by demanding the completion of the representative system through Women's Suffrage, Working Class Representation in Parliament and Proportional Representation. Basically his belief, like those of Burke and Madison and Locke and Harrington, is in a balanced constitution, balanced in its representation of living social interests. It is the *precise opposite* of Rousseau's concept of Democracy as inspired by *volonté générale*—'general will'—which, although not always fully enlightened, is always right. Mill's is basically a rationalistic, not an emotional, political philosophy. His attitude is entirely in accord with Lincoln's doubt—strange though the light shed upon it by the Civil War may be—whether any man is good enough to direct the life of another without his consent (save to protect the natural rights of another).

The practical conclusion of Mill's argument would appear to be one of individual rights and vindicated liberties modified by a free, benevolent sense for the happiness of the greatest number and by some kind of social group liberty, guild socialism or corporativism as outlined by Figgis, Cole and Bertrand Russell. This could only result in anarchism with a people too politically immature—Mill does not doubt there are such—for liberty. This individualism Mill so little considered inconsistent with either social legislation or Socialism [non-Marxist] that, in his *Autobiography* (1873), he styled himself a Socialist.

The Nineteenth Century is chiefly concerned with the third great fight of Democracy—after the Parliamentarian one of Personal Freedom from Arrest by Power of the Purse against Kings (and, in America, from chattel slavery) and that of Religious Freedom—that for Freedom of the Vote, Freedom to control the Oligarchs and the Law through the Ballot-Box, which begins with Chartism and the Great Reform Bill of 1832 and concludes with the XIX Amendment (1920) in America and with the granting of Women's Suffrage, in the Acts of 1918 and 1928, in Britain. But Mill already looks forward to the fourth fight of Democracy, Freedom to Work (not Starve) for the common man—Freedom against Pluto-crats through Social Control guaranteeing Economic Security, of which the struggle begins with the British Factory Acts of 1833 and 1847.

It was by this progress and with these safeguards that Mill hoped to build the land that Tennyson described:

> "It is the land that freemen till,
>   That sober-suited Freedom chose,
>   The land, where girt with friends or foes,
> A man may speak the thing he will."

§ vi

The tragic problem of Cromwell and of Lincoln is worth studying in the light of the issues of our own time. Both men deeply and sincerely believed in liberty—liberty of conscience and expression. Both men were freely accused by their oppo-nents of dictatorship—of being 'King Oliver' or 'King Lin-coln.' Neither was in a position where he could walk deli-cately around the difficulties without brushing against the issues of anarchy—even for conscience' sake—and of authority. Lincoln at least was a convinced democrat. And both shewed that this love of liberty is not inconsistent with vigorous strong government in time of war. Not only were, in Lin-coln's case, the constitutional forms of Democracy preserved, although invigorated with a new spirit, but sight was never lost of the goal and object of Democracy, not only in con-stitutional form but in social substance.

The issue with the Locke-Mill theory of a socially balanced constitution is different and more difficult. Such a balance, in a pre-revolutionary or war situation, it would appear impos-sible to maintain. Mill himself states that representative government is not especially fitted to weld together "a multitude of insignificant units." If government is to do this, it must depart from some of Mill's principles of balanced, or proportional, representative control. The job is to act, not debate. What it can do, which an "irresponsible monarchy" (even when claiming impartiality between classes) may not do, is to enshrine in the tradition for which it fights this notion of balanced claims, practical, utilitarian compromise, minority rights and electoral control. War is necessarily a centralizer.

What, however, of minority rights in peace-time? What of the desirable social ideal itself? Suppose that a minority wishes to conduct itself in a fashion inconsistent with the desired mode of living of the majority. Better—suppose that the majority propose for themselves a mode of life which presumes economic and moral (or what, today, is called 'ideological') uniformity, which the alien, heterogeneous minorities render, by *their* way of living, confused and imperfect? The Liberal theorists habitually thought of the problem as one of the adjustment of individual to individual; but this is unduly to simplify the matter. If we consider not some solicitor's view of legal property rights or some grocer's trade demands, but issues of education, of morals and of national unity, the matter assumes a more momentous form. What is to be done with the immoralist, the heretic? Is it sufficient to say that each group, large or small, may conduct its own common life in its own way so long as it does not coerce, but respects, the equal liberty of the other? Is it sufficient to say that every minority, however small, may do this? Does this rule apply to restrain majority Churches? Or majority Parties (the secular Churches of today)? Or even majority Parties when in control of the government of the State? Is the State *only* to act to defend the totality in war or individual rights in peace? Shall it not defend the near-totality or majority, in *its* chosen scheme of living, in peace? Does not individualism ignore the moral, socialistic importance of common action and the common life in society that, as organic, or religious, is more important than individuals . . . or minorities? Can we attain spiritual or social peace this way?

To this, by implication, reply has already been given. The moral basis of Democracy is respect for the personal rights— natural rights, if one will—of each individual under natural law. The majority, however honest, has no right to dragoon the minority merely for *the sake of moral uniformity*. It does not *know* enough. As J. S. Mill said, "The sole end for which mankind are warranted, individually or collectively, in interfering with the liberty of action of any of their number is self-protection." And Thomas Paine can add: "He who takes nature for his guide, is not easily beaten out of his argument." *If these inherent rights of a man as such, moral rights arising from the irrepressible claims of his permanent nature, be denied, including his right to choose his own social ideal and to consent, then, although many forms of government may be suitable in the world, for the ends of common life there is no intrinsic reason why Democracy should be one of them*. It is not patently the most efficient for propagandizing an ideal. Democracy may be wrong. But, if Democracy is right, coercion of the minority by the majority may be a utilitarian measure of self-defence but it *cannot* be an ideal principle. *The totalitarian State, just because it uses force, is not the ideal*.

If, however, there is a *revealed ideal scheme* of society according to which all men had better live, then clearly it will be better if government is in the hands of the Party oligarchy that has this revelation. Government should be "from above," by the few who are "fully conscious" . . . who "know." For these purposes, Democracy is mere bad, weak government. Apart from such certain knowledge, on the one hand, or at least passive consent, on the other, majority will is mere force; and no majority Democracy can make it other. It has no claim to allegiance save, as Hobbes said, in fear.

Democracy must, then, maintain personal freedom; it must maintain the rights of minorities; it must admit the right to be wrong; it must maintain the right to organize opposition Parties (that is the core, the kernel, the hub) that may some day control the State, provided these Parties themselves propose peaceful means—nor is it enough to register a vote for one Party, whether one may say 'yes' or 'no' for it, as in Germany or, as in Russia, only 'yes' or 'non-Party.' *This choice of organization is of the essence of Democracy.* It also follows from everything that we have said on Toleration and on Experiment. Jeremy Bentham, in one passage, put the matter neatly:

"The characteristic, then, of an undespotic government—in a word, of *every* government that has any tenable claim to the appellation of a good government—is, the allowing, and giving facility to this communication (of opinion); and this not only for instruction, but for excitation—not only for instruction and excitation, but also for correspondence; and this, again, for the purpose of affording and keeping on foot every facility for eventual resistance —for resistance to government, and thence, should necessity require, for a change of government."

It is well to realize what a *price has to be paid* for Democracy, Toleration and Utilitarian Compromise. Where they obtain, it is impossible to have a symmetrical, united social scheme. Or, if there be such, the unity will be that of all-prevalent variety. There can be, however, a homogeneous, coherent tradition—and variety can lie in it as an aspect of social Freedom. . . . Moreover, it is well to recognize that, in times of social passion and of revolutionary demand, another name for 'variety' will be 'obstruction.' John Strachey does not overlook this point; he criticizes Attlee for it. He is against such 'obstruction' and one gathers that his projected "New Model Party" will suppress it. According to Anglo-Saxon (not French) notions, Democracy tends to be federal and 'compromising,' 'utilitarian' and 'co-operationist' in the very tissue of its structure. Until we recognize this we shall not be able seriously to take stock of the system which we may be called upon to defend. It is idle to pretend that it is peculiar in offering no difficulties in the task of government and the reconciliation of liberty and authority.

In the discussion of Democracy as a governmental system, it is indeed essential to distinguish between the prevalent Anglo-Saxon system, a two-party system that has on the whole been politically successful, and the system prevalent in France and the constitutional systems deriving from her, multi-party systems, which, on the contrary, cannot claim to have been singularly successful.

This, however, does not involve giving a blessing, on the ground of constitutional tradition, to any excess of minority obstructionism, even criminal. What it does mean is that the basic principal of secular, *coercive* government, of government by the *State,* is utility. It never rises higher than the pragmatic. There *is* a vision of justice to which we are under a moral imperative to return, a vision conditioned by Natural Law itself. But our apprehension of this justice is never final, logical or absolute. Nor is our right to coerce. That is the caution always present in the mind of any true democrat. The true doctrine of Democracy follows from the doctrines of Tolerance, Compromise and Co-operation, as these, in turn, from those of Liberty and Experiment. They connect. And they fall together.

Of what kind, then, shall our moral assurance be under Democracy?—what will be the framework of our stable values? Or is our Democracy, not as formula of government but as way of life, the same as that of which Plato said that it was but a popular name for moral nihilism?

CHAPTER VI

Moralism

§ i

> "Who would true valour see
> Let him come hither;
> One here will constant be,
> Come wind, come weather.
> There's no discouragement
> Shall make him once relent
> His first avowed intent
> To be a pilgrim.
>
> "Whoso beset him round
> With dismal stories,
> Do but themselves confound;
> His strength the more is.
> No lion can him afright
> He'll with a giant fight,
> But he will have a right
> To be a pilgrim."

So sang Mr. Valiant-for-Truth, and went on his way in pilgrimage to Beulah. But from the enticements of Madame Bubble, or this vain world, he prayed to be delivered. "She would have drawn thee into many foolish and hurtful lusts, which drown men in destruction and perdition (1 Tim. vi. 9)."

The moralism of England and New England has often become hypocrisy. Against this 'canting hypocrisy' the Eighteenth Century saw a revolt to tolerance and the damning of 'enthusiasm.' But the moralism itself, since the Puritans, and indeed since Langland, is part of the very tradition. Only by it does the full tradition become intelligible. It has several facets, as we shall see, but it is not mistaken to see in it a unity.

English mysticism never strains its nerve as much as the Spanish; it is less self-analytic; it has less of the richness of a great philosophic tradition behind it to surmount. It walks in homespun and has, in such a man as John Bunyan (1628–88), constant contact with the shrewd prudence of common life. The characteristic of much English mysticism, especially the Protestant, is moralistic, rather than religious in the sense of any experience of immediate divine union. It walks God-fearingly, reassuring itself that those once in grace can never fall from it, and yet with an instant consciousness of sin. It is individualistic (with a reservation about the habit of forming 'Societies' that I will mention later); and the metaphor of the pilgrim is apt.

Although the pilgrims might move together (Christian went alone, in Bunyan's *Pilgrim's Progress*), each is conscious that he bears his own soul in his own hands and that no man can save his brother. The pilgrim lived knowing that this night his soul might be required of him by the Eternal Maker and that he proceeded to the Judgement Seat alone, not excused by the commands of Caesar nor by the will of the multitude, which men follow to do evil. The great Cardinal of the Nineteenth Century, Newman, in his *Dream of Gerontius,* writes:

"Some angel, Jesu! such as came to Thee
In Thine own agony . . .
Mary, pray for me, Joseph pray for me, Mary pray for me."

But John Henry Newman, like the poets Vaughan and Traherne, represents a minor tone contributing to, but unrepresentative of, the whole, filled with the religious consciousness

rather than (if we may, as we should, distinguish them) the
sternness of the moral consciousness.

John Bunyan was released from Bedford jail, where he
had been imprisoned as a preacher for conscience' sake, under
a pardon also granted to various Quakers. He scandalized his
stricter Baptist brethren by his tolerance for those of that sect.
The authentic English note is heard again in the *Journal* of
John Woolman (1720–72), of Northampton, New Jersey,
Quaker, a man much exercised over the rightness of keeping
slaves and to whom Slavery Emancipation owes as much as
to any. The moral life, unlike the religious life that seeks to
discover the ecstasy of the *visio beatifica* and union, is practical. We may remark, in the *Journal,* the practical note following that of spiritual conviction:

"After some farther Conversation, I said, that Man having Power
too often misapplied it; that though we made Slaves of the Negroes, and the Turks made Slaves of the Christians, I believed that
Liberty was the natural Right of all Men equally: Which he did
not deny; but said, the Lives of the Negroes were so wretched in
their own Country, that many of them lived better here than
there: I only said, there are great odds, in regard to us, on what
Principle we act. . . . Having thus travelled through Maryland, we
came among Friends at Cedar-Creek in Virginia, on the 12th Day
of the fifth Month; and the next Day rode, in Company with several Friends, a Day's Journey to Camp-Creek. As I was riding
along in the morning, my Mind was deeply affected in a Sense I
had of the Want of divine Aid to support me in the various Difficulties which attended me. . . .

"I was troubled to perceive the Darkness of their Imaginations;
and in some Pressure of Spirit said, the Love of Ease and Gain is
the Motive in general for keeping Slaves, and Men are wont to
take hold of weak Arguments to support a Cause which is unreasonable; and added, I have no Interest in either Side, save only
the Interest which I desire to have in the Truth: and as I believe
Liberty is their Right, and see they are not only deprived of it, but
treated in other Respects with Inhumanity in many Places, I be-

lieve He, who is a Refuge for the Oppressed, will, in His own Time, plead their Cause; and happy will it be for such as walk in Uprightness before Him: And there our Conversation ended.
. . .

"These are the People by whose Labour the other Inhabitants are in a great Measure supported, and many of them in the Luxuries of Life: These are the People who have made no Agreement to serve us, and who have not forfeited their Liberty that we know of: These are Souls for whom Christ died, and, for our Conduct toward them, we must answer before Him who is no Respecter of Persons."

Later Friend John Woolman came to England, and travelled to York, which "looked like Home to me," and, as Friends record, "he had a Dream, and saw himself in the Northern Parts [of England], and that the Spring of the Gospel was opened in him much as in the beginning . . . as George Fox and William Dewsberry, and he saw the different States of the People, as clear as he had ever seen Flowers in a Garden." And, as Woolman says, in his *Remarks:*

"People may have no intention to oppress, yet by entering on expensive Ways of Life, their Minds may be so entangled therein, and so engaged to support expensive Customs, as to be estranged from the pure sympathizing spirit.

"As I have travell'd in *England,* I have had a tender Feeling of the Condition of poor People, some of whom though honest and industrious, have nothing to spare towards paying for the Schooling of their Children.

"There is a Proportion between Labour and the Necessaries of Life, and in true Brotherly Love the Mind is open to feel after the Necessities of the Poor. . . .

"Labour in the right Medium is healthy, but in too much of it there is a painful Weariness; and the Hardships of the Poor are sometimes increased through Want of a more agreeable Nourishment, more plentiful Fewel for the Fire, and warmer Cloathing in the Winter than their wages will answer.

"When I have beheld Plenty in some Houses to a Degree of

Luxury, the Condition of poor Children brought up without learn-ing, and the Condition of the Weakly and Aged, who strive to live by their Labour, have often revived in my Mind, as Cases of which some who live in Fulness need to be put in Remembrance."

Elsewhere John Woolman writes (as he also practised): "reading the Life and Doctrines of our blessed Redeemer, the Account of the Sufferings of Martyrs, and the History of the first Rise of our Society, a Belief was gradually settled in my Mind, that if such, as had great Estates, generally lived in that Humility and Plainness which belongs to a Christian Life . . . so great a Number of People might be employed in Things useful, that Labour, both for Men and other Crea-tures, would need to be no more than an agreeable Employ." And this pilgrim of God, having come to York, died there and was interred in the Quaker burying-ground, in the year 1772.

John Wesley (1703–91), sometime Fellow of Lincoln Col-lege, Oxford, is a more complicated character, no less con-cerned with inner salvation, not indifferent to the condition of the people, whether Cornish miners or the Red Indians of Georgia among whom he missionized, but with a detectable deference to authority as by law established which he held it no part of religion to criticize.

In Wesley, like Luther and unlike Woolman, the religious and politico-practical aspects of life remain distinct. Prison and workhouse reform, so that "nothing offends eye or ear," is an exception to the general preoccupation with Methodist revivalism, to the exclusion of other interests, which had dom-inated Wesley's life since, in 1738, he visited the Moravian pietists in Germany. Earlier in the same year Peter Böhler, the Moravian, in Oxford had told him, "My brother, my brother, that philosophy of yours must be purged away." Whether, in 1742, preaching on his father's tomb in Epworth churchyard, or during the subsequent forty-nine years of ministry, Wesley proceeded to disprove the popular belief that an Englishman is unable to abandon himself to emotion. That emotion—harnessed to a remarkable constitution, not enervated by "the softness of a genteel education" and tempered by the training of a strong-minded and obstinate beldame, his mother, who had taught her children "to fear the rod and cry softly" —enabled John Wesley to do with titanic energy a work in England that changed public life. Himself a genius preoccupied with change of spirit, his followers were able to canalize the emotion and to make the social deductions.

Wesley, however, was more than an emotionalist of the Rousseauite type; and the contrast here between the English and French character is interesting and immensely important in its effects. The point is that Wesley believed in the significance of sin; and Rousseau—"a consummate coxcomb," to Wesley—did not. Mrs. Susannah Wesley had taught her children that, "as self-will is the root of all sin and misery, so whatever cherishes this in children insures their after-wretchedness and irreligion; whatever checks and mortifies it promotes their future happiness and piety. This is still more evident, if we further consider, that religion is nothing else than the doing the will of God, and not our own."

Wesley himself writes:

"I casually took a volume of what is called, 'A Sentimental Journey through France and Italy.' Sentimental! What is that? It is not English: he might as well say Continental. It is not sense. It conveys no determinate idea; yet one fool makes many. And this nonsensical word (who would believe it?) is become a fashionable one."

It is interesting, moreover, to observe that Wesley notes in his *Journal* with distaste, as being "both surprised and grieved," what he terms "a genuine instance of enthusiasm";

Law, of the *Serious Call,* is dismissed as "Behmenish, void and vain"; Martin Luther himself "is deeply tinctured with mysticism throughout, and hence often dangerously wrong." Wesley's task was not 'enthusiasm,' but to arouse men to a consciousness of their actual, present, damnation-deserving sin by his words. As Beau Nash said to him at Bath, "Your preaching frightens people out of their wits"—nor did it do so the less because Wesley did not preach Whitefield's Calvinism, but put the issue up to their own free will. Wesley, indeed, denied Nash's charge: "Sir, did you ever hear me preach?" "No." "How, then, can you judge of what you never heard?" "Sir, by common report." "Common report is not enough. Give me leave, Sir, to ask, Is not your name Nash?" "My name is Nash." "Sir, I dare not judge of you by common report: I think it not enough to judge by." Nevertheless, sin and God-fearing, "speaking of death and judgement, heaven and hell," remained the heart of the matter. That gospel Wesley preached through the half-century of his ministry, always "still a wonder to myself . . . never travelling less, by sea or land, than four thousand five hundred miles in a year." Like Charles Kingsley later, emphatically John Wesley was a "muscular Christian," inclined to measure the work of the spirit by mileage:

"Tues. May 5, 1772. In the evening I preached in the new house at Arbroath. In this town there is a change indeed! It was wicked to a proverb; remarkable for Sabbath-breaking, cursing, swearing, drunkenness, and a general contempt of religion. But it is not so now. Open wickedness disappears; no oaths are heard, no drunkenness seen in the streets. And many have not only ceased from evil, and learned to do well, but are witnesses of the inward Kingdom of God, 'righteousness, peace and joy in the Holy Ghost . . .'

"Tues. May 14, 1783. Some years ago four factories for spinning and weaving were set up at Epworth. In these a large number of young women, and boys and girls, were employed. The whole conversation of these was profane and loose to the last degree. But some of them stumbling in at the prayer meeting were suddenly cut to the heart. These never rested till they had gained their companions. The whole scene was changed. In three of the factories, no more lewdness or profaneness were found; for God had put a new song in their mouth, and blasphemies were turned to praise. Those three I visited today, and found religion had taken deep root in them. No trifling word was heard among them, and they watched over each other in love. I found it exceedingly good to be there, and we rejoiced together in the God of our Salvation.

"Fri. 31. As I lodged with Lady Maxwell at Saughton hall . . ."

The trouble with John Wesley was an excessive belief that his acquaintance with the Governor of Guernsey might be an advantage also for the Almighty and "make a more open way for the Gospel" (since he was "one having authority"— I mean, the Governor) . . . or staying with Lady Maxwell; while of famished bodies in Bethnal Green all that can be said is that, considering their conditions, "Who would not rejoice that there is another world?" Nevertheless, there is in Wesley's teaching a burning conviction of the connection between hell and loose living that expresses both the intensity of religious experience and the right Anglo-Saxon moral practicality. It potently fuses the two. Wesley cannot be said to have provided any explanation or philosophy of his experience. He would have disdained to do so. The English hypocrisy, indeed, is the homage rendered by those who do not share this experience but acknowledge its power, to those who do share it but cannot explain it.

The spirit of John Wesley breathed again in a young Wesleyan, born in 1829—so well styled by Mr. St. John Ervine, in his magnificent biography, "God's Soldier"—William Booth. Even more than Wesley, the founder of the Salvation Army moved among the poor; and he was less occasioned to be "moved with compassion for the rich." Booth, like Wesley, had a passion for the salvation of souls; but Mr. Ervine seems to me right in selecting Booth as also typical of certain moralistic qualities of the English (and Anglo-Irish) character that he admires. There was, moreover, a Messianic quality in Booth, due perhaps to a strain of Jewish ancestry. Bramwell Booth, his son, was to receive titles of honour from royalty, and William himself, Doctor of Law of Oxford, was entertained by President McKinley, who told him that he "quite endorsed the doctrine that without the grace of God in the heart there was little hope of permanently reforming the people." The mighty who had rejected Bunyan had learned their lesson in Wesley and Booth. Nevertheless, the work of the Army remained primarily among the very poor. To them Booth went with "something about fighting and less about trumpets. . . . Make some more words . . . with some fight in them!" Booth explained his principles, that he had held from the beginning:

"I looked upon the world around me as being in actual rebellion against God; and I always felt even in my boyhood days that the glory of God trailed in the dust, that He was mocked, and scorned, and hated, as when on earth, and I was led to sympathize very much with Him, and said in my young heart that these revels ought to be subdued to His authority.

"I came to realize that . . . the men and women around me in consequence of their rebellion 'were in great danger of damnation,' and 'that all their miseries, present and to come, were the results of their rebellion against God.'"

This realization, however, was connected with a clear and vivid picture of the social conditions which aided the devil in his work. In *Darkest England* Booth wrote:

"Were it not that I utterly repudiate as a fundamental denial of the essential principle of the Christian religion the popular pseudoscientific principle that any man or woman is past saving by the grace of God and the power of the Holy Spirit, I would sometimes be disposed to despair when contemplating these victims of the Devil. . . . For thousands upon thousands of poor wretches are, as Bishop South truly said, 'not so much born into this world as damned into it.' The bastard of a harlot, born in a brothel, suckled on gin, and familiar from earliest infancy with all the bestialities of debauch, violated before she is twelve, and driven into the streets by her mother a year or two later, what chance is there for such a girl in this world—I say nothing about the rest? Yet such a case is not exceptional."

There are many who may regard the work of the emotional Salvation Army—with its semi-humourous insistence (in Booth's *Darkest England*) that human beings are entitled to what Booth called "the Cab-Horse-Standard," food, warmth, cover—and of the tabulatory Charity Organization Society alike as radically erroneous methods of coping with the problem of poverty in a capitalist civilization. That, however, was not the general view in Britain or America. And the sincerity of the mood of the Army was beyond question. An authentic expression of it will be found in the words of Catherine Booth on what she believed to be her death-bed:

"I feel at this moment, I could put all my children into their graves, and go to a workhouse bed to die, sooner than I could see those first principles of The Salvation Army, for which I have lived and struggled, traduced, undermined, and sacrificed. I am surer than ever that they are the *right* principles; indeed, that they are the only principles by which to push successfully the salvation of the world. . . . I thank God that, notwithstanding all the defects and imperfections I see in my life and work as I look back upon them from this bed, I can say that by His grace I have ever kept the interests of His Kingdom first, and have never withheld anything He required of me in order to help forward the salvation of the world. And my prayer for all of you is that you may be able, when you come as near the end, to say the same."

Salvation was "helped forward" through 'the Army.' For the Wesleys it was helped forward through 'the Societies.' For John Woolman it was helped forward through 'the Society'—'Friends.' Individualists and pilgrims although all these men were, yet in a remarkable fashion they solved the great dilemma of individualism by finding moral assurance for their lives *through,* if not only *in,* an intimate community of their free choice. Both Wesley in his lifetime and the Army were accused of being 'jesuitical,' a charge entirely inept save on the one score: that Wesley and, still more, Booth were personal dictators. However, unlike the Jesuit generals (and this on principle) they succeeded, as Cromwell succeeded, in combining the prerogative due to their personality with respect for other men's conscience. ('Friends,' more typical I suggest, had no such patriarchate.) Free joint personal assurance—the common sense of the like-minded—was the source of their moral energy. They discovered, as the Quakers also discovered, the significance of *the voluntary community*—of community by choice. Out of that sprung their living enthusiasm. Individualist in their pursuit of salvation, they were social in the application they sought to give to it and, because social, practical.

§ ii

Joseph Butler (1692–1752), Bishop of Bristol and then of Durham, once rector of Haughton and Stanhope, "the reverend father in Christ, pious, simple, candid, liberal, so that scarcely though dead shall his memory pass away," is a very different figure from John Bunyan—the Bishop Palatine and Anglican Prelate from the "inspired tinker," the Baptist preacher of Bedford. And yet not so different. Butler was the son of a shopkeeper, a Presbyterian dissenter. And there is a certain sober quality in all his work so that, although Butler would have pleased Locke by his distaste for 'enthusiasm,' yet where Butler and Bunyan agree we may be assured that we have the core of Englishry. And in this Englishness we find the view, in both cases, more than English, and universal. The character, not the content, is English:

"That *mankind is a community*" [says Butler in his *Sermons*] "that we all stand in a relation to each other, that there is a public end and interest of society which each particular is obliged to promote, is the sum of morals. . . .

"As to that love of our enemies which is commanded, this supposes the general obligation to benevolence or good-will towards mankind . . . because that we have the habitual temper of benevolence is taken for granted.

" 'But if lower instances of injury may lessen our benevolence, why may not higher, or the highest, destroy it?' The answer is obvious. It is *not man's being a social creature,* much less his being a moral agent, from whence *alone* our obligations to good-will towards him arise; there is an obligation to it prior to either of these, arising from his being *a sensible creature*—that is, capable of happiness or misery. Now this obligation cannot be superseded by his moral character. What justifies public execution is, not that the guilt or demerit of the criminal dispenses with the obligation of good-will, neither would this justify any severity; but that his life is inconsistent with the quiet and happiness of the world. . . .

"From hence it is easy to see what is the degree in which we are commanded to love our enemies, or those who have been injurious to us. It were well if it could as easily be reduced to practice. It cannot be imagined that we are required to love them with any peculiar kind of affection. But suppose the person injured to have *a due natural sense* of the injury and no more; he ought to be affected towards the injurious person in the same way any good men, uninterested in the case, would be; if they have the same just sense, which we suppose the injured person to have, of the fault; after which there will yet remain real good-will towards the offender.

"Now what is there in all this which should be thought impracticable? I am sure there is *nothing in it unreasonable.*"

Placidly, and with dry humour, the good bishop justifies God's ways to man; discovers in His commands "nothing unreasonable"; sees men as a community and man benevolent; but withal a tempered, sober benevolence that does not forget either, on the one hand, the pleasure and misery of the creature or, on the other, the wider "quiet and happiness of the world." He has discovered his flying arch from happiness for the one to happiness of the greater number. He discovers this through benevolence . . . not excluding public executions. The end of man may be, in the wording of the honoured formula, "to praise God and glorify Him for ever," but the *majorem gloriam Dei* and the vision of God that is the reward of the saints are never permitted to take wings and soar to speculative heights out of touch with "the due natural sense . . . of any good men."

I have a partiality for Bishop Butler. It seems to me that he, too, was a good man. There is a calmness in his judgements, and a shrewd, benevolent sanity that suits his times; one would that it suited ours. Nevertheless, it is to be confessed that his appeal to conscience as final is itself less than final, and his philosophical arguments scarcely carry through. They justify Gallic criticisms of English thinking—although it cannot be said that French philosophy from Malebranche to Cousin does any better than the countrymen of Bacon and Hobbes, Locke and Berkeley, Hume and Bentham and Mill, James and Dewey, Whitehead and Russell. And, if unsatisfying, the appeal to 'common-sense,' 'due natural sense,' is at least both significant and typical.

John Locke had been least happy, of all his philosophy, in dealing with the problem of ethical values. It is a dangerous gap. He speaks of a demonstrable science of ethics springing from axioms or basic propositions concerning the nature of God and of man. On this somewhat rash statement he received the congratulations of no less a man than Leibniz.

But, in other passages, we find that the test of value and vice is identical with the law of God—there is an "unchangeable rule of right and wrong, which the law of God hath established." Locke rides off telling us that no one, not brutish, can doubt that God has given such a law. In part, it appears that it is of revelation and obeyed for the good old Hobbesian reason of pains and pleasures—that it will be the worse for us if we do not—as it also will be if we do not follow that public opinion that awards praise and blame. "Good and evil is nothing but pleasure or pain" (*Essay,* xx. 2, xxi. 42).

In part the moral law is declared by the light of nature, and we are left with the admirable Hooker's tests, of symmetry, universality and measure or fittingness (an aesthetic test, as it was for Plato, and, later, for Hume); of rationality; and of ancient and general tradition in the world. We may presume, with Hooker, "the will of man to be obstinate, rebellious and averse from all obedience," but there are still "the sacred laws of his nature" (Hooker, *Ecclesiastical Polity,* i. 5). The following of desires and natural impulses alone, for Locke, does but upset everything. We may build a bridge from Locke's empirical metaphysics to his 'natural rights' politics, although it will span some verbal ambiguities, if we stress this injunction to 'consider' the 'idea' of man by the only available methods "derived from sensation and reflection," and to study his permanent nature, in terms of which solely we can understand the lasting satisfaction of his desire for "happiness and that alone."

Butler carries us several stages further. By his theory that men follow true self-interest, which yet can be coincident with the *general happiness,* he makes a bridge between Locke and Bentham. He writes:

"Self-love, then, though confined to the interest of the present world, does in general perfectly coincide with virtue, and leads us to one and the same course of life. But whatever exceptions there are to this, which are much fewer than they are commonly thought, all shall be set right at the final distribution of things. It is a manifest absurdity to suppose evil finally prevailing over good, under the conduct and administration of a perfect mind. . . . Conscience and self-love *if we understand our true happiness,* always lead us the same way. Duty and interest are perfectly coincident."

This manifestly was not logically good enough for Bentham, any more than it would have been for Hobbes. Bentham felt he could improve on Butler; and that conscience could be bettered as a guide, with self-love so much clearer in its pointings. It is significant of the century that even the great Bishop Berkeley (1685–1753), the idealist philosopher, said almost the same thing as Butler: "Self-love being a principle of all others the most universal, and the most deeply engraved in our hearts, it is natural for us to regard things as they are fitted to augment or impair our happiness; and accordingly we denominate them good or evil."

The philosophic Bentham (1748–1832) alleges that we must follow pleasure and self-interest all the time. Hutcheson (1694–1746), however, the professor of moral philosophy in Glasgow University, had said that the moral evil of a given action "is as the Degree of misery, and the number of Sufferers; so that, that Action is best, which accomplishes the Greatest Happiness of the Greatest Number." Imparted through the writings of Dr. Priestley, the 'Greatest Happiness Principle' came as a revelation to Bentham. It supplied the missing piece in the puzzle. From the principle of Utility, a commonplace to Dr. Johnson, interpreted in terms of self-love, one moved on to it as a social principle. Bentham failed to notice that the dictum 'I should pursue *my* pleasure,' might be a reason why the majority should pursue *its* pleasure, but gave no moral or intelligent reason why the minority should make *sacrifice* of its. In so far as Bentham met this difficulty, he could only do it by positing, like Butler, altruism or 'benevolence' as an emotion requiring its pleasurable satisfaction in all human beings—an answer more optimistic than realistic.

John Stuart Mill, the disciple, comments even severely upon Jeremy Bentham, the founder of Utilitarianism:

"What Bentham's functional truths could do, there is no such good means of shewing as by a review of his philosophy. . . . In many of the most natural and strongest feelings of human nature he had no sympathy; from many of his graver experiences he was altogether cut off; and the faculty by which one mind understands a mind different from itself, and throws itself into the feelings of that other mind, was denied him by his deficiency of Imagination. . . . A moralist on Bentham's principles . . . what will be his qualifications for regulating the nicer shades of human behaviour. . . .

"Nothing is more curious than the absence of recognition in any of his writings of the existence of conscience, as a thing distinct from philanthropy, from affection for God or man, and from self-interest in this world as in the next. . . . The feelings of moral approbation or disapprobation properly so called, either towards ourselves or our fellow-creatures, he seems unaware of the existence of; and neither the word self-respect, nor the idea to which that word is appropriated, occurs even once, so far as our recollection serves us, in his whole writings."

J. S. Mill is here writing in a condition of emotional crisis and under the influence of Thomas Carlyle, and does less than justice to the initiator of the greatest movement for social reform, especially law reform, in the history of the

country. Bentham had, in fact, discussed conscience by implication, in his discourses on the "principles of sympathy and
antipathy." However, what is significant is that the wheel has
turned full circle and that, with J. S. Mill's criticism, we are
back at conscience and with Bishop Butler. We may talk with
Locke about "the twilight of probability" and we may make
calculations with Bentham about "the greatest happiness"; but
there is some principle *more than probable to ourselves* (perhaps aesthetic) in our nature—and was not Hooker wise in
referring us back upon the consensus of men of *vision* ever
since Sophocles?—by which we comprehend what is stable
and abiding happiness. Butler writes:

"Either there is a difference between right and wrong or there
is not. . . . If it be not, there is no reason for any concern about it;
but if it be true, it requires real fairness of mind and honesty of
heart. And if people will be wicked, they had better of the two be
so from the common vicious passions without such refinements,
than from this deep and calm source of delusion [self-deceit],
which undermines the whole principle of good, darkens that light,
that 'candle of the Lord within' which is to direct our steps, and
corrupts conscience, which is the guide of life."

It may be felt that the good bishop has a certain Hano-
verian optimism and Protestant intellectual facility which
would be none the worse for consideration of a few of the
problems, debated through the centuries, of casuistry. He
makes himself, however, clearer and deeper by his contrast,
entirely in the style of Locke, of true self-love with mere passion. "If passion prevails over self-love, the consequent action
is unnatural, but if [true] *self-love prevails over passion,* the
action is natural . . . if we will act conformably to *the economy
of man's nature, reasonable self-love must govern* . . . *our
nature—that is, the voice of God within us—carries us to the*

exercise of charity and benevolence in the way of compassion or mercy . . . this is that humanity which is so peculiarly becoming to our nature and circumstances in this world":

"The natural supremacy of reflection or conscience being there established, we may from it form a distinct notion of what is meant by *human nature,* when virtue is said to consist in following it, and vice is deviating from it.

"For the conclusion of this let me just take notice of the danger of over-great refinements . . . morality and religion must be somewhat plain and easy to be understood; it must appeal to what we call *plain common sense,* as distinguished from superior capacity and improvement, because it appeals to mankind. Persons of superior capacity and improvement have often fallen into errors which no one of more common understanding could. . . . *The extravagancies of enthusiasm and superstition do not at all lie on the road of common sense;* and therefore, so far as they are original mistakes, must be owing to going beside or beyond it . . . the proper advice to be given to plain honest men, to secure them from the extremes both of superstition and irreligion, is that of the son of Sirach: 'In every good work *trust thy own soul;* for this is the keeping of the commandment' (*Eccles.* xxxii. 23)."

§ iii

In the case of Benjamin Franklin (1706–90), *philosophe* and somewhat odd Presbyterian, the morality as well as the features of Jeremy Bentham were anticipated and portrayed. There are the same vices, a commercial and Philistine set of values, and the same virtues of robust common-sense and self-discipline, in the author of the *Autobiography* and of the American version of 'Poor Robin's Almanack,' *Poor Richard's Almanack,* as in the utilitarian philosopher. There is also a marked tendency to identify thrift and godliness. That the conjunction of qualities is favourable to the advancement of invention and science, Franklin's own life proves, with his achievements in what he terms "the electric branch of natural philosophy," i.e. electricity. Of his *Almanack* Franklin himself says:

"I therefore filled all the little spaces that occurr'd between the remarkable days in the calendar with proverbial sentences, chiefly such as inculcated industry and frugality, as the means of procuring wealth, and thereby securing virtue; it being more difficult for a man in want, to act always honestly, as, to use here one of those proverbs, it is hard for an empty sack to stand upright."

In the *Almanack* itself, for 1758, this worldly wisdom is summarized in terse phrases:

"And now to conclude. Experience keeps a dear school; but fools will learn in no other, and scarce in that! for it is true, We may give Advice, but we cannot give Conduct, as Poor Richard says. However, remember this! They that won't be counselled, can't be helped! as Poor Richard says: and farther, that, If you will not hear reason, she'll surely rap your knuckles."

An individualistic, home-spun, plebeian creed. Nevertheless, Franklin as a young man aspired after a society, a kind of Samurai group after the conception of Mr. H. G. Wells, an aristocracy of the free and well-intentioned, to be called the United Party for Virtue. It is remarkable that, as an elder statesman who looked back on a Revolution and whose sagacity was respected throughout Europe, in 1788 Franklin still was "of the opinion that it was a practicable scheme . . . as I have thought that one man of tolerable abilities may work great changes . . . if he first forms a good plan and . . . makes the execution of that same plan his sole study and business." Actually Franklin, in his 'Junto' and elsewhere, was assiduous in working through clubs and the like societies.

It is also noteworthy that he changed his early free-thinking views, which had been after the style of Paine; and characteristic why he changed them:

"My London pamphlet, which had for its motto three lines of Dryden:

> " 'Whatever is, is right, though purblind man
>   Sees but a part o' the chain, the nearest link:
>   His eyes not carrying to the equal beam
>   That poises all above;'

and from the attributes of God, his infinite wisdom, goodness and power, concluded that nothing could possibly be wrong in the world, and that vice and virtue were empty distinctions, no such things existing, appear'd now [by the test of moral backslidings] not so clever a performance as I once thought it; and I doubted whether some error had not insinuated itself unperceiv'd into my arguments, so as to infect all that follow'd, *as is common in metaphysical reasonings.*"

In brief, Franklin anticipated the famous Hegelian argument that "what is is what ought to be," and rejected it in advance on good Anglo-Saxon pragmatic grounds.

No less pragmatic in temperament, wider in appeal, more pathetic in mood, is the most characteristic of all Anglo-Saxon moralists, "that great man" for Wesley, his dearest friend to Burke, Dr. Samuel Johnson (1709-84). Just as in the *obiter dicta* of Franklin are to be found such remarks, topical for our days, as that it is "indiscreet to print scurrilous reflections on the governments of neighbouring states," so among those of Johnson will be found the observation that "it is difficult to negotiate where neither will trust." However, in the *History of Rasselas*—which Johnson, in his poverty, wrote off to pay for his mother's funeral with the £20 that it earned —we find a more adequate expression of his philosophy:

"Of the uncertainties of our present state, the most dreadful and alarming is the uncertain continuance of reason. . . . All power of fancy over reason is a degree of insanity. . . . I can only tell that I have chosen wrong. I have passed my time in study *without ex-*

perience; in the attainment of Sciences which can, for the most part, be but remotely *useful* to mankind."

This attitude has its almost necessary consequence in Johnson's view of Rousseau, recorded in Boswell's *Life:*

"JOHNSON. 'Rousseau *knows* that he is talking nonsense and laughs at the world for staring at him.' BOSWELL. 'How so, Sir?' JOHNSON. 'Why, Sir, a man who talks nonsense so well must know that he is talking nonsense' . . .

"They make a rout about universal liberty, without considering that all that is to be valued, or indeed can be enjoyed by individuals, is private liberty."

The Doctor, it may be felt, was a greater man than his philosophy. Passages, however, in the *Journal to the Hebrides* and the *Life* shew a mood that transcends the Augustan cold of the Eighteenth Century and anticipates the romantic social sentiment of the Nineteenth, and yet in a fashion that remains classical, restrained and pious rather than Rousseauistic and enthusiastic. There is no reason to suppose that Johnson would have disagreed with Robert Burton (1577–1640), in his *Anatomy of Melancholy,* when he wrote: "Now for prophets, dreamers, and such rude, silly fellows, the best means to reduce them *ad sanam mentem* is to alter their course of life, and with conference, threats, promises and persuasions, to intermix physic. . . . We have frequently such prophets and dreamers amongst us, whom we persecute with fire and faggot: I think the most compendious cure, for some of these at least, had been in Bedlam." In the *Journal* Johnson says:

"Whatever withdraws us from the power of our senses; whatever makes the past, the distant or the future predominate over the present, advances us in the dignity of thinking beings. Far from me and from my friends be such frigid philosophy as may conduct us indifferent and unmoved over any ground that has been dignified by wisdom, bravery, or virtue. That man is little to be envied whose patriotism would not gain force upon the plain of Marathon, or whose piety would not grow warmer among the ruins of Iona."

Boswell, in the *Life,* records a similar comment upon a spend-thrift Scottish laird who was ruining his estates and his family's reputation in the countryside:

"Nay, Madam, it is not a preference of the land to its owner; it is a preference of a family to an individual. Here is an establish-ment in a country, which is of importance for ages, not only to the chief, but to his people; an establishment which extends up-wards and downwards; that this should be destroyed by one idle fellow is a sad thing."

The torch of moral conviction, the conviction of a pilgrim, individual yet permeated with social sense, Johnson passed on to Edmund Burke, his friend: "Sir, . . . I must be in a wretched state, indeed, when your company is not a delight to me."

§ iv

It was Lord Acton who wrote: "Burke at his best is England at its best." Despite Burke's vindications of the rights of the American colonists, no attempt, it can be maintained, could well be more inept than to try to join together Thomas Jeffer-son and Edmund Burke, or Edmund Burke and Jeremy Bentham, into the plan of one, consistent Anglo-Saxon philos-ophy or outlook. It yet happens that all three in fact were, or believed themselves to be, lineal descendants, in the spirit, of John Locke. Our purpose, moreover, is not to shape a philosophy of the schools, complete with questions, conclu-sions and demonstrations—a *Summa contra Gentiles* of the English. The statement seems well warranted that English, and even Anglo-Saxon, civilization throughout four centuries has preserved and developed certain characteristics recognizable by other nations, however much on all remaining points Englishmen or Scotsmen or Americans or Canadians may differ among each other as much as they differ collectively from Latins or Slavs. Those characteristics of the Anglo-Saxon mind, at least as manifested in Great Britain, Burke (Norman-Irish although he be by descent) has undoubtedly contributed to express, form and make definite.

When we come to a study of our present discontents Burke's work will be seen as significant, no less in its errors than in its justice. "Right as to two" (America and Ireland), "wrong as to one" (France), was Gladstone's verdict. It is by his general quality of judgement that Burke must be appraised and valued, and not for any systematic or profound philosophy. A land governed by philosophers recalls to him Swift's satire in *Gulliver's Travels;* his highest praise of a policy is with the words *"this was to understand human nature."* For him philosophers and human nature tend to be put in antithesis, especially "the cannibal philosophers of France."

Speaking on American affairs, in 1774, in a fashion entirely typical, Burke said:

"They (the Americans) and we, and their and our ancestors, have been happy under that system. . . . Do not burthen them by taxes: you were not used to do so from the beginning. Let this be your reason for not taxing. These are the arguments of States and Kingdoms. Leave the rest to the schools, for there only may they be discussed with safety. But if, intemperately, unwisely, fatally, you sophisticate and poison the very source of government by urging subtle deductions and consequences odious to those who govern, from the unlimited and illimitable nature of supreme sovereignty, you will teach them by these means to call that sovereignty itself in question."

Here Burke expresses a wisdom that the metaphysical Stuarts never knew. To this pragmatism, as an Anglo-Saxon or Anglo-Celtic characteristic, we shall have occasion to return. The pragmatism, however, in Burke, is cloudy; wears an aura of mysticism; has a Celtic quality; and yet is represented as the fruit of a just marriage between reason and the instinct of simple men. "Man is by nature reasonable"; but *"Under the direction of reason,* instinct is always right." Burke is, after all, a contemporary of Rousseau, and these men were less dissimilar than they themselves imagined.

Government is not constituted in virtue of natural rights which may, and do, exist in total independence of it. Government is only a contrivance of human wisdom to provide for human wants (and men have a right that their wants shall be provided for by this wisdom). Government "ought to conform to the exigencies of the time." "What in the result is likely to produce evil is politically false: that which is productive of good, is politically true." As for the rhetoric about resistance and revolution, "it renders the habit of society dangerously valetudinary; it is taking periodical doses of mercury sublimate, and swallowing down repeated provocatives of cantharides to our love of liberty." "The State ought to confine itself to what regards the State, or the creatures of the State: namely the exterior establishment of its religion; its magistracy; its revenue."

Repeatedly, Burke reverts to this theme of the evils of political metaphysics and the mischief that "the coxcombs of philosophy" do. The philosophy of the intellectuals of the French Revolution is a "barbarous philosophy which is the offspring of cold hearts and muddy understandings." "Nothing can be conceived more hard than the heart of a thoroughbred metaphysician. It comes nearer to the cold malignity of a wicked spirit than to the frailty and passion of a man." The truth is that Burke habitually meant, instead of the contrast of philosophy and human nature to which he refers, a contrast of scepticism and prescription. He has a conservative distrust of "great lights lately obtained in the world." Despite all his contempt for coxcombs who ignored experience, Burke was himself not an especially successful politician, as his own career demonstrates, and was moved to dismay and moral fury when he discovered that the innovators' denunciations were more practically competent to stir popular feeling than his own rhetoric of common-sense—were, in brief, better demagogic propaganda.

In the statement, "they (the Americans) and we have been happy under that system . . . leave the rest to the schools," there were not only anti-metaphysical, but Tory, implications which entitle Burke—the man once indicted by George III as among those who were to be deemed "not his friends but his enemies" and who styled Henry VIII "one of the most decided tyrants in the rolls of history"—to his place as the father of modern Conservatism. The phrase is highly significant: "I have, for one, been born in this order of things, and would fain die in it." British liberty was rather "a possession to be secured than a prize to be contended for." For "the professors," on the contrary, it was "a war or a revolution, or it is nothing." These implications become clearer in his writings on parliamentary reform and on the French Revolution. "This constitution in former days used to be the admiration and the envy of the world; it was a pattern for politicians. . . . As to Englishmen, it was their pride, their consolation. . . . Now all its excellencies are forgot, its faults are now forcibly dragged into day, exaggerated by every artifice of representation."

This reverent view could scarcely have been expressed more absolutely by Mr. Justice Braxfield himself who said, in 1793, briefly: "The British Constitution is the best that ever was since the beginning of the world and it is not possible to make it better." It contrasts, not too favourably, with the words of one of the greatest of the American Founding Fathers: "Some men look at constitutions with sanctimonious reverence, and deem them like the ark of the covenant, too sacred to be touched. They ascribe to the men of the preceding age a wisdom more than human, and suppose what they did to be beyond amendment. I [Thomas Jefferson] knew that age well; I belonged to it, and laboured with it. It deserved well of its country. It was very like the present, but without its experience. . . . I think that moderate imperfections had better be borne with . . . but I know also that laws and institutions must go hand in hand with the progress of the human mind." Burke, nevertheless, gave expression, however rhetorically, to that profound conviction which we have already noted in Milton—that England had so far reached political maturity and had so far proven her political course by experience, that it was not for her to follow among the nations, when political ideas and the genius that creates them were at issue. Burke's instinct was not wrong when he declared that "I am sure that I shall not be misled when, in a case of constitutional difficulty, I consult the genius of the English constitution." He thereby shewed an historic sense too lacking in the age of Dr. Priestley and William Godwin.

Burke's respect for the "British Constitution," even in its abuses, is to be explained as of a piece with his profound reverence for tradition. He fought for the cause of Catholic emancipation in Ireland because the Irish were his own people; Catholicism was his mother's faith; and because Ireland and Catholicism were for him replete with memories. He fought for the cause of the American colonists because their object was security in their ancient condition. "We view the establishment of the English colonies on principles of liberty, as that which is to render this kingdom venerable to future ages. . . . Those who have and who hold to that foundation of common liberty, whether on this side or on your side of the ocean, we consider as the true and the only true Englishmen."

In his *Reflections on the French Revolution,* Burke makes his position still more clear. The English Revolution, of 1688, was made "to preserve our ancient, indisputable laws and liberties, and that ancient constitution of government which is our only security for law and liberty. . . . What we did was, in truth and substance, and in a constitutional light, a revolution, not made, but prevented. . . . We wished at the period of the Revolution, and do now wish, to derive all we possess as an inheritance from our forefathers." Burke was prepared to defend the English, unlike the French, Revolution for the reasons, and with the safeguards, given by Sir Robert Walpole: "Resistance ought never to be thought of, but when an utter subversion of the laws of the realm threatens the whole frame of our constitution, and no redress can otherwise be hoped for." Not unaware of the hypocrisy of defending revolutions only when over and when monuments have been raised above their dust, Burke nevertheless insists that his argument is substantial. Mere passive obedience was "a dangerous, exploded principle." The great lawyers of England were "industrious to have the pedigree of our liberties." Burke has, however, to record that the Act declaring the throne vacant stated that James II had clearly broken the original contract between King and people.

The famous doctrine, however, of the social contract undergoes a significant change in the hands of Burke, as it did in those of Rousseau. The British conservative and the French collectivist thinkers never came nearer to agreement than on this issue. Both were romantic, mystic, filled with a sense for the community, opposed to the atomism of the political protestants of the preceding century. Nevertheless (and it is note-worthy) Burke, in set phrase, declines "the philosophy of vanity" of Rousseau—and rightly, since his own tradition owed nothing to the Genevese. "We are not the converts of Rousseau; we are not the disciples of Voltaire." Rousseau's philosophy is optimistic, emotional while yet intellectualist and abstract, revolutionary, anti-Catholic. Burke's philosophy is full of a religious pessimism. It is in touch with that of the high churchmen—not only with Dr. Johnson who advised, in *Rasselas,* the reflection that each of us is "but one atom in the mass of humanity," but also with the subtler, Pascalian spirit of Law who wrote: "When we are at the top of all human attainments we are at the bottom of all human misery, and have made no further advance towards true happiness than those whom we see in the want of all these excellencies." Burke's philosophy is one of an impassioned reason, but a reason that finds its wisdom immanent in history—a philosophy, profoundly Catholic, conservative of a tradition that Burke believed included all the nobler values of personal freedom and social loyalty.

In a memorable passage Burke turned from the Eighteenth Century and the old mythology of "Original Contract" to the Nineteenth Century and to anticipation of the new-mode mythology of the "Social Organism":

"Society is indeed a contract. Subordinate contracts for objects of mere occasional interest may be dissolved at pleasure—but the state ought not to be considered as nothing better than a partnership agreement in a trade of pepper and coffee, calico or tobacco or some other such low concern, to be taken up for a little temporary interest, and to be dissolved by the fancy of the parties. . . . It is a partnership in all science; a partnership in all art; a partnership in every virtue, and in all perfection. As the ends of such a partnership cannot be obtained in many generations, it becomes a partnership not only between those who are living, but between those who are living, those who are dead, and those who are to be born. Each contract of each particular state is but a clause in the great primeval contract of eternal society. . . ."

The contract has ceased to be one between free individuals. Burke would probably have endorsed the statement of the good Dr. Price that "civil liberty (it should be remembered) must be enjoyed as a right derived from the Author of nature only, or it cannot be the blessing which merits this name"— as all authority is from Above, so is all true liberty—but the rights of social authority enjoy for Burke a more awful sanction than any which derive from some expedient and contingent contract among the temporary population at any time inhabiting a land. The contract has become an inescapable obligation written out across the pages of human history.

Consistently enough, Burke anticipates what, a full century later, is to become a famous doctrine of the Oxford idealist philosophers. Most questions "which regard our duties in life, are to be determined by our station in it. . . . Neither the few nor the many have a right to act merely by their will, in any matter connected with duty, trust, engagement or obligation. . . ." God "having disposed and marshalled us by a divine tactic, not according to our will, but according to His . . . virtually subjected us to act the part which belongs to the place assigned to us." The duties of this station will be observed by those who recall that European civilization has been built on two principles, "the spirit of a gentleman and the spirit of religion." Burke quotes from Persius:

"Quantum elargiri debet? Quem te Deus esse
    Jussit?—et humana qua parte locatus es in re?" [1]

As for the pert philosophers of revolution, they are like grasshoppers. They "make the field ring with their importunate

[1] "How much charity? Whom did God ordain you to be
    And in what human station are you in fact placed?"

chink, whilst thousands of great cattle, reposed under the shadow of the British oak, chew the cud and are silent."

There is in Burke much of the genuine obscurantist. His age was one which paid for its Augustan equanimity this price—that it was terrified of probing the more disquieting doubts of life and revered reason at the cost of never putting her to any searching test. Inquiry was impiety, where common-sense and established religion alike prescribed contentment. To this corrosion of the bright metal of thought even the least Philistine of Eighteenth-Century writers, no less than tidy Pope and honest Johnson, fell victim. But Burke's warning words, concerning the meaning of duty, to the optimistic hedonists—no one can say "facile," who recalls Condorcet writing in his prison cell, before execution, his *Esquisse d'un Tableau historique des Progrès de l'Esprit Humain*—were never cheap and do not fade.

Burke's exposition of the principles of government is throughout characteristically English (if not characteristic of English philosophy) in its moral tone; but it is also—and this is new—social (if erratically so) rather than individualistic. He is concerned with what will satisfy "the moral tastes of every well-born mind." He has a compelling sense of the continuity of the generations: "well-born" is not an empty phrase and has no allusion to the privilege of hereditary aristocracy. "I am well aware that men love to hear of their power, but have an extreme disrelish to be told their duty. . . . Men are qualified for civil liberty in exact proportion to their disposition to put moral chains upon their own appetites. . . . It is ordained in the eternal constitution of things that men of intemperate minds cannot be free. Their passions forge their fetters." Let us add that Burke explicitly (and obviously sincerely) disclaims the view, later maintained by the Duke of Wellington and such men of the world, that religion exists to keep the lower orders in their place. He does not agree with Lord Melbourne that "things have come to a pretty pass if religion is to interfere in the affairs of private life." As little as Thomas Arnold, of Rugby, had he belief in the possibility of division between politics and any vital religion. The eminent "would find it difficult to make others believe in a system to which they manifestly gave no credit themselves."

His belief in the natural rights of each man does not amount to any confidence that he should enjoy an equal share in political direction. "The effect of liberty to individuals is that they may do what they please: we ought to see what it will please them to do, before we risk congratulations which may soon be turned into complaints. . . . To flatter any man, or any part of mankind, in any description, by asserting that in engagements he or they are free whilst any other human creature is bound, is ultimately . . . to subject the *sovereign reason* of the world to the auspices of weak and giddy men." There is, on the contrary, a natural demand for leadership, and in every healthy society that demand is satisfied. That leadership, moreover, must be personal. Burke makes his position patent in phrase after phrase:

"Whatever each man can separately do, without trespassing upon others, he has a right to do for himself; and he has a right to a fair proportion of all which society, with all its combinations of force and skill, can do in its favour. In this partnership all men have equal rights; but not to equal things. . . . The restraints of men, as well as their liberties, are to be counted among their rights. . . . It is said, that twenty-four millions ought to prevail over two hundred thousand. True: if the constitution of a kingdom be a problem in arithmetic. . . . The will of the many, and their interest, must very often differ; and great will be the difference when they make an evil choice. . . . You do not imagine that I wish to confine power, authority and distinction to blood, and names and titles. No, sir. There is no qualification for government but virtue and wisdom, actual or presumptive. . . . A perfect democracy is the most shameless thing in the world. . . . Some decent, regulated pre-eminence, some preference (not exclusive appropriation), given to birth, is neither unnatural, nor unjust, nor impolitic. . . . When you separate the common sort of men from their proper chieftains ["a natural aristocracy, without which there is no nation"] so as to form them into an adverse army, I no longer know that venerable object called the people in such a disbanded race of deserters and vagabonds." ["The people" . . . by which term "it is plain they mean their own faction."]

"To qualify us for that [English] pre-eminence, we had then a high mind and a constancy unconquerable; we were then inspired with no flashy passions, but such as were durable as well as warm, such as corresponded to the great interests we had at stake. This force of character was inspired, as all such spirit must ever be, from above. . . . As well may we fancy that of itself the sea will swell, and that without words the billows will insult the adverse shore, as that the gross mass of men will be moved, and elevated, and continue by a steady and permanent direction to bear upon one point, without the influence of superior authority or superior mind."

As a description of such princes of the people as Harley, Montague and Churchill this last passage is mere deception. As a description of the Puritans it is not inept.

Behind the fine phrases, however, on duty and excellence and leadership, there lies a mood, not so much of reaction, as of non-comprehension. Burke takes refuge in a tragic pietism too congenial to his temperament, instead of sharpening his mind upon that study of economic means which might have mitigated the tragedy. His attitude to property and land ownership shews a tenderness at variance with the severity of his own moral principles. There is indeed a plain confusion in his own thought. He writes, "If we command our wealth, we shall be rich and free; if our wealth commands us we are poor indeed." But this is left as a mere impersonal moralization. "My opinion is against this most momentous of all meddling on the part of authority; the meddling with the subsistence of the people." It was a duty "manfully to resist the very first idea, speculative or practical, that it is within the competence of government, taken as government, or even the rich, as rich, to supply the poor those necessaries which it has pleased the Divine Providence for a while to withhold from them." The province of the magistrate did not even extend to enjoining charity: "his interference is a violation of the property which it is his office to protect."

It lies, it appeared to Burke (himself always in debt), in the nature of things and in accordance with divine law that some men are born poor and some (he tritely adds, "not to be envied") rich. "Poor rich man," he comments, with his "few and idle years." Burke, one feels, had never suffered in his stomach or in the stomachs of his children: his sorrows were genteel and treasured sorrows. God, once again, is brought in to quell inopportune human ambition. There is, apparently, unalterable "social economy by which so many wretches are inevitably doomed." After all, were not these the years of Whitfield and of the preaching of predestination to damnation by an inscrutable destiny, strangely called the justice of God? "If it were not," Burke adds characteristically, "generally pernicious to disturb the natural course of things, and to impede, in any degree, the great wheel of circulation which is turned by the strangely directed labour of these unhappy people, I should be infinitely more inclined forcibly to rescue them from their miserable industry, than violently to disturb the tranquil repose of monastic quietude." Not the monks but the makers of a commercial civilization were, for Burke, the enemies of man—but he proposed to interfere with neither. To inquire, when we are speaking of the just title to property, concerning the use to which it is being put appears to him "a sort of profaneness." No reason is assigned for this reversion to the least morally defensible kind of individualism. It is, indeed, not always clear that "the little platoon" to which Burke urges attachment is not a class, *beata possidens*. The state "suffers oppression" when such men as tallowchandlers, "individually or collectively, are permitted to rule."

The thought of the succeeding century and a half, despite the doctrines of Adam Smith, Cobden and Bright, was not to confirm Burke's judgement here. In America individualism, reinforced by the tradition of the Supreme Court in interpreting the Constitution, was to make the rejection of economic commercialism more hesitant, but it did not succeed in maintaining its connection (as was hoped by a few keen-sighted writers such as Jefferson) with an obstinate ruralism. In Burke's own day men who, for different reasons, cannot themselves be said to be cardinal builders of the Anglo-Saxon tradition, Thomas Paine and William Godwin, began the purge of conservative economic complacency. Burke's work is an essential part of that tradition, but not his judgement upon the condition of the poor. In his writings on the French Revolution, expressing views in no small part resultant from that judgement, Burke exposed a still more ample target to his critics.

The Revolution, a movement so ruthless to his especial gods, outraging his conservative preferences and his reverence for traditions, roused Burke to unmeasured fury of denunciation—denunciation of it and of its apologists, "the dashing Machiavellian politicians." Even Arthur Young was able to write in his earlier years, "The true judgement to be found of the French Revolution must surely be gained from an attentive consideration of the evils of the old Government; when these are well understood—and when the extent and universality of the oppression under which the people groaned, oppression which bore upon them from every quarter—it will scarcely be attempted to be urged that a revolution was not absolutely necessary to the welfare of the kingdom." But no stern reflections on the moral case for improving the lot of the common man, no mere politic considerations of the pace at which popular resentment would advance in the land of Louis XIV, are permitted to deflect or moderate the storm of Burke's obsessive indignation.

In its earlier stages, he maintains, the Revolution was carried forward by lawyers of no great repute, "men not taught habitually to respect themselves," in an assembly of the *Tiers Etat,* "in which was scarcely to be perceived the slightest traces of what we call the natural landed interest of the country." The more temperate spirits were merely "men who would usurp the government of their country with decency and moderation." Impatiently he refused to discuss the details of a scheme by which men ascended from "parochial tyranny to federal anarchy," under the guidance of "litigious attorneys and Jew brokers." The wilder furies who promoted the Revolution did not stop short of cannibalism. In the issue, France had become a society after the likeness of

"a den of outlaws upon a doubtful frontier; of a lewd tavern for the revels and debauches of banditti, assassins, bravoes, smugglers, and their more desperate paramours, mixed with bombastic players, the refuse and rejected offal of strolling theatres, puffing out ill-sorted verses about virtue, mixed with the licentious and blasphemous songs proper to the brutal and hardened course of life belonging to that sort of wretches."

On Robespierre's death he could only comment that he "could rather bear the stench of the gibbeted murderer than the society of the bloody felons who yet annoy the world." The Revolution was "one of the greatest calamities that had ever fallen upon mankind." Its authors were "the revolution harpies of France, sprung from night and hell"; its mood was "a drunken delirium from the hot spirit drawn from the alembic of hell." In an apostrophe which the acid Sir Philip Francis dismissed, to Burke's mortification, as "pure foppery," Burke declared that "the age of chivalry is gone. That of sophisters, economists and calculators has succeeded; and the glory of Europe is extinguished for ever." He concludes in memorable words—words applied not to Marxist or Fascists, but to Jacobins:

"It is with an armed doctrine that we are at war. It has, by its essence, a faction of opinion and of interest, and of enthusiasm, in every country. To us it is Colossus which bestrides our Channel . . . for they never have abandoned, and never will they abandon, in peace, in war, in treaty, in any situation, or for one instant, their old, steady maxim of separating the people from their government."

Definitely Burke declines to draw up any balance of accounts between the good and the ill of the French Revolution—and this intransigent moralism demands consideration when we are confronted with the yet vaster Russian Revolution of our own day, which arouses equally passionate partizanship and hates. Burke is an interventionist in what is today called "the warfares of ideologies"; and declines to believe that there can be any third course instead of intransigent opposition to what he saw red in detecting as evil beyond mitigation or excuse. "The first intuitive glance, without any elaborate process of reasoning, will show that this method of political computation would justify every extent of crime." The means, in brief, urges Burke (by no means superficially) condition the ends. The historical consensus of mankind has decided that the French Revolution conferred such benefits on the common man that it is to be reckoned (despite excesses, at the least uncalled for in happier lands) on the credit side of history. Edmund Burke risks his reputation for political judgement by repudiating any such computations, whether in the interests of "monarchical or democratic tyranny." In these writings on France Burke is yet prepared (and here lies the contradiction) to advocate taking the initiative in war, with all its atrocities and cumulative crimes against the civilized temper—to intervene—rather than to risk the success of revolution. "Those whose known policy is to assassinate every citizen whom they suspect to be discontented by their tyranny, and to corrupt the soldiery of every open enemy, must look to no modified hostility."

It is perhaps precisely here that Burke is wrong; and it may be that neither revolution nor war is ever worth while. That has, however, not been hitherto the common opinion of mankind. It is clear that the atrocity of revolution is always evil in itself. The *consensus universalis,* however, has not been found to favour that absolute view of morality according to which it were better, as Cardinal Newman maintained, for the world to perish than for one sin to be committed— a view here, in effect, advocated by Burke to colour an argument in his own favour. It has preferred the road of the lesser evil, whether revolution or war, under the directive guidance of the maxim of the happiness of the greater number. That the "sophistic tyrants" of Paris whom Burke so bitterly condemns—men who "occupied all the avenues to opinion," exercising a revolutionary censorship—had once masters and rulers who confined this spirit of revolt within "dungeons and cages," Burke himself has to admit. The violence of revolution was but an index of how steeply, contrariwise, the pendulum of conduct had been held back. For the rest, the French Revolution, as Burke confesses with dismay, had shewn for the first time in history, by example, that "the natural equality of man and the sovereignty of the people" were, like modern totalitarianism, "a thing feasible in practice"—however much ending in The Terror, Thermidor and Bonaparte.

Burke has firmer ground in his complaint, like Conservatives today in relation to the Third International, in that "England is not left out of the comprehensive scheme of their malignant charity." Burke feared the agitators, whether in sympathy with Lord George Gordon or with Danton and Robespierre. "They are the rival follies which mutually wage so unrelenting a war; and which make so cruel a use of their advantages, as they can happen to engage the immoderate vulgar on the one side or the other in their quarrels." "Shall we . . . choose for our teachers men incapable of being taught, whose only claim to know is that they have *never doubted?*"

Speaking of the partizans of the tricolour cockade, he writes:

"Those whose principle it is to despise *the ancient, permanent sense of mankind,* and to set up a scheme of society on new principles, must naturally expect that such of us who think *better of the judgement of the human race than of theirs,* should consider both them and their devices as men and schemes upon their trial. They must take it for granted that we attend much to their reason but not at all to their authority. . . . Their confederations, their spectacles, their civic feasts, and their enthusiasm, I take no notice of; they are nothing but tricks. . . . Mahomet [and here also a modern parallel suggests itself] hid, as for a time he was, in the bottom of the sands of Arabia, had his spirit and character been discovered, would have been an object of precaution to provident minds."

The French Revolution, sustained by like prophets, is one "of doctrine and theoretic dogma." "I cannot love the Republic":

"In the modern world, before this time, there has been no instance of this spirit of general political faction, separated from religion, pervading several countries, and forming a principle of union between the partisans of each. But the thing is not less in human nature. The ancient world has furnished [in Athens and Sparta, heading the democratic and aristocratic interests] a strong and striking instance of such a ground for faction. . . . *There are several who are persuaded that the same thing cannot happen in England. . . . Let us only suffer any person to tell us his story, morning and evening, but for one twelve month, and he will become our master."*

At times Burke comes very near to the grotesque whimsy of Montesquieu who declared (doubtless with memories of Tacitus) that the English had found their constitutional liberties "in the woods." It was an age that idealized "the iron barons" of King John. Human liberty is seen, not as something growing, but as something pre-existent, if not in a solitary state of nature or in Eden, then in the pristine, if social, splendour of a past age of the forefathers. Burke's respect for tradition here perverts his nascent historic sense. Occasionally his view of history becomes merely a still-life view. Incidentally, in typically Anglo-Saxon fashion, "liberty," for Burke, is always thought of as plural—"liberties." With singular insight he puts his fingers on the limitations of this liberty—according to a later phrase, "this bourgeois liberty," without yet in any way recognizing these limitations to be such. To the French common people these boasted liberties of a Pym and Hampden do not, he admits, appeal. The people of that vain nation are rather proud of the plenitude of their king's power. "They had felt nothing from *lettres de cachet*. The Bastile could inspire no horrors in them. This was a treat for their betters." Whether Burke be right or wrong in his description of Parisian popular feeling, undoubtedly he here indicates why, in a later century, the privileges of British liberalism were to wane in their appeal. To

Burke this insensibility was merely proof of the political immaturity or ineptitude of the French populace.

A deeper fount of Burke's conservatism was his belief in original sin, that is, a belief that one corrupt, half-brutish humanity, which might save itself through rational attention to duty, obedience and discipline, was not for the most part destined, in the universal scheme, for happiness here and merely fell into licentious and anarchic depravity if individuals presumptuously pursued it. To flatter the poor and tell them that they can greatly change their state is "nothing less than fraud and wicked folly." "Patience, labour, sobriety, frugality, and religion, should be recommended to them; all the rest is downright fraud." Burke does not, however, deny value to the "animal happinesss" of good food, health and the like. The truth is that his moral pietism, and great words about duty and the primeval contract between all members of our race, are strangely confounded with the crassest economic individualism just coming into vogue but having (alas! for Burke) no other forefather than Thomas Hobbes. Burke is a transitional writer and the confusion is natural. His pious apathy, however, about the cry of the children in the "dark Satanic mills" of Britain or about the lot of the French *metayer* and serf is an anaesthesia induced by an economic metaphysic of his own. There is, for him, an Economic Destiny confounded, as by Archbishop Whately a generation later, with God's Law:

"It is plainly," writes Burke, "more the farmer's interest that his men should thrive than that his horses should be well-fed. [Burke had neither visited the negro plantations of the Carolinas nor, apparently, read Cato on the theory of slave labour.] On the other hand, if the farmer cease to profit of the labourer, and his capital is not continually manured and fructified, it is impossible that he should continue that *abundant* nutriment, and clothing, and lodging, proper for the *instruments* he employs.

"It is therefore the first and fundamental interest of the labourer that the farmer should have a full incoming profit on the product of his labour. The proposition is self-evident, and nothing but the malignity, perverseness, and ill-governed passions of mankind, and particularly the envy they bear to each other's property, could prevent their seeing and acknowledging it, *with thankfulness to the benign and wise Disposer of all things, who obliges men whether they will or not, in pursuing their own selfish interests, to connect the general good with their own individual success."*

In brief, the maxim of enlightened self-interest is the clue to economic conduct. It springs from a moral philosophy that acquiesces in too facile a synthesis between individual happiness and social duty. What is false in the uncritically optimistic theory of Burke explains what is at fault in his prematurely pessimistic political theory. The lot of man can be improved if we are not too indolent to change the principle, or too interested to change the practice, of his economic circumstance. It is the romantic in Burke which leads him to ride away on a horse, as the knight of the bleeding heart, on some chivalrous errantry, when he should be soberly advancing on foot to the capture of the sooty bastions of vulgar oppression.

Burke's emotional judgement, at fault, must be corrected by that of others of his countrymen, not in most matters so representative. That of Wordsworth changed; and that of the young Shelley rather illuminated than illustrated the common opinion. When Napoleon came, British opinion consolidated into obstinate hate. Until then, as Burke knew to his chagrin, it by no means echoed with unanimity his verdict. Blake shares with Burke his uncertainties about the spheres of reason and emotion—uncertainties which Pope never knew, with his devotion to instinct, the best of philosophers, and to a Nature prim and trim. "If Men were Wise," enigmatically writes Blake, "the most Arbitrary Princes could not hurt them. If they are not Wise, the Freest Government is compelled to be a Tyranny." But, over the issue of the Revolution, the imagery of the orator is met by the opposed splendour of the poet. Cataract battles against cataract to channel the stream of our tradition.

There are denunciations, in Blake's *French Revolution,* by "the ancientist Peer, Duke of Burgundy . . . red as wines from his mountains," and by the Archbishop of Paris, against that day when

"The priest rot in his surplice by the lawless lover, the holy beside the accused,
The king, glowing in purple, beside the grey plowman, and their worms embrace together."

Nevertheless, victory was not with them.

"The noise of trampling, the wind of trumpets, smote the palace walls with a blast,
Pale and cold sat the king in the midst of his peers, and his noble heart sunk, and his pulses
Suspended their motion; . . .
     . . . shaken the forests of France, sick the kings of the nations,
And the bottoms of the world were open'd, and the graves of archangels unseal'd;
And the enormous dead lift up their pale fires and look over the rocky cliffs."

It may be suspected, however, that the cause for Blake's approval of the French Revolution had little to do with the luminous dawn of emancipating reason. For Blake, "the road of excess leads to the palace of wisdom":

"The giants who formed this world into its sensual existence, and now seem to live in it in chains are in truth the causes of its life and the sources of all activity; but the chains are the cunning of weak and tame minds which have power to resist energy."

"Is this the Female Will, O ye lovely Daughters of Albion,
To Converse concerning Weight and Distance in the Wilds of
Newton and Locke?"

"But the Spectre, like a hoar frost and a Mildew, rose over Albion,
Saying, 'I am God, O Sons of Men! I am your Rational Power!
Am I not Bacon and Newton and Locke who teach Humility to
Man,
Who teach Doubt and Experiment? and my two wings, Vol-
taire, Rousseau?

Where is that Friend of Sinners? that Rebel against my Laws
Who teaches Belief to the Nations and an unknown Eternal
Life?
Come hither into the Desert and turn these stones to bread.
Vain foolish Man! Wilt thou believe without Experiment?'
So spoke the hard cold constrictive Spectre."

"Like dr. Priestl[e]y and Bacon and Newton—
Poor Spiritual Knowledge is not worth a button."

§ v

Let us attempt to summarize what is perhaps incapable of
summary. What are the common characteristics of Anglo-
Saxon morality, if there be anything that is characteristic?
The common qualities in the outlook of Hooker and Locke
and Butler, Franklin, Hutcheson, Bentham and Mill are indeed clear and demonstrable enough:—the stress upon human
nature as a constant; upon the prerogative rôle of reason; the
always slightly hedonistic stress on the notion of happiness;
the distrust of fine arguing about some recondite 'real happiness' decided upon by a few spiritual know-alls; and this happiness for the greater number, all counting equally; utility;
distrust of enthusiasm and approbation of common-sense; belief that there is such a common 'sense'; optimistic belief in
the universality of benevolence; reference to humanity.

The common quality between Bunyan and the Puritans

and John Wesley is again clear—and, even, in the stress on conscience, between Butler on the one side, and Wesley on the other. Much more difficult is it to see a similarity between the sober benignance of Butler and the passion of Burke, the new Tory, enemy of the Revolution. Not only the medium is different but—although both of them believed themselves to be good Lockians—the content. Burke anticipates the Oxford Idealists and Bradley's doctrine of 'My Station and its Duties.' Blake, again, has qualities in common with a proto-Fascist such as the sado-masochistic D. H. Lawrence; and his Twentieth-Century revival coincides with Lawrence's post-war vogue. It is easier to see connection between Blake and Burke (who only occasionally, in his economics, lapses into moral individualism) than betwen Burke and Butler—and Blake is in explicit reaction from the mood of Locke and Butler.

We come nearer an answer if we note Burke's reaction to Rousseau; his enthusiastic repudiation of enthusiasm; his *empiric stress* and distrust of the *a-priori;* his approximation to the position of Dr. Johnson with his sense of sin; his stress upon tradition, slow change and caution inspired by a sober and even sombre estimate of humanity. There is nothing, in all that, which Hooker would have rejected.

Indeed, Burke gives an answer to the question that the Benthamites were, for a generation, with varying success to propound. What is the greatest number? Those who enter into the contract between the generations—between the living, the dead and the unborn—those, for Burke as for the Oxford moralists, are the greatest number. And is the contract between the generations of humanity or of my nation? That neither clearly answered; but talked vaguely of 'Society'—certainly *not* of the State.

We can come yet nearer to an answer if we consider that

the common characteristic of Anglo-Saxon moralism is precisely its morality. By that I mean that it is moral, *not* religious, so far as the two may be contrasted. Even its mysticism never strays far from practical conduct, and remains
typical. Its concern is with this personal conduct rather than
with mass emotion, even of love. On the other hand—and
here Butler is significant and representative—there is a deep
belief that the distinction is a clear one, to the uncorrupted
mind, between right and wrong. Morality is eternal and final,
even if the comprehension of it is necessarily incomplete.

Benevolence, further, is the key-word rather than the ardour
of charity. Charity tends to be something to be organized. The
approved religion, even when not 'established,' more makes a
man stand on his feet to *do* things than brings him to his
knees to *feel* them. And yet these 'works' are not prescribed
for the whole society by authority but are the fruits of an individual sense of duty after examination of conscience in all
sobriety. Exhibitionism, 'enthusiasm,' are the great vices. Not
'good citizenship' so much as 'public spirit' is approved; and
not even public spirit so much as personal morality, as a
standard of personal behaviour for men, whether alone or
together.

We here reach the core of the whole matter. If anywhere
the Anglo-Saxon Tradition can be attacked, it is just here—
in its moralism; in its too ready theory of conscience; and
in a repudiation of speculation which is often repudiation of
vision. Quite simply, the suppositions of the Anglo-Saxon Tradition are individualistic—even if the qualified individualism
of a Hooker—and the springs of individualism are moralistic.
Concern is for the adventure of the individual soul, 'doing
his duty.' The springs of totalitarianism are enthusiastic, almost 'Buchmanite.' Socialism can be interpreted either way—
whether as the economic completion of the emancipation of

the common man or as the first stage in the realization of the totalitarian community as 'Social Organism.' In view of the clamour in these days for a new religion, a political religion, heated by mass enthusiasm, a brief comment may not be irrelevant on this issue.

For the purposes of the criticism of this Anglo-Saxon Tradition let me take a striking modern example from the opposite school—Professor Macmurray's *Clue to History* (1938). Those of us who are Communists—but of the order of the Palestinian colonists in Esdraelon today or of Noyes and Owen and their co-operators or of the Benedictine Rule—are under a debt to Professor Macmurray for having raised the issue of religious Communism in so fresh a fashion.

His book is a work of high imaginative quality, illuminating the contours of thought and deeper patterns as such work alone does. Disturbing, it is not easy. Like Mr. Heard, in his *Social Substance of Religion,* Professor Macmurray is preoccupied with the need for being 'in tune' with the community. His argument is that Christianity must be understood in terms of Jesus, and that Jesus was through and through Jewish. But, says Professor Macmurray, the Jew has *not* the merely practical consciousness of the Roman and *not* the speculative consciousness of the Hellene, *but* the religious consciousness. "Christianity is essentially Jewish." Judaism is "the only religious culture that history has produced." The scholar may object that Professor Macmurray is a 'judaizer' who not only brusques the authority of the Church. I do not imagine that this is likely to deter him, or the censure of the Churches. The Churches are "practical negations of the Christian intention." Macmurray totally ignores such inconvenient manifestations in early Christianity as Ebionitism and the Marcionites who damned the Old Testament. The fight, in the history of Christianity, between 'judaizer' and 'hellenizer' is nothing novel. Harnack's great seven-volume *History of Dogma* goes in the scales against Macmurray's theory. The stylist may object to being told that "the characteristic expression . . . of the religious consciousness is Religion." These are small flies in the spikenard.

Professor Macmurray freely indulges in such statements as that belief in God is no test of religion; that Jesus and the Old Testament were uninterested in individual immortality; and that Marxist materialism and atheism may conceal a deeper Christianity. I am prepared to swallow all this. Jesus is, for him, the Jew and the Marxist preaching love, which means equality, of which Marx has explained the content. The oppressed Jewish people is Messias that shall come, equalizing the world, perhaps through revolution. The prophecies of Isaiah were of a 'people.' Jesus' intention was that His commands should be obeyed and His kingdom realized in this world. Messias could come here and now, if men willed it. The other-worldly idealists radically misinterpret Christ.

Professor Macmurray then shews the red flag—or, if this is ambiguous, let us say the cloven hoof. Let us grant his argument about Christ, the Marxist, fulfilling, through the Chosen Jew, His purpose. As I said in *Preface to Action* (1934), I quite decline to regard this thesis as a pack of nonsense. Gleefully Macmurray salutes his 'inspired' fellow-visionary, Adolf Hitler, saying the same thing the reverse way round. What then? We are invited to share the religious consciousness: "All primitive societies are religious." So far Macmurray goes with Gerald Heard. They want to set the clock back—millennia. They have the Nicodemus-complex for return to the womb of history. Further, Macmurray says, Christ discovered the secret of personality, *but* this secret involves rediscovering ourselves, not individualistically, but in community. There is *"this totalitarian character of the re-*

ligious consciousness." Apparently Professor Macmurray is Hegelian enough to find freedom in the mere conformance of our intention with our destiny. I see no clear indication that we are to *choose* our community (as Heard, the pacifist, allowed). That is the crux. We are to be Marxist revolutionaries, which seems, in history, to preclude such bourgeois choosings. The truth is one, and known. It is well to recall that he who would found a Kingdom of Heaven on Earth by *force* will also found a Kingdom of Hell. There are yet hopeful words, implying tolerance, about "the bases of a free, human commmunity. . . ."

Further, we are told that the Jewish religious consciousness does not divorce thought and action; is moved by emotion; recognizes that the speculative reason moves nothing. Some time ago Professor Lancelot Hogben wrote an excellent little book called *The Retreat from Reason* (1936). This shews the need for it. Here, in Professor Macmurray's book, is a recipe for primitive emotional intoxication. I regret to say that I find this to be a program of reaction, the more fatal for being profound. I recall Locke's quotation, in his chapter on "Enthusiasm," from *Hudibras:*

> "An ignis fatuus that bewitches,
> And leads them into pools and ditches."

Certain notes will be remarked here—apart from Professor Macmurray's identification of Jesus with a special definition of the spirit of Judaism:—the stress on the primitive consciousness; the stress on the totalitarian nature of this consciousness, including such conforming abandonment as seems to exclude need for choice [observe that the Greek word 'heretic' means a 'chooser,' whereas of *choice* Locke says, "in this consists freedom," and the faculty to pursue that good which is our happiness]; the assumption that other fallible men are competent, like parents, to select our 'good' for us; and the stress on emotion which will issue in action, justified or damned by its intention, not by its immediate fruits. Freedom is capacity to do the destined Will of God, already known to those chosen few who have grasped the certain clue in history—just as Fichte grasped it; and as Hegel, in his Dialectic of History, also stole the Golden Fleece of final knowledge; and as Marx took the clue over from Hegel.

The tendency in the Anglo-Saxon world has been to admire a morality to the extent to which, abandoning a cloistered virtue, it became adult, mature, able to face facts and *removed* from the primitive. Here the exhortation is to *return* to the primitive. For the individual child there are no empiric facts, since he lives in a world of his own dreams where the demand is that all should obey his will—what can be expected to obey this will, and what cannot be expected to obey, is not differentiated. Truth very really is 'my truth'; the real world has not yet distinguished itself from the dream-world of *wish*. It is so also with the somnambulist—even, like Herr Hitler, the self-announced somnambulist politician. In the history of the race, in the childhood of humanity, it is so with a primitive, infantile people, each one of whose members is protected from external reality by the shell made of the corporate opinion of his clan or tribe. For the tribe itself, at a later stage, magic controls reality. Not until maturity in individual or race is reached, as Lippmann has pointed out in his *Preface to Morals* (1929), does man come to admit the facts in order scientifically to study them, and then to control or face them.

"Unless ye become as little children ye shall in no wise enter into the Kingdom of Heaven." We may interpret that as an admonition against what good Bishop Butler called self-deceit and arrogant pride. Or we may take it as confirming this exhortation, stressed by Macmurray and Heard, to return to the primitive consciousness. I prefer the first interpretation. Certainly the Anglo-Saxon Tradition has been one of praise for the virtue of impersonal disinterestedness and of the moral sternness that is ready to face facts without illusion. For that matter, mass enthusiasm has not been the characteristic of the *élites* either of Communism or of southern Fascism, any more than of the Jesuits, although it precisely was the characteristic of Rousseauism and Jacobinism. If we choose the second of the alternatives, then I suggest that Heard's interpretation of a religion of love focused in small *voluntary* groups is much to be preferred to Macmurray's, which can be interpreted as advocacy of a crusade in which zeal for liberty and equality replaces the characteristic spirit, the mood, of charity.

I do not wish to minimize the truth of Professor Macmurray's contention that what matters is, not dreams about ideals, but the intention to act. Recognition, however, of the *real conditions* of action does not characterize either the primitive or the totalitarian mentality. That requires the empiric mentality. We must equip ourselves as men, not as children seeking our mother in the form of this or that society.

I do not, however, wish to obscure an admission: the difficulty raised by Heard and Macmurray is quite fundamental. They are recalling a religion of love, but, above all, a *religion*. A mass religion can, of course, release tremendous, if temporary, streams of psychic energy, almost hypnotic force. There is release from the gnawing of that sense of expulsion from the Eden of tribal sympathy that is, anthropologically speaking, the real Original Sin of self-consciousness. The typical expressions, nevertheless, of the Anglo-Saxon mind through the centuries, even in Wesley (for all his respect for the Moravians) in his attitude to Behmen [or Boehme], is *moralistic, methodistic,* a kind of common-sense asceticism. That Heard regards as merely a manifestation of individualism, a sublimation of the impulse of power-seeking—even as immortality-seeking is power-seeking—and a foment of ego-istic, militaristic aggressiveness bound to bring civilization down in flames. (Alternative systems seem to me equally likely to have this effect and, especially, those systems which advocate mergence in the consciousness of the society *so long as that society remains based upon, or designed to use, force.*)

However, on the one hand, one notes that even the Puritans, stern moral individualists, found their especial historic expres-sion in an army—an army of the saints—intent on one pur-pose. Again, the Wesleyans found characteristic expression in the *group-life,* the 'class-meeting.' Wesley notes the advice of the man who told him: "Sir, you wish to serve God and go to heaven. Remember that you cannot serve Him alone. You must therefore find companions or make them. The Bible knows nothing of solitary religion." On the other hand, our advocates of the like-minded group look with especial favour on that almost exclusively Anglo-Saxon phenomenon, the Quakers. The characteristic Quaker doctrine of "the Inner Light" is certainly *not* totalitarian. The spirit moving on the Society calls for the entirely *free witness* of the individual. The Society of Friends seems to indicate more clearly than may be seen elsewhere how the Anglo-Saxon mind can effect for itself a reconciliation between moralism and religion.

In the modern world Parties have taken the place of sects and Churches. They are the new *Churches,* Communist and Fascist, just as the old *Parties* were Jesuit and Calvinist. These like-minded bodies give to the 'little man' the purpose and vicarious importance for which, in a cold world, his soul, if stirred beyond material pleasures, cries out. "Why am I so un-important? Need I be? I will march with the Führer or with Comrade Stalin." Undoubtedly such bodies, as also close re-ligious or national groups, Jesuits, Jews, even Scotsmen . . .

have been history's favourite vehicles of power. We do well to reflect on the sociological significance of this, if our object is to achieve something. There can be what Walt Whitman calls "an institution of the dear love of comrades." Unhappily, these Parties are almost all, at the lower level, concerned with the acquisition of power and, at the higher, with the forceable regulation for good of their neighbours. We need a renewed Society of Friends. I agree with Gerald Heard that religion can evolve a higher, because a wider, vital consciousness or intense sense of brotherhood—and that it need not necessarily merely become dead or react to the primitive. "The future of religion," he writes, in his *Social Substance of Religion,* "is the future of an illusion only if religion cannot evolve"—and become the spirit that moves to actual fraternity in cumulative effort among men, for Man, in the context of God.

"This religion [of other-worldliness, as excuse for conventional acceptance] has actually become a dope. This the charitic religion [of fraternity] cannot be, for its whole basis is self-forgetfulness, love, and the acceptance of a salvation in this life. It therefore is not opium. Rather it is the only real food of the soul and its communion. For this communion starts at the base, in psychology, and with a right psychology produces naturally the fruit of that spirit, a sane and perfect economics. The economic communism has already revealed its psychic unsoundness. It is driven not by love, but by hate, and to attain even an appearance of its ends it has to use ever more force. If the ordinary man does not feel that love for his fellows, then he will never be a Communist. If he does feel that love, then there is no need for a proletarian dictatorship to transform him. There is only one problem before the world, but it is one which, if unsolved, humanity has failed (and fortunately shews at last power and intention to destroy its ghastly self): that is to create and sustain charitism."

I submit, indeed, that there is another concrete, objective problem, which I shall not hesitate to include within the same field; and that is, quite literally and materially, "to scale the stars." Beside "the heart within" I shall place "the stars above." I shall judge a civilization by whether it is likely to generate the scientific curiosity, patience, energy and courage requisite to attempt this. This present ant-heap of earth is growing far too small; and unless man is to recognize himself as only an ant and to perish of lack of will to go on, he must make the greater spatial adventure, as one among his spiritual Columbus-farings of adventure.

To revert: the weakness of Heard is that his small monastic groups are nowhere very clearly related to the great catholic world of action, whereas the weakness of Macmurray is that his program of intention is not too obviously related to choice and charitism—the preservation of charity.

These, however, are high flights; and only Lionel Curtis, in his *Civitas Dei,* has winged his way up to them from specifically English soil. I am, however, convinced that neither can Anglo-Saxon civilization be understood nor its future be rightly shaped unless these reflections are present in the quieter and inner places of our minds: Needed, a recall to religion, not in any superficial, conventional sense. Needed, a new and sterner Commonwealth mood. Needed, a communism of communalism. Are those right who declare that this devotion can now *only* be found in the Communist—or the Fascist—Parties, as 'new-style' parties, church, religions? That all the rest is 'dead'? Or not? . . . Needed, a new Society of Friends, to give depth of spirit and resolution again to the frame of English moralism. These issues, however, raise speculations irrelevant to this present book.

CHAPTER VII

Public Spirit

§ i

"God is our guide! from field, from wave,
From plough, from anvil, and from loom;
We come our country's rights to save,
And speak a tyrant faction's doom:
We raise the watch-word, liberty;
We will, we will, we will be free!

"God is our guide! no swords we draw,
We kindle not war's battle fires;
By reason, union, justice, law,
We claim the birth-right of our sires:
We raise the watch-word, liberty,
We will, we will, we will be free!"

The verse is nothing remarkable. It was written in pencil
on a scrap of paper and handed to the crowd at Dorchester,
on March 17, 1834. George Loveless, the writer, a labouring
man of the parish of Tolpuddle, in Dorset, England, and his
companions, all agricultural workers, were then sent back to
the prison, handcuffed, under sentence of transportation to
Australia for seven years for the offence of unlawful conspiracy by entering into a sworn trade union to maintain
wages. After the Anti-Combination Acts of 1799 and 1800,
not until 1871 did trade unions in Britain cease to be unlawful
conspiracy. Indeed, serfdom, called bluntly by the lawyers
'slavery,' had not ceased in the Scottish mines until the Act
of 1775—and was then abolished as 'discouraging the supply
of labour.'

In the summer of 1777 or thereabout a boy of fourteen, in blue smock and red garters to keep his stockings up, was to be seen sweeping the lawn of Kew Gardens, London, around the famous Pagoda there. He was the son of the innkeeper of 'The Jolly Farmer,' Farnham, where the landlord and his customers were accustomed to toast the health of George Washington and success to the Americans. He had come to Kew to see the world, and later he was to see Canada, France and America. His name was William Cobbett (1763–1835), later to be well known, as the editor and chief author of *The Political Register,* the best-read 'weekly' of its day. At his death *The Times* wrote:

"Take this self-taught peasant [there were still peasants in England in those days] for all in all, he was perhaps, in some respects, a more extraordinary Englishman than any other of his time. . . . By masculine force of genius, and the lever of a proud, confident, and determined will, he pushed aside a mass of obstacles, of which the least and slightest would have repelled the boldest or most ambitious of ordinary men. He ended by bursting that most formidable barrier which separates the class of English gentlemen from all beneath them. . . . The first general characteristic of his style is perspicuity, unequalled and inimitable. A second is homely masculine vigour. A third is purity, always simple, and raciness often elegant. His argument is an example of acute, yet apparently natural, nay, involuntary logic, smoothed in its progress and cemented in its parts, by a mingled storm of torturing sarcasm, contemptuous jocularity, and slaughtering invective. . . . He was a man whom England alone could have produced and nurtured up to such maturity of unpatronizing and self-generating power."

The Times wrote with a not uncustomary complacency, and yet with an admission almost too frank for discretion, about the reality of class barriers in Britain. About these Cobbett, once (like Edgar Wallace) a 'ranker' in the Army, expressed himself in a vein, unmistakable and in no wise complimentary:

"How often has my blood boiled with indignation at seeing this fine, this gallant, this honest, truehearted and intelligent young man [his comrade in arms, Sergeant Smaller], standing with his hand to his hat before some worthless and stupid sot of an officer, whom nature seemed to have designed to black his shoes. And does not the English Army contain many a Smaller *now?*"

Cobbett, however, had wider causes of trouble to explore than the case of the honest, gallant Sergeant Smaller. The battle for Political Democracy was in process, in his own days, of being won; but the battle for Economic Democracy—of Democracy as a way of life, in which men lived equally save so far as the common social advantage or difference of talent, not accident or acquisitiveness, dictated otherwise—this battle was only just beginning. The iron of the Industrial Revolution had entered into men's souls. Before that Revolution there is little evidence of any widespread sentiment of resentment between little masters and their journeymen. Now the consciousness of economic status difference—class difference, the seed-plot of class war—begins.

"The sole food of the greater part of them," writes Cobbett in 1830, in his *Political Register,* "has been for many years, bread, or potatoes, and not half enough of these. They have eaten sheep or cattle that have died from illness; they have eaten garbage, such as a lord or a loan jobber would not give to his dogs; children have been seen stealing the food out of hog-troughs; thousands of them have died for want of food; three men were found dead last May, lying under a hedge, and, when opened by the surgeons, nothing but sour sorrel *(oseille sauvage)* was found in their stomachs, and this was within a few miles of a palace, which had cost millions of pounds sterling of the public money! The spot on which these poor creatures expired was surrounded with villas of rich Jews and stock-jobbers, living in luxury, and in the midst of pleasure-gardens, all the means of which living they derived from the burdens laid on the working people." Cobbett began a protest, economic rather than political, which is not yet irrelevant in days when the United States counts its unemployed by the million and in Britain they padlock themselves to monuments to make more conspicuous their complaint. Here is the running sore of our own days. What does our moralism propose to *do?*

Cobbett's protest was economic; but his remedy in terms of social justice was political. Nor, even in these blackest years of reaction of the Nineteenth Century, had he doubt that normal forms for registering that protest were available against the works of the too ready disciples of the Classical Economists and what was understood by practical business men to be their philosophy of lucre.

"In proceeding now [1816] to examine the *remedies* for your distresses, I shall first notice some of those, which foolish, or cruel and insolent men have proposed. Seeing that the *cause* of your misery is the *weight of taxation,* one would expect to hear of nothing but a *reduction of taxation* [*tariff*] in the way of remedy; but, from the friends of corruption, never do we hear of any such remedy. To hear them, one would think, that *you* [the labourers] had been the guilty cause of the misery you suffer; and that you, and you alone, ought to be answerable for what has taken place. The emissaries of corruption are now continually crying out against the *weight* of the *Poor-rates,* and they seem to regard all that is taken in that way as *a dead loss to the Government!* Their project is to deny relief to all who are *able to work.* But what is the use of your being able to work, if no one will, or can, give you work? To tell you that you must work for your bread, and, at the same time, not to find any work for you, is full as bad as it would be to order you to make bricks without straw. Indeed it is rather more cruel and insolent; for Pharaoh's task-masters did point out to the Israelites that they might go into the fields and get *stubble. . . .*

"I know of no enemy of reform and of the happiness of the country so great as that man who would persuade you that we possess *nothing good* and that *all* must be torn to pieces. There is no principle, no precedent, no regulations (except as to mere matters of detail), favourable to freedom, which is not to be found in the Laws of England or in the example of our ancestors. . . .

"[On the other hand] the object of [some] writers is clearly enough seen. Keep all *quiet!* Do not *rouse!* Keep *still!* Keep *down!* Let those who perish, perish in *silence!* It will, however, be out of the power of these quacks, for all their laudanum, to allay the blood which is now boiling in the veins of the people of this kingdom; who, if they are doomed to perish, are, at any rate, resolved not to perish *in silence.* . . ." [1]

No man was less of a radical firebrand than Dr. Thomas Arnold, headmaster of Rugby School—no man more representative alike of the moral sense of the Victorian middle classes and of its limitations. Cobbett, however, had written "it is *men,* and not *machines,* that constitute a nation." Cobbett had managed to touch the moral sense of the representative man and to kindle a public sense that did not abate with the passing of the years and that gave flame to the somewhat cold theme of 'benevolence' of Butler and Bentham. Among "the various causes of our present distress" Dr. Arnold lists

"the natural tendency of wealth to become richer and of poverty to become poorer."

One may with profit note the change—the representative change—in stress of the great doctor's views, which he expressed in June 1831, in the *Englishmen's Register.*

[1] In these references to Cobbett I am indebted not only to Mr. G. D. H. Cole's admirable *Life of William Cobbett* (1927), but also to the excellent anthology by Mary Palmer, entitled *Writing and Action* (1938). I also wish to call attention to an anthology by an author beyond rival suited for the task: *England's Voice of Freedom* (1929), by Henry W. Nevinson.

"The hearts of men are in [God's] hand no less than the stars of Heaven; and He will no more permit the one to destroy the social system by their vices, than He will let the other derange the order of the universe by their irregular wanderings. Therefore, if the right of property be founded on justice, and is according to God's will, and necessary to the well-being of mankind, as I have shown that it is, it never will be overthrown; and although its abuses will and ought to be removed, yet it will in itself stand fast till the world itself shall perish."

One recalls the pious style of Burke. Towards the end, however, of that critical year, 1831, Arnold writes:

"The high Aristocrat is but echoing the language of the worst Jacobin; except that the Jacobin is the more consistent of the two. Both would pull down the higher of two unequal classes, instead of raising the lower; but whilst the Jacobin would reduce all ranks to the lowest level, the high Aristocrat would reduce all but his own. To both is the doctrine of the good and the wise utterly opposed. Our business is to raise all, and to lower none. Equality is the dream of a madman or the passion of a fiend. Extreme inequality, or high comfort and civilization in some, co-existing with deep misery and degradation in others, is no less also a folly and a sin. But an inequality where some have all the enjoyments of civilized life, and none are without its comforts,—where some have all the treasures of knowledge, and none are sunk in ignorance, that is a social system in harmony with the order of God's creation in the natural world."

By 1840, in his essay on the "State of the Working Classes," the transition of emphasis to one of urgency is complete with this sincere conservative of good-will, as fully endowed with moral sense as any man of his day and having in him more than most men of those sentiments which all typical men had:

"Something must be done to restrain the enormous accumulation of property in single hands, *to facilitate its acquisition and secure its possession to the mass of the community*. Men must clearly distinguish between small tenancies and small properties;

the former, as in Ireland, are but a source of servility, wretched-
ness, and crime; the latter, as in Norway, and in every other
country where they have ever existed, have been a source no less
sure of independence, comfort, and virtue."

§ ii

The protests of Cobbett against the social injustice begotten
of the callous pursuit of wealth by certain captains of industry
were not founded on isolated instances. Marx was to collect
many more, not indeed so much from personal experience in
Britain as from the reports of the factory inspectors of a bourgeois government. These, by their honest public spirit, while
supplying Marx in his researches in the British Museum with
the material of his indictment, contradicted by their performance his psychological theory of society as based in its structure dominantly on class interest. When we stand on the verge
of the Revolution that will succeed the next war, it will be
well to bear this in mind, if passion will permit it. Marx saw
the abuses but not the social conscience, other than his own,
that exposed them. At this same time Thomas Carlyle (1795–
1881), who influenced Engels, and Carlyle's friend and admirer, John Ruskin (1819–1900), were also busy with the work
of exposure and of stirring public spirit to a recognition of the
claims of social justice. "This one voice of Carlyle's," says Ruskin, "has been the only faithful and useful utterance in all
England." Carlyle it was who ventilated "The Condition of
England Question."

"This largest of questions, this question of Work and Wages,
which ought, had we heeded Heaven's voice, to have begun two
generations ago or more, cannot be delayed longer without hear-
ing Earth's voice. 'Labour' will verily need to be somewhat 'organized,' as they say,—God knows with what difficulty. Man will
actually need to have his debts and earnings a little better paid
by man; which, let Parliaments speak of them or be silent of

them, are eternally his due from men, and cannot, without pen-
alty and at length not without death-penalty, be withheld."

Carlyle's own methods of settling the issues of social justice
were not so much those of public spirit springing from moral
recognition of the evil as of ukase by a Führer voluntarily
chosen. The virtues of Benevolent Despots were always very
patent in the eyes of the 'stern child of Ecclefechan,' himself
something of a licensed public scold. He quotes, in *Past and
Present,* with approval the comment, "There is but one reform
for the Foreign Office—to set a live coal under it." For the rest,

"How true is this of Crabbe: Men sit in Parliament eighty-
three hours per week, debating about many things, Greek questions, Portuguese, Spanish, French, Egyptian and Æthiopian questions; dexterously writing despatches and 'having the honour to
be.' Not a question of them is at all pressing in comparison with
the English question. Pacifico the miraculous Gibraltar Jew has
been hustled by some populace in Greece: upon him let the British Lion drop, very rapidly indeed, a constitutional tear. Ra-
detzky is said to be advancing on Milan;—I am sorry to hear it,
and perhaps it does deserve a despatch, or friendly letter, once and
away: but the Irish Giant, named of Despair, is advancing upon
London itself, laying waste all English cities, towns and villages;
that is the interesting Government-despatch of the day!"

In his passage Carlyle is one point right and one point
wrong as a guide to the authentic tradition, the well-known
characteristics. Concern for the misery at our gates, yes! But
concern for human under-dogs the world over, and ourselves
as world-leaders, world-crusaders, world-school-mistresses and
world-moralists, has always, for good or evil, whether in Washington or Westminster, been our characteristic. Humanity we
have always appropriated as our business. It has not made us
loved, but it is, I fear, too late to change.

"This lesson will have to be learned—under penalties! England will either learn it, or England also will cease to exist among

Nations. England will either learn to reverence its Heroes, and discriminate them from its Sham-Heroes and Valets and gas-lighted Histrios; and to prize them as the audible God's-voice, amid all inane jargons and temporary market-cries, and to say to them with heart-loyalty, 'Be ye King and Priest, and Gospel and Guidance for us': or else England will continue to worship new and ever-new forms of Quackhood,—and so, with what resiliences and reboundings matter little, go down to the Father of Quacks! Can I dread such things of England? Wretched, thick-eyed, gross-hearted mortals, why will ye worship lies, and 'Stuffed Clothes-suits created by the ninth-parts of men'!"

It is no more easy to find consistency in Carlyle than in Charles Kingsley. The message, however, of *Alton Locke* and the general tendency of the Christian Socialists are clear enough. And so is the message of Carlyle. Maybe we need a new Carlyle with his call for Oliver *Redivivus,* a new sage of Chelsea. If there is to be competition, it must not be cash competition between man and man in the same society . . . and *this* determining the structure of that society. It must not be the rule of Plugson of Undershot. But Anglo-Saxony must be a society of men, not of machines—not an aggregate of machines and unemployed.

"I consider that a cash-account, and balance-statement of work done and wages paid, is worth attending to. Precisely *such,* though on a smaller scale, go on at all moments under this Sun; and the statement and balance of them in the Plugson Ledgers and on the Tablets of Heaven's Chancery are discrepant exceed-ingly;—which ought really to teach, and to have long since taught, an indomitable common-sense Plugson of Undershot, much more an unattackable *un*common-sense Grace of Rackrent, a thing or two!—In brief, we shall have to dismiss the Cash-Gospel rig-orously into its own place: we shall have to know, on the thresh-old, that either there is some infinitely deeper Gospel, subsidiary, explanatory and daily and hourly corrective, to the Cash one; or else that the Cash one itself and all others are fast travel-ling! . . .

"Certainly it were a fond imagination to expect that any preaching of mine could abate Mammonism; that Bobus of Hounsditch will love his guineas less, or his poor soul more, for any preaching of mind! But there is one Preacher who does preach with effect, and gradually persuade all persons: his name is Destiny, is Divine Providence, and his Sermon the inflexible Course of Things. Experience does take dreadfully high school-wages; but he teaches like no other! . . .

"'Men cease to regard money?' cries Bobus of Hounsditch: 'What else do all men strive for? The very Bishop informs me that Christianity cannot get on without a minimum of Four thousand five hundred in its pocket. Cease to regard money? That will be at Doomsday in the afternoon!'—O Bobus, my opinion is somewhat different. My opinion is, that the Upper Powers have not yet determined on destroying this Lower World. A respectable, ever-increasing minority, who do strive for something higher than money, I with confidence anticipate; ever-increasing, till there be a sprinkling of them found in all quarters, as salt of the Earth once more. The Christianity that cannot get on without a minimum of Four thousand five hundred, will give place to something better that can. Thou wilt not join our small minority, then? not till Doomsday in the afternoon? Well; *then,* at least, thou wilt join it, thou and the majority in mass!

"But truly it is beautiful to see the brutish empire of Mammon cracking everywhere; giving sure promise of dying or of being changed. A strange, chill, almost ghastly day-spring strikes up in Yankeeland itself: my Transcendental friends announce there . . . that the Demiurgus Dollar is dethroned. . . . A deep feeling of the eternal nature of Justice looks out among us everywhere,— even through the dull eyes of Exeter Hall. . . . Of all our Cant, all condemnable, how much is not condemnable without pity . . .'"

John Ruskin is a figure of a very different cut from Carlyle. Here is an artist without pretensions to be the 'hero or prophet.' Like William Morris, his protest against the hallelujahs to the Industrial Revolution is that of a man whose humanism is offended by the crass vulgarity of those whom Matthew Arnold denounced as 'the Philistines.' The issue is one of more than mere 'good taste.' It is one of 'good manners' in the profoundest, Chinese sense of the term—in the widest sense of the vision of the good life. It is an issue of the Hellenic vision of 'the excellent' that the English individualists, raking for money, too often had forgotten. It is an issue of the Christian vision; of human values against material values; of an exaltation of justice as the impartial right of each man to receive in accordance with his worth and not according to his force, as a successful plutocrat, to buy service. The emancipation begins for 'a nation of shopkeepers' from the grocer's values that had tended to dominate, not its older, feudal aristocrat leaders, but the new, crude and arrogant middle-class.

In *Unto this Last,* Ruskin writes:

"The real science of political economy, which has yet to be distinguished from the bastard science, as medicine from witchcraft, and astronomy from astrology, is that which teaches nations to desire and labour for the things that lead to life: and which teaches them to scorn and destroy the things that lead to destruction. . . . Government and co-operation are in all things the Laws of Life; Anarchy and competition the Laws of Death. . . .

"*These are not, observe, merely moral or pathetic attributes of riches, which the seeker of riches may, if he chooses, despise;* they are, literally and sternly, material attributes of riches, depreciating or exalting, incalculably, the monetary signification of the sum in question. One mass of money is the outcome of action which has created,—another, of action which has annihilated,—ten times as much in the gathering of it; such and such strong hands have been paralyzed, as if they had been numbered by nightshade: so many strong men's courage broken, so many productive operations hindered. . . . That which seems to be wealth may in verity be only the gilded index of far-reaching ruin; a wrecker's handful of coin gleaned from the beach to which he has beguiled an argosy; a camp-follower's bundle of rags unwrapped from the breasts of goodly soldiers dead; 'the purchase-prices of potter's fields, wherein shall be buried together the citizen and the stranger.'

"And therefore, *the idea that directions can be given for the gaining of wealth, irrespective of the consideration of its moral sources,* or that any general and technical law of purchase and gain can be set down for national practice, is perhaps the most *insolently futile* of all that ever beguiled men through their vices."

As one of the greatest of French bankers said to me not many weeks ago (and surely the saying is significant of the normal conscience): "The trouble with the imperialist is that he cannot bring himself to make concessions of interests when it is necessary for the peace of the world, and the trouble with the capitalist is that he cannot bring himself to sacrifice wealth *in time* to save social peace." There is the prophecy, the warning and, at the same time, by the very recognition of folly, the augury of better.

Ruskin's conscience was not a solitary voice but representative enough. Romilly and the 'Benthamee' reformers, whom Carlyle despised, had yet in fact cleared up the Augean stables of the law in the first half of the century. Chadwick, another Benthamite, spent laborious years on poor law and, above all, on health reform and in inculcating 'the Sanitary Idea.' Lord Shaftesbury had laboured at the work. Much yet remained to be done in checking the ravages of *laissez-faire*. Samuel Plimsoll, as late as 1873, uttered his protest against insuring unseaworthy ships and then sending them to sea, veritable coffins. " 'Oh! Mr. Plimsoll, you should have been here yesterday; a vessel went down to the sea so deeply loaded, that everybody who saw her expects to hear of her being lost' . . . I hate to appeal to class feelings or prejudices, but class jealousy can only be allayed by justice, not by ignoring murderous wrong." Be it added that Plimsoll had the satisfaction of seeing a provisional Act put through in the self-same year as he distributed his pamphlet.

Ruskin points out that if the public conscience was impotent to teach the mutual obligations of human beings, the typhus would teach it. Infection demanded no social passports. In sharp contrast, however, to the Utilitarian morality, Ruskin insists upon the social force of the vision of the good rather than upon the penalties of the evil. The bland Adam Smith declares: "It is the fear of losing their employment which restrains his [the workman's] frauds, and corrects his negligence." Ruskin comments, "What an entirely damned state of soul any human creature must have got into, who could read with acceptance such a sentence as this." It should be added that Chadwick and Ruskin were both nearly crushed by an obdurate opposition, with its typically English suspiciousness of novelty as evil in itself. Bentham, dazed by the same opposition, overcame it by sheer length of life; Carlyle overcame it by a superior power of vituperation and by a happy knack of calling stupid men damned blockheads and finding that they answered to the call.

Ruskin brings the benevolence, upon which even Adam Smith pinned his faith with the impersonal calm of the Augustan Eighteenth Century, to a focus in human instances:

" 'Five years ago' deceased applied to the parish for aid. The relieving officer gave him a 4-lb. loaf, and told him if he came again he should 'get the stones'. That disgusted deceased, and he would have nothing to do with them since. They got worse and worse until last Friday week, when they had not even a halfpenny to buy a candle. Deceased then lay down in the straw, and said he could not live till morning.—A Juror: 'You are dying of starvation yourself, and you ought to go into the house until the summer.' Witness: 'If we went in, we should die. When we come out in the summer we should be like people dropped from the sky. No one would know us, and we would not have even a room. I could work now if I had food, for my sight would get better' . . .

" 'Why would witness not go into the workhouse?' you ask.

Well, the poor seem to have a prejudice against the workhouse [industrial farm] which the rich have not; for of course everyone who takes a pension from the Government goes into the workhouse on a grand scale; only the workhouses for the rich do not involve the idea of work, and should be called play-houses. But the poor like to die independently, it appears; perhaps if we made the play-houses for them pretty and pleasant enough, or gave them their pensions at home and allowed them a little introductory peculation with the public money, their minds might be reconciled to it."

Cobbett and Carlyle and Ruskin are rather making here a tradition than echoing it. Cobbett indeed looks back upon an earlier age of rural co-operation as Carlyle looks back, in *Past and Present,* on the Catholic civilization of his great Abbot Sampson. But Carlyle looking to Germany, and Ruskin to Italy, reintroduce a connection with the general tradition of European Humanism that had been lost ever since St. Thomas More. They do, indeed, more than this, as we shall see later.

As I write this I find in a London newspaper *(Daily Herald)* within two days three illustrations alike of the continuity of the problem and of the growth—however still inadequate— of the tradition that settles the decencies and right attitude.

25th Jan. 1939.

Won't be 'Burden to State'

Threatened with eviction, but determined not to be a burden on the State, Mr. and Mrs. M. Long, of Bath-road, Harmondsworth, Middlesex, have for more than a week been living with six of their seven children in an empty house, eating and sleeping in one room on bare floorboards.

They have sold all their furniture.

"These two mattresses are the only things we have not sold," Mrs. Long said to the *Daily Herald* last night as six of their children lay asleep on one mattress.

"We have been living in this house for seven years, but through continued unemployment my husband got behind with the rent. A court eviction order was made against us in December, and we were told to find another house.

"We were due to leave here on January 13, but though my husband has tramped for miles he cannot find another house, as we have so many children.

"To avoid having our furniture put out in the street we have sold it, and are struggling to get enough money to pay off what we owe.

"It has been suggested that my children should go into an institution, but my husband and I are determined that they shall not be a burden on the State. My husband has at last managed to get a job.

"I have a boy of eight, twin boys of six, twin girls of four, a girl of two, and a baby of three months. The baby is being cared for by a friend."

25th Jan. 1939.

Workless Invade Banquet
By Our Own Correspondent
Brighton, *Tuesday*

Carrying banners inscribed, "You feast while we starve," eight members of the National Unemployed Workers' Movement walked into the Royal Albion Hotel banqueting room to-night.

In that room members of the Brighton branch of the Wine and Food Society were eating their Normandy dinner.

The leader of the men, Anton Mile, recently back from fighting in Spain with the International Brigade, said to the forty members of the Society: "We have not had a bite to eat all day. We want you to invite us to join you."

The managing director of the hotel, Mr. J. F. Edens, provided the men with a three-course meal in another room.

26th Jan. 1939.

Sympathy from Magistrate to Workless

"Everybody sympathises with the position of the unemployed. Through no fault of your own you are passing through a time of hardship.

"You are entitled to draw public attention to your grievances, but you must adopt constitutional methods to do it and not unconstitutional methods such as holding up traffic."

Magistrate J. B. Sandbach, K.C., said this at Marlborough Street police court yesterday.

He was addressing Richard John Wood, aged 28, of Albany Road, Camberwell, S.E., and Patrick Kelly, aged 40, of King's Cross Road, W.C., who were bound over on charges of obstruction following an unemployed "lie-down" demonstration in Oxford Street, W., on January 17.

One wonders whether Mr. Sandbach supposes that the great industrial Trusts adopt no other methods, in the way of publicity and pressure, in constraining their Parliamentary representatives than by writing them a polite 'constitutional' letter (what has the Constitution got to do with it, Mr. Sandbach—do you mean 'legal'?) full of mathematical figures and information. Do you, Mr. Sandbach? And how shall men without money in their pockets advertise their case? For myself, I would pay to enable the unemployed, with their coffin, peacefully to parade daily through Bond Street, London, or down Fifth Avenue, New York. And I would remind legislators that photographs of this tribute to their lethargy will surely appear the next day, with compliments to Democracy, in the *Berliner Illustrirte Zeitung* and in the *Moscow Daily News*. But I would ask the unemployed to consider that compulsory labour is not much better, and to reflect on their dinner in Brighton. As for the hotel-keeper, I would make him a Member of Parliament.

It will be noted that Mrs. Long's offence appears to be that of having too many children. The National State has not yet made up its mind in Britain or the United States, if it wants more children, just *how much* it will pay for them. It still adopts the old Liberal attitude: "The advantage is mine, the responsibility yours." Signor Mussolini has done better. When hotel-keepers reject families with too many children, the hotel-keeper loses his licence and his Party ticket. He becomes what the Germans call *staatsfeindlich*.

Unless free Democracy can do better by public spirit, in the actual elimination of unemployment, than totalitarian dictatorships, red or black, do by regimentation of labour in the name of the totality, free Democracy will yield to the totalitarianism that Carlyle, at least, so much admired, in its more moderate and embryonic form, in the rule of the Benevolent Despots.

William Morris (1834–96), another artist and poet, drew more firmly the lines that Ruskin had sketched; reinforced the argument by a persuasiveness and public-spirited energy of his own; defined more sharply the nature of the forming tradition—even for the young undergraduates who were building roads under Ruskin's instruction or for the future civil servants whom T. H. Green was teaching at Oxford, and even more for the slowly organizing trade unionists who were finding their mental feet.

"I feel sure that the time will come when pople will find it difficult to believe that a rich community such as ours, having such command over external nature, could have submitted to live such a mean, shabby, dirty life as we do.

"No, it is not Absolutism and Democracy, as the French Revolution understood those two words, that are the enemies now: the issue is deeper than it was; the two foes are now *Mastership and Fellowship*. This is a far more serious quarrel than the old one, and involves a much completer revolution. The grounds of conflict are really quite different. Democracy said and says, men shall not be the masters of others, because hereditary privilege has made a race or a family so, and they happen to belong to such race; they shall individually grow into being the masters of others by the development of certain qualities under a system of authority which *artificially* protects the wealth of every man, if he has acquired it in accordance with this artificial system, from the interference of every other, or from all others combined.

"The new order of things says, on the contrary, why have masters at all? Let us be *fellows* working in the harmony of association for the common good, that is, for the greatest happiness and completest development of every human being in the community."

Another poet put Morris' complaint, against the starvation of life under the domination of acquisitive and commercial standards, in brief words. Browning wrote:

> "Each life's unfulfilled, you see,
>   It hangs still patchy and scrappy;
> We have not sighed deep, laughed free,
>   Starved, feasted, despaired, been happy"—

Men starved (literally, as Ruskin shewed) and despaired all right; but these only. The triumphant advance lay in the new moral determination that these things should not be.

§ iii

The politicians spoke with a voice no less uncertain than the poets, and spoke from the most unexpected quarters.

"I have been the subject of torrents of abuse and of whirlwinds of invective. . . . The working classes of this country are to continue in the future as they have in the past—to order themselves lowly and reverently to all their betters and to do their duty in the state of life to which it shall please God to call them. . . . The proposals which I have made are not directed against any class or any individual. I have had two objects in view. In the first place I want to see that the burthen of taxation is distributed according to the ability of the taxpayer, and in the second place I want to increase the production of the land and I want to multiply small owners and tenants. *All this clamour about confiscation and blackmail and plunder is so much dust raised by men who are interested in maintaining the present system* and who are either too prejudiced to read my proposals or too stupid to understand them. Let them keep their invective for some better occasion—for more apposite uses.

"If it be blackmail to propose that the rich should pay taxation in equal proportion to the poor, what word is strong enough to describe the present system under which the poor pay more than the rich?

"If it be confiscation to suggest that land may be acquired at a fair value for public purposes, what language will fitly describe the operations of those who have wrongfully appropriated the common land and have extended their boundaries at the expense of their poorer neighbours, too weak and too ignorant to resist them?

"If it be plunder to require the restitution of this ill-gotten property I should like to know what we are to say to those who perpetrated the original act of appropriation. . . . *I hold that the sanctity of public property is greater even than that of private property,* and that if it has been lost or wasted or stolen, some equivalent must be found for it and some compensation may be fairly exacted from the wrongdoer."

The words are those of Mr. Neville Chamberlain's father, Joseph, in 1885. They deserve to be put beside the following utterance of President Roosevelt:

"The true friend of property, the true conservative, is he who insists that *property shall be the servant and not the master of the commonwealth;* who insists that the creature of man's making shall be the servant and not the master of the man who made it. The citizens of the United States must effectively control the mighty commercial forces which they have themselves called into being.

"There can be no effective control of corporations while their political activity remains. To put an end to it will be neither a short nor an easy task but it can be done. . . . We grudge no man a fortune in civil life if it is honourably obtained and well used. It is not even enough that it should have been gained without doing damage to the community. *We should permit it to be gained only so long as the gaining represents benefit to the community.*

"No man should receive a dollar unless that dollar has been fairly earned. Every dollar received should represent a dollar's worth of service rendered—not gambling in stocks, but service rendered. The really big fortune, the swollen fortune, by the mere fact of its size acquires qualities which differentiate it in kind as well as in degree from what is possessed by men of relatively small means. . . .

"But I think we may go still further. *The right to regulate the use of wealth in the public interest is universally admitted.* Let us admit also the right to regulate the terms and conditions of labor, which is the chief element of wealth, directly in the interest of the common good. The fundamental thing to do for every man is to give him *a chance to reach a place in which he will make the greatest possible contribution to the public welfare.* Understand what I say then. Give him a chance, not push him up if he will not be pushed. Help any man who stumbles; if he lies down it is a poor job to try to carry him; but if he is a worthy man, try your best to see that he gets a chance to shew the worth that is in him. *No man can be a good citizen unless he has a wage more than sufficient to cover the bare cost of living,* and hours of labor short enough so that after his day's work is done he will have time and energy to bear his share in the management of the community, to help in carrying the general load. We keep countless men from being good citizens by the conditions of life with which we surround them. . . .

"National efficiency has many factors. It is a necessary result of the principle of conservation widely applied. In the end it will determine our failure or success as a nation. National efficiency has to do, not only with natural resources and with men, but it is equally concerned with institutions. The state must be made efficient for the work which concerns only the people of the state; and the nation for that which concerns all the people. *There must remain no neutral ground to serve as a refuge for lawbreakers, and especially for lawbreakers of great wealth, who can hire the vulpine legal cunning which will teach them how to avoid both jurisdictions.* . . .

"*I am for men and not for property,* as you were in the Civil War. I am far from underestimating the importance of dividends; but *I rank dividends below human character.* . . .

"Those who oppose all reforms will do well to remember that

ruin in its worst form is inevitable if our national life brings us nothing better than swollen fortunes for the few and the triumph in both politics and business of a sordid and selfish materialism."

The author of this speech of 1910 was a Republican—Theodore Roosevelt. . . .

The relation between Liberty and Equality we have already discussed in our earlier chapter. As for "rich man's liberty" as an intransigent argument against social justice—a 'natural right' but not urged (as Locke would have urged it) as a natural right of property for each and all: what Lincoln called "liberty in the wolves' dictionary"—the comment is illuminating of one of the greatest judges who ever sat on the American Supreme Court bench. Mr. Justice Holmes, in *Lochner* v. *New York*, 1904, declared:

"The other day we sustained the Massachusetts vaccination law. . . . The decision sustaining an eight-hour law for miners is still recent. . . . A liberty of the citizen to do as he likes so long as he does not interfere with the liberty of others to do the same [the liberty of all to go to the devil together], which has been a shibboleth for some well-known writers, is interfered with by school laws, by the Post Office, by every State or municipal institution which takes his money for purposes thought desirable, whether he likes it or not. The Fourteenth Amendment does not enact Mr. Herbert Spencer's *Social Statics.*"

After the declarations of Chamberlain and Theodore Roosevelt, those of a Socialist such as Blatchford, editor of *The Clarion,* whose *Merrie England* (1894) sold to the extent of over two million copies, wear the clothes of a modest moderation:

"Here again I differ very much from the Manchester School. "My ideal is frugality of body and opulence of mind. I suggest that we should be as temperate and as simple as possible in our use of mere bodily necessaries, so that we may have as much time as possible to enjoy pleasures of a higher, purer, and more delightful kind.

"Your Manchester School treat all Social and Industrial problems from the standpoint of mere animal subsistence. They do not seem to think that you *have* any mind. With them it is a question of bread and cheese and be thankful."

Blatchford continues with a statement on the unemployment issue that has a closer resemblance to the stark system of contemporary Russia, with its recognition of compulsory labour corps as (in Trotsky's words) "of the A B C of Marxism," and to the *ipsissima verba* of Marx, than to any Jerusalem-in-England Utopia of Morris:

"So long as it is possible for a willing worker to be forced into idleness, so long will there be reason for the giving of alms.

"Why do we relieve a tramp on the road, or a beggar in the street? It is because we are never sure that the man is a loafer; because we always fear that his penury may be due to misfortune, and not to idleness. But under Socialism this doubt would disappear. Under Socialism there would be work for all. Therefore, under Socialism every man who was able to work would be able to live. This fact being universally known, no able-bodied man could exist without work. A beggar or a tramp would be inevitably a loafer, and not a hand would be held out to help him.

"The answer to the able-bodied beggar would be, 'if you are hungry go and work.' If the man refused to work he must starve.

"The answer, then, to the question of what Socialists would do with the loafers is, that under Socialism we should oblige the loafer to work or perish; whereas, under present conditions, we either made him a 'gentleman' or a pauper, or a beggar, or a thief; in any one of which capacities he is allowed to live in idleness upon the labour of other men.

"Tell me, is it not true of England to-day that the idlest are often the richest, and the most industrious the poorest among the people?"

Along with solid truth, Blatchford, it may be felt, combines an overstatement of his case if his object is to get back to a 'Merrie England.' While England should be a hive of industry, Blatchford, unlike Ruskin, does not exclude a species of economism that would make it a very unpleasant speed-up workhouse. However, he has the excuse that, like Roosevelt, he is concerned with efficiency. He corrects himself in another, significant passage, and swings into line with the general trend:

"The ideal of British Society to-day is the ideal of individual effort, or competition. That is to say, every man for himself. Each citizen is to try as hard as he can to get for himself as much *money* as he can, and to use it for his own pleasure, and leave it for his own children.

"That is the present personal ideal. The present national ideal is to become 'The Workshop of the World.' That is to say, the British people are to manufacture goods for sale to foreign countries, and in return for these goods are to get more money than they could obtain by developing *the resources of their own country for their own use*.

"My ideal is that each individual should seek his advantage in co-operation with his fellows, and that the people should make the best of their own country before attempting to trade with other countries."

§ iv

"Smile at us, pay us, pass us; but do not quite forget,
For we are the people of England, that never has spoken yet,
There is many a fat farmer that drinks less cheerfully,
There is many a free French peasant who is richer and sadder
    than we . . .
Only you do not know us. For we have not spoken yet."

G. K. Chesterton's words, in an otherwise not especially remarkable, halting poem, are a warning and a hope. The statement of the issue of social justice has indeed, during this last century, taken in Anglo-Saxony a shape so far uniform in the mouths of more outstanding speakers that we are, here also, entitled to state that a tradition has formed. There are recognized values and decencies, violated a century and a half ago, and now affirmed. There is a condemnation, again quoting Chesterton, of an economic vulgarism that stamped the last century—vulgar because insensitive and inhuman:

> "That perfect dullness counting hands
> That have no man or woman,
> That fullness of the commonplace
> That can despise the common"—

—lines that the Catholic poet and distributivist wrote on a certain noble lord of recent elevation, head of the Port of London Authority. To speak of any traditional answer concerning the mode of social justice is more hazardous. We are left with an appeal to public spirit against private money-scratching, and a belief in what can be done by voluntary co-operation. We are left with disputed and Party answers. At the turn of the century, in the Edwardian period, Kipling attempted an answer in terms of co-operation on the basis of nationalism and imperialism. Others find it in an exhortation to an international economic movement and that the "workers of the world unite." Those who sing Kipling's *Recessional* or Elgar's *Land of Hope and Glory,* in fact move others, by reaction, to sing the *Internationale* or *The Red Flag*. Not tradition but division is apparent. In Britain only Blake's *Jerusalem*—

> "And did the Countenance Divine
> Shine forth upon our clouded hills?
> And was Jerusalem builded here
> Among these dark Satanic Mills?"

—focuses emotion into unity, as it is still focused in the West, not only by *America,* but by the *Battle Hymn of the Republic:*

"Mine eyes have seen the glory of the coming of the Lord;
 He is trampling out the vintage where the grapes of wrath are
  stored;
 He hath loosed the fateful lightning of His terrible swift sword:
  His truth is marching on!

"He hath sounded forth the trumpet that shall never call retreat;
 He is sifting out the hearts of men before His judgment-seat;
 Oh, be swift, my soul, to answer Him; be jubilant, my feet!
  Our God is marching on!

"In the beauty of the lilies Christ was born across the sea,
 With a glory in His bosom that transfigures you and me:
 As He died to make men holy, let us die to make men free,
  While God is marching on!"

Here is not the season to inquire whether every nation does not speak of "Unser Gott," or to deplore it. Rather praise be that they do—for here, so long as the Grand Tradition of human civilization is preserved as it has been passed on by the lips of the sages, a pledge and warranty is given that mankind is one, that what they fight for is its richness, and that all else, whether it be of nation or class or race, is parricide and civil strife. Whatever be the case with political governments and ambitious men, the common people of mankind are much the same, in hopes and fears, pleasures, pains, joys and sorrows, on either side of frontiers. Goethe said that, as the core of his wisdom, a century and a half ago; and it is still true. Until, however, the world-empire is refounded or the world-commonwealth built, national allegiance to that world-ideal, inter-national and *supra-national* but not anti-national, must perforce take, for the interim, a national character and quality.

An admirer of William Morris draws a picture of the England—itself no longer, any more than Virginia, a sovereign political unit—that is for him focus of community and of community allegiance:

"The sounds of England, the tinkle of the hammer on the anvil in the country smithy, the corncrake on a dewy morning, the sound of the scythe against the whetstone, and the sight of a plough team coming over the brow of a hill, the sight that has been seen in England since England was a land, and may be seen in England long after the Empire has perished and every works in England has ceased to function, for centuries the one eternal sight of England. The wild anemones in the woods in April, the last load at night of hay being drawn down a lane as the twilight comes on, when you can scarcely distinguish the figures of the horses as they take it home to the farm, and above all, most subtle, most penetrating and most moving, the smell of wood smoke coming up on an autumn evening, or the smell of the scutch fires: that wood smoke that our ancestors, tens of thousands of years ago, must have caught on the air as they were returning home with the result of the day's forage, when they were still nomads, and when they were still roaming the forests and the plains of the continent of Europe. These things strike down into the very depths of our nature, and touch chords that go back to the beginning of time and the human race, but they are chords that with every year of our life sound a deeper note in our innermost being."

Shall we praise ourselves? To what else did Virgil or Horace recall the minds of the great Romans, but to the hearth and the farm and the countryside? These things have always been the roots of living—to them have responded "chords that go back to the beginning," not only of us, but of "the human race." Why should we not thus praise ourselves in that which unites all men of deeper feeling?

"The place where a great city stands is not the place of
    Stretched wharves, docks, manufactures, deposits of produce
      merely.
Nor the place of ceaseless salute of new-comers, or the anchor-
    lifters of the departing.

Nor the place of the tallest and costliest buildings, or shops,
    selling goods from the rest of the earth,
Nor the place of the best libraries and schools, nor the place
    where money is plentiest. . . .

"Where no monuments exist to heroes but in the common words
    and deeds,
Where thrift is in its place, and kindness is in its place, . . .
Where the city of the faithfulest friends stands,
Where the city of the cleanliness of the sexes stands,
Where the city of the healthiest father stands,
Where the city of the best-bodied mothers stands,
There the great city stands."

Walt Whitman (1819–1892) will not be accused of losing in
provincial patriotism sense for the democratic unity of the
common man or the fraternity of the human kind. Totalitarian militarism and mechanical collectivism are not the qualities of the man who so admirably declared that "a great city
is that which has the greatest men and women." Beneath the
curmudgeonism of the English countryside and the rush of
the great town, the impersonal splendour and glory of power
of Manhattan, alike, lies a kindliness of man to man, a gener-
osity, in the American and the English character which the
poet could perceive. Whitman, however, was the last person
to decline to acclaim

    "A new song, a free song . . .
      By the wind's voice and that of the drum . . .
      With the banner and pennant a-flapping."

Loyalism to the Great Society—and loyalism to the littlest
platoon, the intimate, sweet community; as Plato said, "community of pleasures and pains"—loyalism to internationalism
that is supra-nationalism, does not exclude loyalism to nation
and commonwealth, nor is it anti-nationalism. Where to find
the community upon which to pivot social justice; how to

place well and truly community within community, loyalty within loyalty, cumulative, stronger; how to vitalize the sacrificing sense of human justice, the public spirit that looks outward—there is the issue.

And for us the answer must come in terms of our own tried tradition, that commands the emotions. In terms of a philosophy of five centuries, that is a tradition, whereby we can give a reason for the faith that is in us. In terms of experiment that is ceaseless and unashamed, because modest about truth, in new social forms. In terms of tolerance and self-respecting compromise that keeps life sweet. In terms of passion for justice that has discovered other men to be of like clay, with like passions, failings, rights as ourselves. In terms of morality that orders a man humbly in self-pride and with discipline and contempt of self-seeking indulgence. In terms yet of liberty that asserts the right of each, preventing none to discover if he is able new treasures of civilization and of the spirit, as inventor, scientist, artist, poet, and as plain, common man of self-respect who will work out his own morality and who will be free from being spied on, delated, terrorized by jacks-in-office.

Men have fought for a land, the actual black acres that their fathers have ploughed, their property, or the place where their own houses have stood and the little shrines. Men fight for their interests and from simple loyalty to their fellows—their "we-group"—if attacked . . . attacked by "the men on the other side of the mountain." But the significant turning-points of history have been where men, as the vehicles of ideas, have fought as they do actually fight before our eyes today, whether for race or class or nationalism or internationalism. Ideas make history, and men today die by reason of ideas. Our tradition is one uniformly hostile to fanaticisms. That, if any, is its message. But that too—a tradition federal, unaggressive, aiming to live and let live—may itself be challenged whether it shall be suppressed from the earth and denied its contribution, its also, to human progress in right manners. Whether Anglo-Saxon civilization shall grow stronger to contribute, as bearer of the greatest of human hopes, or shall be suppressed into negligibility, we may decide this—not prematurely or rashly, but possibly—we may decide this to be the issue. Is it defence or disruption? This issue also, whether in Mount Vernon or in Arden, new Plymouth or old Plymouth, can be met. Lawrence Whistler at the invitation of Lutyens, to be read round the earth's girdle, but written on a pane of glass in the public room of an inn, up in Cockington, where the old West Saxon village looks down towards the Devon sea, has given the answer:

> "Drake left a drum to Englishmen,
> And bade them beat and wake him when
> Perils upon his England come
> But now where can we find that Drum?

> "You who stand and closely peer,
> Curious to read what's written here,
> And see the light of English skies
> Silver the glass, and bless your eyes,
> Think of the England old and green
> You wander and are happy in,
> And if the hour of perils come,
> Find, in your own loud heart, that Drum."

III

CONCLUSION

"I am sure I shall not be misled when . . . I consult the genius of the English constitution. . . . We want no foreign examples to rekindle in us a flame of liberty; the example of our ancestors is abundantly sufficient to maintain the spirit of freedom in its full vigour."

EDMUND BURKE.

"You must act lively. Do it without distraction. Neglect no means."

OLIVER CROMWELL.

CONCLUSION

§ i

The Anglo-Saxon Way of Life

In the preceding pages we have given substance to the notion of Anglo-Saxony by describing that tradition which alone gives the whole a common character—a tradition contributory to civilization, not limited in significance to certain lands, not even peculiar in all its qualities to those lands, but there alone, continuously through centuries maintained and become native to them.

That tradition is a unity. The notes that we have enumerated —of humanism, of personality, of experiment, of liberty, of tolerance, of accommodation, of federalism, of democracy, of moralism and of public spirit—are not isolated and disconnected items. They constitute a theme and follow appropriately each from each. Humanism, with its stress upon the ideas of reason, of humanity as the total of reasonable beings, of personality as the quality of those beings with moral choice, is the buckle connecting the Anglo-Saxon Tradition with the wider tradition of Western Europe, and indeed with a Grand Tradition in history that transcends even these limits. The Renaissance, however, which saw the new shaping of Humanism also was the Age of Exploration, Discovery, Experiment.

The notions alike of Personality and of Experiment give birth to the notion of Liberty in personal life, intellectual and social; and from Liberty logically follows the concept of Tolerance. These, translated into social life, mean 'live and let live'; Accommodation within the civil order, not dogmatic intransigence as men of *a-priori* principle; Federation between political units rather than Caesarism and centralization. Democracy, not as a mystic enthusiasm for majority rule, but as a system of discussion, opposition and utilitarian balance, where yet each personality shall count for one, and hence, as a practical matter, where the rule of a majority that does not abuse its power is recognized as best—this system follows, as appropriate, from the preceding Tolerance, Accommodation and Empiricism raised to human virtues.[1]

If, however, liberty of discussion and tolerance are to be enjoyed, it follows complementarily, as Bertrand Russell has shewn, that there must be some *common sense of community,* some agreement on fundamentals. Under autocratic régimes that agreement is procured by imposition of authority, by propaganda on the one side and by intimidation on the other. Under other systems it is procured by externally imposed *law* and ukase. The alternative is that it shall be procured by tacit agreement on custom and by *self-imposed discipline.* Anglo-Saxon moralism may be charged with hypocrisy, the homage

---

[1] I deliberately emphasize the word 'empiricism,' since the customary attack on the Anglo-Saxon Tradition—e.g. the Leninist attack—accuses it of 'opportunism.' The assumption, of course, is that there is no philosophy of principle, but only moment to moment self-seeking government action, in countries of this tradition. We have not the advantages of the Hegelian omniscience. Needless to say, we are not justifying a self-seeking opportunism that rejects connected thought because it may be inconvenient for profits in its conclusions. We are saying, on the contrary, that connected thought may issue in a damnation of dogma (lauded as alone being 'principle') as obscurantist and hostile to progress, and in praise of the experimental mood (designated as 'opportunism') as most favourable to that progress and to the practical co-operation upon which progress depends in the face of metaphysical obstinacies such as often merely serve to screen self-will.

that virtue pays to vice, and it certainly is not the same thing as mystical religion. Its destruction, however, whether by ridicule or by the assertion that no one community any longer exists—the Marxian thesis of *stasis* or class war (which in turn inherits from the bad psychology of Hobbes and his disciples, the Classical Economists)—leaves, as Russell says, the conclusion (Marxist also, as touching the interim) that tolerance and personal liberty of discussion must cease to exist save within a dogmatic framework. Freedom and tolerance have possibility within some framework of cohesion. *Tradition, with its moral sanctions however strong, or Coercion—these are the alternatives*.

Granted an accepted morality, with its assumptions of cooperation and of willingness to accept discipline, then the building up of a just social order consonant with the tradition can be left to Public Spirit. It is significant, as Madame Rappard has said, that what in France one refers to as 'citizenship' in Britain one refers to as 'public spirit.' The tradition in France, in its profounder depths, has been split apart by the secularism of the French Revolution.

The keystone of the whole Anglo-Saxon structure, as a philosophic construction or even as a 'way of life,' is a certain Theory of Truth, whether consciously grasped or only habitually held. Paradoxically, we may call that Theory a Distrust of Theory. More precisely, it is a belief that the knowledge of truth is a matter, where we are talking of society and its values, of approximation, experiment and groping. Now, in the quest for certainty, a 'groper' is at a dialectical disadvantage in dealing with a dogmatist. Nevertheless, the 'groper' may be actually nearer the truth, and intellectually the better man, than the dogmatist. The dogmatic school hies itself off to a German professor to get a philosophy ready made:

"Zu fragmentarisch ist Welt und Leben.
Ich will mich zum deutschen Professor begeben,
Der weiss das Leben zusammenzusetzen,
Und er macht ein verständig System daraus." [1]

§ ii

The Latin and Catholic Traditions

I have no desire to provide, over against the present Red and Black ideologies, yet a third. And although I respect the Confucian and Aristotelian 'Middle Ways' and their wisdom, "to provide a Middle Way" is only a very rough description of what we are here seeking to do unless we agree that non-totalitarianism may be 'middle way' between two totalitarian extremes (which, like most extremes, meet). My object is the reverse of trying to draw precise limits. Rather it is to throw a bridge over to other 'cultures,' just as politically I would seek confederation with other units. The object is the spiritual redintegration of culture, on one level, as it is that of the formation again of the *republica mundana,* the World-Commonwealth such as once the Roman Empire held, on the other —the political—level.

The first step in this process is that of finding common terms and common values with French culture with its tradition that has played so mighty a part in continental Europe.[2]

We must not underestimate the difficulty. Latin culture has a long history, and in its French form it wears a shape precise, self-conscious, rather arrogantly confident that *"la civilisation c'est la France."* Before we tax "the German professor" with

---

[1] "The world and life are far too fragmentary.
I will hie me off to a German professor,
Who knows how to put Life together again,
And make an intelligent System out of it."

[2] A project that finds its political equivalent in Mr. Streit's scheme for the 'Union Now' of a North Atlantic Federation.

being the especial maker of dogmatic systems such as the Fascist and Marxist, we do well to recall that of the four outstanding systems of modern philosophic thought that evoked the immortal criticism of dogmatism by Immanuel Kant, two were French and one Jewish (that of Marx's predecessor, Spinoza). The best junction for the discovery of agreed values is to be found in that Humanism which is common ground both to the Anglo-Saxon and to the French, and especially the French Catholic, tradition. I have already referred to the work of M. Jacques Maritain and to his discussion of the problems of discipline and freedom. The common values between predominantly Protestant Anglo-Saxon Tradition and French Catholicism may perhaps be found, as we have suggested, in respect for reason, respect for personality, and belief in free moral choice of one's social allegiances—the notion of the part to be played [a Catholic, rather than a French trait, this] by the voluntary society. We need not indeed look so far afield as France. The work of Irish thinkers may serve to provide a buckle—as Burke in some measure once did—between Anglo-Saxon and Catholic thought.

No one can read Umanuno's great book on *The Tragic Sense* without perceiving the profound difference between even the very quixotism of the Anglo-Saxon, adventuring with a Raleigh or dreaming with a Shelley but never without thought about something to be done in this world, and the quixotism of Spain, with its belief that only the vision beyond accomplishment is the vision splendid and with its profound contempt for the useful and for accommodation. Here pain and tragedy are the boasts of the dignity of the human spirit. Nowhere does the 'moralism' of the Anglo-Saxon spirit as something non-mystic, utilitarian and almost secular stand out more sharply than in contrast with the Spanish spirit. This last can only be reined in from passionate excesses, that seem to the

Anglo-Saxon to verge on the morbid, by the rational spirit of Catholicism, a spirit Latin and Roman, forebear of our own and with which it is possible to make common terms in the present battle of civilization. Madariaga, however, and Ortega y Gasset alike point the Spanish people to the recovery of the mood of Humanism, howbeit a disciplined Humanism.

It is Ortega y Gasset who writes, in his *Revolt of the Masses* (1930):

"I can now sum up the thesis of this essay. The world today is suffering from a grave demoralization which, among other symptoms, manifests itself by an extraordinary rebellion of the masses, and has its origin in the demoralization of Europe. . . .

"Only the determination to construct a great nation from the group of peoples of the Continent would give new life to the pulses of Europe. . . . To my mind the building up of Europe into a great national State is the one enterprise that could counterbalance a victory of the 'five years' plan.' . . . Communism is an extravagant moral code, but it is nothing less than a moral code. Does it not seem more worthy and more fruitful to oppose to that Slavonic code a new European code, the inspiration towards a new program of life."

It is only in terms of Humanism that common ground can be found between the Anglo-Saxon Tradition and that European tradition that talks the same language of ideas from Galicia and Brittany to Poland and Slovenia, if not further east into the once Byzantine lands of the old Eastern Roman Empire. Here can be found a common spiritual nerve in any united front of Occidental civilization. All else is mere shuffling alliances and unstable power-politics.[1]

Renan's anatomy of nationalism is recalled to us by Ortega. In that demonstration Renan points out two components: a

[1] I use this word, on which I have commented elsewhere (*Story of the Political Philosophers,* chap. 22), to indicate that the politics of co-operation, as distinct from that of domination, rests on a communal understanding due to sharing of common values in ideas and habits.

plan of common life with an enterprise in common; and the adhesion of men to that common enterprise. If we do not share the outlook that makes the enterprise possible that "will light up the continental horizon as with a new and flaming constellation," how shall we resist those who have these new Islamic faiths? Especially how will young men resist, by repeating dead conservative pieties about liberty, democracy and individualism, these crusading religions of action and the sword? "If Europe persists in the ignoble vegetative existence of these last years, its muscles flabby from want of exercise, without any plan of a new life, how will it be able to resist. . . . It is simply a misunderstanding of the European to expect that he can hear unmoved that call to a new *action* when he has no standard of a cause as great to unfurl in opposition." So wrote Ortega y Gasset before the fascisization of Spain. Under the control of an unimaginative, upper-class conservatism comfortably determined to see no change, and of a cowardly, bourgeois middle class frightened to see any visions, no view on life will appear vivid enough to surpass that which stirs to action Marxian and National Socialist. And the disunited Western Powers, so led, will perish, and deserve to perish, as the Carthaginians did of old. If that is to be avoided, there must be renewal of control and an expulsion from their high seats of the dead men, and of the busy little men who run rapidly in circles round them; expulsion of the repeaters of slogans, half-disbelieved by the men who incant them; and expulsion of those who chew platitudes.

§ iii

The Challenge from the Totalitarian Ideologies

The Anglo-Saxon Tradition is challenged, and it is challenged not only by accidental collocations of powers, but by what Edmund Burke called "armed doctrines." The Anglo-Saxon typically is a man who does not recognize an idea until it is thirty years old, and, if he does, he endeavours to escape hastily from it. He will, however, in this crisis of history, not be permitted to do this. The armed doctrines claim, each of them, to possess a theory, a dogmatic theory, and assert that their theory is dogmatically right. It is not enough, then, to plead "let sleeping dogs lie." The dogs are awake and barking—they lie in quite another sense. It is necessary that one's own beliefs should vindicate themselves and, from apologetic defence, that we should at long last take the offensive.

Over against the sweep of Germain claims we must state what it is for which we stand. As to Russia, although Germany may make Russia into our ally, this must be said: *either* the U.S.S.R. is no longer an active Marxian Communist Power, in which case the difference of our views may inoffensively be stated, *or,* with its talk of an "imperialist war" from which its own war aims are detached, the U.S.S.R. is still an active Communist Power, in which case it is important that our different view *should* be stated.

That Marxism is a doctrine—and a doctrine that once, at least, claimed the initiative as theory of world events—is self-confessed and in no dispute. No platitude is more idle or superficial than that Fascism is not also a doctrine. The excuse given is that the doctrine follows the action. An ignorance of Fichte and Nietzsche and Wagner, not to speak of such local prophets as Stefan Georg and Sorel, and the preparatory influence of Marxism on such a professional Marxist as Mussolini, is assumed by those who propagand this happy, lazy view. It is childish to suppose that Machiavellianism, because a practice of power as its own justification, is not also a theory of power as of life. Machiavelli was no such fool.

This theme is backed up by the assertion that Fascism can

have no theory—I disregard here Marxists who would *like* it to have no theory, because unallowed for in their philosophy —because its theory is chiefly negation. Was not Marxism also chiefly negation; and the Christianity of the creeds, with their development by negation of heresy?

Fascism is a theory that denies the all-sufficiency of the *economic* thesis about the founts of power and substitutes a thesis of personal power, tinged if one will by Bergsonism, decorated with a cult of Woden and a complete demonology, but as old as the ancient opponents of Plato and their theories. Their theories will be found discussed by Plato and the evolution of their actions described by Aristotle. It is not at all new or even surprising. But it *is* a theory and one of the most attractive. It is also one of the oldest. "Power is its own justification. It *is* virtue and vitality. Take power as a nation (for the Folk is a Social Organism)—or take it as a leader. Transvalue values. Break the Natural Law and replace it by Will. And ye shall be as gods. Ye shall not surely die."

This is no place to engage in a protracted critique either of National Socialism or of Marxism. It is enough to make the radical nature of the challenge plain. That the challenges issued by the Red and the Black forces have a certain similarity is perhaps not remarkable. I have already alluded to the chance, the five per cent. chance, of an understanding between Germany and Russia, not finally removed by any temporary arrangement but dictated by interest and by the Russian certainty of, and chance of advantage from, German defeat and revolution.[1] More certain is it that both philosophies stem

[1] Cf. p. 29. In certain diplomatic quarters (not friendly to Germany), the percentage of chance is placed higher than in the text. I attach no especial importance to Dr. Peter Drucker's statement, in *The End of Economic Man* (1939), that "only a war within the very near future could prevent . . . the alliance between Germany and Russia." There is, however, weight in French opinion that, if Russia had not been promised a military alliance

from a common origin in German Hegelian philosophy, in the Fascist case modified by Fichte, Nietzsche and Sorel, in the Marxist case by Spinoza, Feuerbach and Marx himself.

"To leave an error unrefuted," according to Hyndman, was, for Marx, "to encourage intellectual immorality." In this Marx had the advantage of knowing what was the truth. "Hegel's dialectic is the basis of all dialectic, but only after it has been stripped of its mystical form, and it is precisely this which distinguishes my method." The contempt of Lenin for the would-be Communist who despised theory appears in passage after passage. It is not only necessary to study theory. It is necessary to conclude with the right theory.

"You must, and you certainly will, understand that once a member of the party is convinced of the absolute incorrectness and harm of a certain preachment, he is in duty bound to take a stand against it." (*Letter to Gorki.*)

"Non-partisanship in philosophy is only a contemptible cloak of servility to idealism and fideism." (*Materialism and Empirio-Criticism.*)

The warning of Stalin is definite: "The tendency of the practical people to turn up their noses at theory runs contrary to the whole spirit of Leninism and involves serious damage in its practice." In this connection a recent letter in the *New*

---

and direct defence (instead of mere defence of Poland) by the Western Powers, it would have been arranged with Germany to stand aloof during war, and wait, in this fashion, for the West to exhaust itself. Those who fight along with Russia at least have this advantage, as I had the opportunity four years ago of saying to M. Litvinov, of having revolution on their side. *What kind* of revolution, however, in the event (which it must be our object to prevent) of war, is less clear; whether Communism followed by Fascism in the West; or Communism in Middle Europe; or Cromwellian. If the last, it will depend upon Anglo-Saxon will. It will also depend upon the clarity of Anglo-Saxon objectives in freedom, equality and compulsory peace, order for all, security for the common man, opportunity for initiative. *Et pactum servare.*

Statesman (June 19th, 1937) from a Marxist recently returned from Moscow, Mr. Pat Sloan, has interest:

"Let me deal with some of the points in Mr. Sewell's letter.

"First, freedom of the press, through the abolition of the dependence of the press upon property, was achieved in the Soviet Republic in 1917–1918 and the new Constitution alters nothing in this respect.

"Secondly, the Soviet authorities accept the scientific conception of Nature and Human Society formulated by Marx, Engels and Lenin, and called Dialectical Materialism. According to this conception the 'economics of Communism' and 'metaphysics of Marxism' cannot be isolated as suggested by Mr. Sewell.

"A professor who *advocates* an antiquated pre-scientific philosophy as against a scientific one may be as powerful a reactionary force as a soldier in an army of intervention. How many minds in Britain to-day are kept from ever establishing contact with Marxism by the simple process of loading them to capacity with the works of Plato and other philosophers? These works play, not a neutral, but an anti-Marxist role in such circumstances and Marxists recognize this fact. Philosophy is not, as Mr. Sewell seems to think, neutral ground.

"Thirdly, when the Soviet authorities do not encourage those professors who advocate pre-scientific ideologies, and in fact replace them by real scientists, they are exercising no more of an 'inquisition' than the British University that employs a scientist, and not an astrologer, as professor of astronomy. Or does Mr. Sewell advocate the employment of some astrologers for this job, in the interests of Real Freedom?"

This attitude is not peculiar to Marxism. Italian Fascism has no less definitely staked its claim to be regarded as a systematic doctrine. Apart from popular slogans such as that *Mussolini ha sempre ragione* ("Mussolini is always right"), we have the considered statement of the *Dottrina Fascista*:

"Fascism is now a completely individual thing, not only as a regime, but as a doctrine. And this means that today Fascism, exercising its own critical sense upon itself and upon others, has found its own distinct and peculiar point of view."

That point of view is not one that involves the toleration of other points of view. The attitude of German National Socialism was expressed, as long ago as 1931, by the then Reichstatthalter of Thuringia: "In future in Thuringia there must be one political faith only. . . . The National Socialists claim the right to be intolerant in view of the necessity for uniform thinking and acting in the nation as a whole." The same theme has since been more authoritatively stated by Dr. Goebbels, in April 1934, and not modified since:

"National Socialism cannot be judged right in this and wrong in that respect. As we, the National Socialists, are convinced that we are right, we cannot tolerate any other in our neighbourhood who claims also to be right. We deny the right to those who have no share in the responsibility and the burden of the work. . . . There is no freedom of the individual; there is only freedom of peoples, nations and races, for these are the only material and historical realities through which the life of the individual exists."

This theme is, of course, not peculiar to Fascism. Mr. John Strachey, the Marxist, in his book *What Are We To Do?* sketches the character of his New Model Parties in various lands, especially Britain and the United States, that are to realize the Marxist program:

"They do not tolerate within their ranks the coexistence of more than one ideology. . . . In this refusal to tolerate the coexistence of incompatible opinions, the new model parties are simply asserting the claim that Socialism [Marxism] is scientific."

Stalin's remarks are relevant here: "The party, the Communist Party, is the basic instrument of the dictatorship of the proletariat . . . the leadership of one party, which does not share and cannot share this leadership with other parties, constitutes the fundamental condition without which a more or less lasting and developed dictatorship of the proletariat is inconceivable."

This policy, radically incompatible with Bentham's definition of democracy and good government, when taken in its total framework,[1] and indeed incompatible with the Anglo-Saxon notes of tolerance, experiment, liberty and even respect for individual personality and moral choice, at once theoretically issues in and practically follows from the doctrines of the Revolutionary Vanguard common to Fascism and Marx-Leninism. Mr. Strachey continues:

"The distinguishing characteristics of political parties built upon the new model are as follows. First, they possess the ideology which we have called scientific socialism (p. 251). . . . The first socialists who appear in capitalist society are very rarely wage-workers at all; they are nearly, although not quite always, of the middle class."

This attitude is confirmed by Lenin himself. "The history of all countries bears witness to the fact that the working-class by its own powers alone cannot achieve more than the trade union consciousness. . . . The working-class is unable to develop a [Marxist] social consciousness of its own. It can be impregnated with it only from the outside."

There is a need for a Revolutionary Vanguard. Lenin continues: "A party is the vanguard of a class, and its duty is to lead the masses, *not* to reflect the average state of mind of the masses." "Revolution is the most authoritarian thing in the world." "Comrade Tanner and Comrade Ramsay tell us that the majority of the British Communists do not agree to unite; but must we always agree with the majority?"

"To suppose that in any serious revolution the issue is decided by the simpler relation between majority and minority is the acme

[1] Cf. p. 224.

of stupidity. . . . Freedom of the press and assembly under bourgeois democracy is freedom to conspire against the toilers, freedom for the capitalists to corrupt and buy up the press [also the Hitlerite charge]. I have explained this in the press [*sic*] so often that I find it a bore to repeat it. It is not verbal recognition that is needed, but a complete rupture in deeds with the policy of reformism, with prejudices about bourgeois freedom and bourgeois democracy, the genuine pursuit of the policy of revolutionary class struggle. . . . Today, however, this same revolution in the interests of Socialism [Marxism] demands the absolute subordination of the masses to the single will of 'the leaders' of labour."

Signor Mussolini has reached comparable conclusions about the need for and nature of revolution.

"I understood now [1909] that the Gordian Knot of Italian political life would only be undone by an act of violence. . . . Liberty only flourished for half a century. It was born in 1830 in reaction against the Holy Alliance. It is the logical, and indeed historical, forerunner of anarchy. Today the Liberal faith must shut the doors of its deserted temples, for the peoples of the world realize that its worship—agnostic in the fields of economics and indifferent in the field of politics and morals—will lead, as it has already led, to certain ruin. Whoever says Liberalism implies individualism, and whoever says Fascism implies the State . . ."

This revolutionary will must not only affect religion, whether in the direction of atheism in Russia or neo-paganism in Germany. It must also determine morality. "Is there such a thing as Communist morality?" writes Lenin. "Of course there is. . . . We say that our morality is *wholly subordinated* to the interests of the class struggle of the proletariat. We deduce our morality from the facts and needs of the class struggle of the proletariat." In this connection, the injunction of Herr Hitler, in *Mein Kampf,* will be recalled:

"not to seek out objective truths so far as it may be favourable to others, but uninterruptedly to serve one's own truth."

The consequences of this subordination of the moral values of human personality to the immediate needs of particular societies are a spiritual totalitarianism and, indubitably, great practical efficiency—"forty thousand men marching like clockwork as one," as Signor Mussolini has said. *Pravda*, in welcoming in its editorial, the XVIIIth Russian Communist Party Congress, wrote:

"Our party comes to the congress united, *monolithic* and mighty as never before. It is strong in the iron unity of its ranks and in its supreme devotion to the cause of communism and the solidarity of the party ranks around the Stalinist control committee and around Comrade Stalin."

One recalls a declaration of a few years back of Mussolini:

"Fascism is *monolithic*. . . . All the opposition newspapers have been suppressed, all the anti-Fascist parties have been dissolved. The special police already gives signal service. The political bureaux of secret investigation have been created. The Special Tribunal has been created; it functions in a remarkable fashion."

The end and purpose of this ruthless cult of efficiency has been announced, in Italy and Germany, as being the national advancement of their people. Mussolini has described Italy as an authoritatively organized democracy. In Germany the goal used to be described as that of the overthrow of the ruling class, hereditary wealth and 'finance capital.' It was—so said and says German official propaganda—only the steel-master and bourgeois armaments manufacturers, deluding the workers who have nothing to gain, who wanted war. Objectively, the present German system itself has been described as State Capitalism, or again (much less convincingly) as 'armament-finance capitalism.' In Russia the goal is the advancement of the condition of the workers, the classless society and the withering away of the State. There is a distant vision of Freedom on the horizon—as also in Hitler's phrase in *Mein Kampf:* "Human rights are above State rights." Trotsky, however, described how "just as a lamp, before going out, shoots up in a brilliant flame, so the State, before disappearing, assumes the form of dictatorship of the proletariat, i.e. the most ruthless form of State, which embraces the life of the citizens authoritatively in every form. . . ." Moreover, during this interim period that has now lasted twenty years, it is a mistake to suppose that the goal of classlessness involves equality, any more than the disappearance of the State involves the early end of the Dictatorship. Stalin writes:

"Equalitarianism has nothing in common with Marxist Socialism. Only people who have no knowledge of Marxism can think in such a primitive way, as if the Russian Bolsheviks wanted to gather up all wealth together and then divide it up equally. This is the conception of the people who have nothing in common with Marxism. Such is the conception of Communism held by people of the type of the primitive 'communists' of the time of Cromwell and the French Revolution. But Marxism and the Russian Bolsheviks have nothing in common with such equalitarian 'Communists.' [Cf. G. B. Shaw] . . .

"Who is right, Marx and Lenin, or our equalitarians? We may take it that Marx and Lenin are right. But if so, it follows that whoever draws up wage scales on the 'principle' of equality, and ignores the difference between skilled and unskilled labour, is at loggerheads with Marxism and Leninism."

In a work in his period of Bolshevik collaboration Trotsky adds:

"Democratization does not at all consist—as every Marxist learns in his A B C—in abolishing the meaning of skilled forces, the meaning of persons possessing special knowledge, and in replacing them everywhere and anywhere by elective boards. . . . The very principle of compulsory labor service is for the Communist quite unquestionable. 'He who works not, neither shall he eat.' . . . It is necessary once for all to make clear to ourselves that the principle itself of compulsory labor service has just so radically and permanently replaced the principle of free hiring as the socialization of the means of production has replaced capitalist property. . . . If organized economic life is unthinkable without compulsory labor service, the latter is not to be realized without the abolition of the fiction of the freedom of labor, and without the substitution for it of the obligatory principle, which is supplemented by real compulsion."

The realization of ideals has to be relegated to the period after an 'interim' which shews every prospect of being prolonged. From Revolution to achieve Ideals emerges Dictatorship to achieve Revolution; and from Dictatorship emerges the need to take steps to maintain, if need be by force, the forcible Régime. Propaganda supplements force. A leader as symbol of the union of the masses is required, and the inculcation of respect for his directive will. Thus General Goering writes:

"We National Socialists believe that, in political affairs, Adolf Hitler is infallible, just as the Roman Catholic believes that, in religious matters, the Pope is infallible. . . . His will is my law."

Herr Kerrl, of the Ecclesiastical Administration, transcends this:

"As Christ in his twelve disciples raised a stock fortified unto martyrdom, whose belief shattered the great Roman Empire, even so in Germany today we are experiencing the same thing. . . . Adolf Hitler is the true Holy Ghost."

With this can be set the poem published in *Pravda* (August 28th, 1936)—and poems, as Mr. Duff Cooper says about Germany, may be more expressive of the popular mood than mere official utterances:

"O great Stalin, O leader of the peoples,
Thou who broughtest man to birth,
Thou who fructifiest the earth,
Thou who restorest the centuries,
Thou who makest bloom the spring,
Thou who makest vibrate the musical chords.

. . . . .

Thou, splendor of my spring, O Thou,
Sun reflected by millions of hearts."

Germany and Russia are both the lands of great peoples. Any man of good-will must desire to maintain the peace of the world with the aid of both or either of them. In a division of the world into four massive *blocs,* Russia and Germany will dominate two. Spiritually, however, there can be nothing in common between the temper of the Anglo-Saxon Tradition and way of life and the mood of those philosophies. There is indeed explicit antagonism, and the central faith of that Anglo-Saxon Tradition is regarded with contempt by the priests of totalitarian ideologies. Following on Spinoza's criticism of Francis Bacon, and on Hegel, with his criticism, in his *Logic,* of Empiricism, are Marx and Engels, and Lenin. Of the former two, Plekhanov said: "The materialism of Marx and Engels is a kind of Spinozism." Of Lenin it is important indeed to remember that he was not only the man of action but the writer with twenty volumes to his credit, and not only a writer but a philosopher whose 380-page book, *Materialism and Empirio-Criticism,* is directed, as its name implies, as an attack upon the Empiric Tradition in philosophy, upon Mach the philosopher who influenced William James, and especially upon Hume, the prince of British philosophers. It shews how the current runs. There is "an inevitable philosophical alternative (materialism or idealism)." "Only utter ignorance of the nature of philosophic materialism generally and of the nature of Marx' and Engels' dialectical method can lead one to speak of a 'union' of empirio-criticism and Marxism . . . behind the epistemological scholasticism of empirio-criticism [Lenin's choice of words, not mine—*he* thought it all important], it is impossible not to see the struggle of parties in philosophy, a struggle which in the last analysis reflects the tendencies and ideology of the antagonistic classes in modern society." What Lenin omitted to note was the decisive rôle that can be played by the middle, technical and skilled classes in the West.

The antagonism is only less grave as a matter of working accommodation in practical matters. It is indeed true, and should be noted, that Herr Hitler, in *Mein Kampf,* has expressed his desire for the friendship of Britain and Italy, but he there made no such statement about France. Subsequently, indeed, he has declared that he regards the present French frontiers as permanent; but we do not yet know that we are entitled to regard his reference in *Mein Kampf* as an allusion merely to the historic diplomacy, since Richelieu, of France, as dominant in Europe, and not to her integrity as a Power. His persistent conduct can certainly *not* be said to have encouraged confidence. Mussolini has declared that he "absolutely disbelieves in perpetual peace," although he has qualified this by a demand for a "prolonged peace for the sake of European civilization" in the present. There is an explicable indisposition in the West to forget these things.

Similarly, first Marx and then Lenin singled out Anglo-Saxony as the very citadel of the enemy—"the British Government is the purest form of the Executive Committee of the Bourgeoisie" (Lenin); "Development is slow because the British bourgeoisie is in a position to create better conditions for the aristocracy of labour and by that to retard the progress of the revolution" (Lenin); "England cannot be treated simply as one country among a number of other countries. . . . She must be treated as the metropolis of capitalism" (Marx); and the social reformists should be pushed "once for all into the cesspool of the lackeys of the bourgeoisie" (Lenin). The success of the Marxian revolution depends upon its success in Anglo-Saxon lands, and, as Lenin wrote, this in turn depends upon the army and upon Britain being involved in war. Assuredly the Soviet Union cannot be expected to give quarter to our tradition, our institutions or our power as a people if the occasion ever arises when we have to supplicate her aid and not, in the Ukraine, she have to supplicate ours. Marxism, it is true (and should also be noted), is concerned to attack, not Britain or America as such, but the capitalist *system*. Merely it alleges that Anglo-Saxon workers have occupied a privileged and inequitable advantage, in comparison with the world proletariat, owing to the Anglo-Saxon monopoly position. The U.S.S.R. cannot, however, be expected to be especially sensitive to the position of Anglo-Saxon workers, thanks to their historic position, e.g. their fear of famine in highly industrialized lands in the event of revolution, since the Russian workers perforce themselves went through appalling famine conditions. There is disillusion for those who suppose that the U.S.S.R. will ever sacrifice one prop of the régime from consideration for the feelings of 'the Anglo-Saxon aristocracy of labour.' The maintenance of free Democracy, as understood here, it is empty illusion to regard as her task or as other than laughable to any orthodox Marxist. On the other hand, as Ortega y Gasset says: "The European does not see in (Marxist) organization an increase in human happiness."

Can Anglo-Saxon Democracy stand firm in such a world and under such challenges? In the old Hellenic division between societies organized for peace and societies organized for war, the Totalitarian Powers are societies perfectly organized for war—or perfectly with certain, probably fatal, reservations.

It is not for me to say that, granted great statesmanship, they may not will peace. It is not for me to say that, granted skill, they may not be brought to will co-operation, however deep the spiritual cleavage. Merely I submit that this will depend upon the strength, the total strength, the moral strength, of the Western Powers. The instant obligation is to recognize and to draw from the sources of that moral strength. The marching battalions will march in vain if the mind behind them is confused and they do not march with the inspiration of some ideal, the old Cromwellian ideal.

§ iv

Where We Stand

Can the Anglo-Saxon Tradition stand under the challenge? *Can Humanism stand?* It may be, as Señor Fernando de los Rios suggests to me, that the tragedy of modern European culture was the divorce between Reason and Spirit at the Renaissance. I have commented on how that wound may be healed. But for anyone to identify Humanism as a whole with the intellectualism of, for example, Voltaire or with what Blake called "poor spiritual knowledge . . . not worth a button," is to misunderstand the nature of Humanism. It cannot be said that the abandonment of Humanism for narrowly nationalist visions and "blood thinking" has conduced to a better world.

Germany here has her excuse. Devoted to cosmopolitan ideals and the cult of Hellenism in the days of Goethe and Schiller, she found herself swindled. In the days of the French Revolution the French troops entered the Rhineland in the name of the Emancipation of Man, and remained there in the interests of France. That bitterness, springing from betrayal, has endured and will endure until we reach a United States of

Europe, or a new Roman Empire. Reference has already been made to Herr Sieburg's book, *Germany, my Country,* with its story of reaction against a 'civilization' that has spelled French dominance. Similarly, not only Nietzsche, but the spiritual father of the National Socialist movement, Moeller van den Bruck, began as a "good European." He ended as an assertive "Germanizer." In a brilliant book, *The Tyranny of Greece over Germany,* Miss E. M. Butler traces the relapse in Germany from Goethe to Stefan Georg, the occultist poet who did so much, along with Wagner, to inspire Naziism and to put in circulation the Führer-notion. For myself I prefer Goethe to Stefan Georg—and so would Germany, did it not suffer from a morbid sense of having been bilked of its due. There is a distinctive German Gothic mood, and indeed a distinctive German contribution to civilization—but that mood, let us hope, is not the *furor teutonicus.* The last is no mood which will create a new world-civilization. And to do this is our present moral imperative.

The charge against Humanism is that, in respecting personality, it encourages individualism. I shall not quarrel when Adolf Hitler says:

"It should not be forgotten, as a general rule, that *it is not the highest aim of man's existence to maintain a State government,* but to conserve its national character. Human rights are above state rights."

But 'humanity' must here mean the human race. There may be better individuals and worse, better nations and worse. But no one people is so much better that, in a wide aloofness from the rest, it is entitled to arrogate to itself that moral allegiance which belongs to humanity. To have asserted that is the triumph of Humanism. Humanism is not humanitarianism, but it is, since the days when it emerges from Catholic Christianity, supra-nationalism.

Is it, then, that *the note of Experiment* is faulty? Are there not great social experiments? Must (it may be said) experiment always be individual? What of the German autostrades or of the Italian draining of the Pontine marshes? What of the great Russian experiment? Has not Totalitarianism done more than Democracy?

Russia, Germany, Italy are entitled to boast of their experiments. But we also have our way of life. If the argument be that experiments are social as well as individual, then we also, we have our own social experiment. And, as the Totalitarian Powers do not tolerate interference, so we too cannot tolerate interference with our experiment by those who share the totalitarian ideologies. We will carry through our own experiment.

Is the fault with the notes of Liberty and Tolerance? How far are these other names for laxity, indiscipline, and moral indifference?

Is the fault with Democracy itself! Mr. Strachey asks Mr. Attlee in *What Are We To Do?* just when 'respect for minority rights' becomes tolerance of obstructionism. How far is the Anglo-Saxon concept of Democracy, with its discussion, balances and oppositions, another name for obstructionism and not getting things done? So with the Marxist. How far is the French concept of Democracy, with its Rousseauite reverence for the majority, merely a cheap deference to the mass pleasure of the moment? Is not Democracy the triumph of the average, the stupid, the incompetent? What moral value has that? So asks the Fascist. Both are men of action.

It was not for nothing that, having reviewed the connected notes of our Tradition, from Humanism and Experiment to Social Accommodation and Democracy, we passed on to a chapter on the characteristic Anglo-Saxon Moralism, and gave warning that probably our Liberty and Tolerance could never survive without this Moralism. Here, then, is our discipline, a self-discipline, a spontaneous discipline, in the grain and habits of the folk. Do, moreover, the Dictatorships make no appeal to the masses for popularity? Do they not do it every day? And is not our Moralism as dignified, as ethically worth-while, as their Propaganda? Let them answer and reply whether they would not willingly exchange the one for the other if they could. To keep, in crisis, Dignity and Self-Respect is no cheap achievement.

What then? Is there no case to answer? There is. What is it? Briefly that we—that the ideas that ruled Europe and the world for two centuries, that derive from a religious outlook that ruled the world for the greater part of two millennia— have lost the initiative; and have to resume it. How?

It would be futile to sketch some mere dead academic system, to which everyone assented as a piety with his lips, and no one was prepared to live by in his life. Here we have the record of our tradition. Even as record—record of what men, our forbears, have done and suffered for—it is instinct with emotion. It is our task to tear down the walls of dead time and mere erudite record, and to make those men live, to transmit what they felt to how we feel. The dead, I have said, are far better allies, because far greater heroes to lead us into the future, than many, far too many, of those who, officially speaking, are said to live. The dead live. The living are dead and due to be thrust aside.

The task is to translate our 'notes' into the sound of emotion and power. And here one warning and two 'pointers.'

Steadily throughout the Anglo-Saxon Tradition, from Hooker to today, there has been reiterated *the Theme of Equality*. It has not been stressed or made into a grand abstraction as in the French Tradition. The cautious Anglo-Saxon, as we have shewn, whether it be Locke or Jefferson or Mill, has hedged it about with reservations. He did not mean by it equality of talent. Or of capacity for education. Or of dignity. Or a strict economic equality or equality in power. He had a notion of diversities of gifts and a functional social scheme—if classless, still functional. What then did he mean? Here, in the key passages, Locke, whom Jefferson follows, in the Declaration of Independence, refers us back to Hooker. And what did Hooker say (himself echoing the earlier Christian tradition)? Locke tells us that Hooker makes equality "the foundation of that obligation to mutual love among men on which he builds the duties they owe one another." For Hooker they are "of one and the same nature"—and to just this extent that if you prick any one of them he bleeds; that men have, by and large, like pains if not like pleasures; that they are alike human, entitled to sympathy; that there is a basis of duties, values, morals; that these duties transcend races and classes; that the prime moral fact is not that of race or class but of community, if, in evolution, just of "the little platoon," nevertheless, ultimately and over-ridingly, community of humanity itself. The man who repudiates community is evil. That is the gospel of equality.

That gospel can be translated into practice. One must begin somewhere, although one dare not also end there. One does not stay inquiring, "Who then is my neighbour?" but one begins with the neighbour whom in fact one sees. And for those who decline to begin instantly and, by intention and practice, to break down the boundaries of class and race, within two decades the Revolution is in store and blood and slaughter. Let, then, these see to it that they practise their Christianity in time instead of discoursing about it. In Marx's words: "The philosophers have only interpreted the world in various ways; the point, however, is to change it." Any marching movement that is to have power these days must bear on its banners the words: *The End of Classes: The End of Nations.* (No: not 'the end of functions' or 'the end of cultures.') The Marxists have announced these things for their world-federation of Soviets. The National Socialists have announced it with their dream of a restored Roman Reich, and of Commonwealth before Private Wealth. The issue is Caesarism or Federalism; 'Military Communism' or Co-operative Functionalism. But, anyhow, the actual Classless Society and the Union of the World. Diversity of pay by social service alone: the test of need to be the requirements of efficiency. This, then, is the meaning of Equality. One Community. No Faction. No Privilege. No Lumber. No Stucco.

Shall we not *have to do yet more if Democracy is to work?* Ortega y Gasset, again, points out that the weakness of Democracy, however excellent otherwise, is to be measured by the weakness of its electoral system. This has also been the burden of Sir Norman Angell's complaint. Can the system whereby medical doctors are sent to Congress or Parliament because they are adored for the way they cure children's ailments, and the system whereby persons far less qualified than these doctors to cope with a nation's problems are sent to be our legislators because of a popularity far less reputable—is this a system satisfactory, efficient and beyond improvement?

Is—it may indeed be replied—the system of dictatorship better—even in its great days of the Roman Empire when, the principle of legitimate authority being removed, empurpled emperors succeeded each to his assassinated predecessor? Even these medical men and popular journalists, idle young men of more wealth than brains, and retired local trade union officials —they may not be geniuses, but then, also, they will never be Mussolinis or Hitlers, or Lenins for that matter. They are selected by their fellows for likeability, common-sense and judgement. What better qualities would one have?

Only this—that if Liberty is to survive, the Expert side of Government must also be recognized; and the training of the civil servant, certainly as government passes over into business, is far too narrow to enable him to shoulder all this burden. I am not thinking here of scientists and technicians, with their departmental preoccupations—although closer co-ordination here also is required if the best is to be got out of the material available for government. I refer rather to needs for improvements in Congressional and Parliamentary procedure, so that technical measures of wide range do not get thrust upon one side for the sake of more obviously popular and politic bills of momentary appeal. That may mean measures of devolution and of professional or corporative organization. Certainly it requires courage and foresight at the helm, and the knowledge of when to override bureaucratic tradition in the interests of imaginative vision and of instant efficiency in the great crisis where Democracy is at its worst—war.

The chief asset of Democracy, as against Totalitarianism, as a political system contributing to human civilization, is that it provides a mental climate favourable not only to the personal expansion of Smith and Jones but to the intellectual play and decisive experiments of genius. If, when these experiments are made, Democracy is too dumb to tell how to use the fruits of their work, then Democracy's chief asset is wasted and Democracy itself will go into the discard in exchange for the organized war-system of the ant-heap. It is the 'variants' that matter.

If the Democracy of discussion, adjustment and multiplicity of Parties cannot, besides talking of equality, practise it to the extent of providing—not only no unemployment, as in Germany—but a modicum of security for the worker, the workers in fact will wash their hands of what will then be rightly stigmatized as 'bourgeois' Democracy and will prefer Marxian Communism. And they will be right in doing so, with the assistance of our Russian allies. They will do this unless our Democracy knows how to turn heads and pens to work, and technical skill (in what is, after all, a technical issue), to work out with authority better plans so that fear, the hall-mark of a barbarian condition, is removed from the daily life of the common man.

There are many, however, to whom the appeal of Community and Equality, as consequences of membership within the Community, will seem weak and pious. Nothing less than the storms renewed of the French Revolution will convince their slowness that when men demand equality, against inequalities that have become glaring and functionally impossible, they also mean it; and that those of the old order that will not leave the stage will be hustled off it.

Certainly that will be the case—and perhaps no harm—in Britain, if that country has to find its ally and rescuer in the Soviets; as distinct from Anglo-Saxon union. The moves of politics on the set board of history allow few alternative choices to slow-minded players.

There are others to whom the fact that the other man is "also human"—equally human as himself, even if of unequal gifts or opportunities—has sufficient moral appeal for no further argument to be needed. He does not require to have the argument reinforced by the consideration that, a grain less of iodine in his thyroid gland and he himself would be an imbecile. He does not need to be intimidated by class-war threats. The curse of bourgeois civilization, however, let us repeat, is lack of Courage and lack of Imagination. Mankind has to be forced and kicked by war and revolution, not so much because men are evil as because they are stupid and will not move unless made uncomfortable. The great political vice is this stupidity. And the requisite in community life is a vivid and sympathetic imagination for how the other man feels.

A more powerful consideration may, then, have to be brought in to reinforce the appeal to view our Democracy as a movement towards Equality. The most powerful appeal to man is the appeal of Power itself. Upon that all politics turns. What is this Personal Power?

Power is of two kinds—as Engels said; but the Church Fathers said it before him. There is Power over Men—what William Morris called Mastership as over against Fellowship —and Power over Things. Dominion over Men is in its essence evil; and Dominion over Things is in its essence good. The circumstances may change, but fundamentally this remains true.

The error of the Liberals was to believe that an autocrat, a dictator, an emperor, because he held dominion over men so that he could crush their interests, must therefore be regarded as an enemy by them. It is indeed eternally true, and needs to be repeated, that if we trade in our heritage of political liberty and democratic control in return for the pottage of Marxist economic security, we are without defence when the commissars of the new one-party, Totalitarian State, who got into power by promising this bread and circuses, in defence of their own group-power choose later to deprive us, not only of political liberty but of economic security also. So did also the Roman dictators. Nevertheless, men like a tyrant—which the Liberals never allowed for, with their neat theories of utility. Little men, living frustrated lives, always fearing, and fearing ever more to face the facts, have to *live* by and through some other, some great and glorious hero, either in escape-dreamland or, best of all, when myth comes to life in Führer or Duce or Great Red Voyd and Comrade. This is the living appeal of dictatorship. It gives heroic power vicariously by self-illusion and identification.

There is another power—the power over things. If our theme has been right, there is a peculiar association between power over the natural world and scientific invention; between scientific invention and the mental climate of freedom, adventure and initiative. Explorers may go to order over the Arctic ice, but the explorations of the mind do not succeed to a formula. The power over things, springing from technology and invention, is the guarantee of human progress alike in spirit and in material goods. Technology and its requirements confront Dominion and its subjects. The Anglo-Saxon civilization is technological and practical. Who collaborates with it collaborates with a beneficent, not an evil, power. And the duty of each of its sons is to build it higher yet, by knowledge, power to control, and joy in that power.

He who has power to control things, scientist, inventor, technician, has power—the civilization that consistently harbours and honours these men has power—if challenged, also to control men; if challenged, to surpass its opponents in peace and crush them in war. Only for one thing need we envy the Totalitarian States, their inventors. . . . But for how long will these States breed, not cannon-fodder, but inventors?

Of old, Egypt and Athens stood as symbols of two civilizations. Egypt lasted until the power of Rome swindled and conquered the power of Egypt. Athens lasted in Human Civilization itself. Egypt, with its god-kings and its slave-subjects, found its symbol and immortality in great tombs built by the sweat and death of slaves. Its history is that of gold-laden dead kings. Athens had its glory in youth, the springtime of mind, the triumphs of the spirit. Its temper directly, and indirectly through the Renaissance, stimulated discovery and invention. This challenge is with us today. Which are we with? Which tradition is the more glorious? Which is the heir of Humanism and civilization?

It is contemptible to despise Sparta or to ridicule Egypt—idiotic to patronize the self-sacrifice of Leninist Russia or the 'Battalions of Death' of the young men of Nietzschean modern Germany. Let us do as well, as firmly, as proudly, and more richly.

Let us summons ourselves again to confront the magnitude of the moment. And let us again recall the words of the great Puritan of three centuries ago:

"Behold now this vast city: a city of refuge, the mansion house of liberty, encompassed and surrounded with his protection; the shop of war hath not more anvils and hammers working to hammer out the plates and instruments of armed justice in defence of beleaguered Truth than there are pens and heads there . . . methinks I see in my mind a noble and puissant nation rousing himself like a strong man after sleep."

The issue must not be between discipline and wealth. It will be between the discipline of a determined liberty and the discipline of despotism. We are concerned with the future, the dignity and peace of great nations. We must conduct ourselves in a fashion that befits it.